D0103421

SECOND BEST

THE
CRISIS
of the
COMMUNITY
COLLEGE

SECOND BEST

L. STEVEN ZWERLING

McGRAW-HILL BOOK COMPANY
New York   St. Louis   San Francisco   London
Düsseldorf   Mexico   Toronto   Sydney

123456789BPBP79876

Library of Congress Cataloging in Publication Data

Zwerling, L. Steven.
    Second best: the crisis of the community college.

    Bibliography: p. 350
    Includes index.
    1.   Community colleges—United States.
2.   Students' socio-economic status—United
States.   I.   Title.
LB2328.Z93   378.1'543   75-31735
ISBN 0-07-073090-3

To my students and teachers.
There have been many of both.

ACKNOWLEDGMENTS

This book has grown out of a conversation that began over the kitchen table when I was a child and continues to this day. Education was hotly debated in my house: my mother was an elementary school teacher and my father had many ideas about schooling—most of which we argued about then and continue to disagree about today. And though I began life thinking about being an architect-engineer-doctor-writer-etc., I suppose it was inevitable that I in fact became a teacher and administrator. So my first acknowledgment goes to those early influences.

In later life my ideas about education were shaped by my encounters with Mr. Burt Ludwig, my seventh-grade teacher. He taught me the power of motivation for learning and inspired me to become a lifelong reader. In college I recall Lionel Trilling and Moses Hadas; they taught me the magic of a wide-ranging intellect tempered by a deep belief in the importance of feeling.

My work at Staten Island Community College, especially, has been full of the opportunity to try to do what I believed should be done; for this, I gratefully acknowledge the unwavering support of the president, William M. Birenbaum. S.I.C.C. has also been full of encounters with colleagues who often became friends. Dabney Park, Jr. helped shape the design of this book and is coauthor with me of an article which in a slightly different form comprises the introduction. My thanks to him for allowing me to use it here. Joseph Harris, Wendy Guillou, John Schorr, Carl Takakjian, Elinor Azenberg, and Anne Arthur were in on many of the experiences and ideas described here.

I particularly want to mention Ivan Kronenfeld. We have worked together at Staten Island for six extraordinary years. We've been through so much together it would take a chapter to try to sort out where his ideas begin and mine end. Suffice it to say I've learned more about learning from him than anyone else.

Roger Ekins and Patricia Bertini read an earlier version of this and their detailed comments helped set me right in too many places to mention. Florence Bergin typed and retyped all of this and thereby deserves my gratitude. Joyce Johnson, my editor at McGraw-Hill, not only did what had to be done to get this published in the first place, she also is responsible for much of the life you may find here.

My wife Lisa wasn't all that happy with me during the year and a half that it took to complete this; many dinners and weekends were spoiled. But we're still together, and her criticism and help with the manuscript helped me keep things straight. My love to her for that.

In spite of all this help and nurturing, whatever remains awkward or wrongheaded is my final responsibility.

CONTENTS

"It's not a very attractive job from the college teaching point of view."

Claude Campbell, Secretary,
Faculty Union
City University of New York
(Staten Island Advance, 1975)

"All I want to know is why I have to hold my humiliating job—teaching [community] college students that sentences start with big letters and end with punctuation. . . . Being hired to teach journalism at my college is like being hired to coach track in a paraplegic ward."

John Medelman (1975)

INTRODUCTION*

Angelo Liberato is a second-generation Italian-American born in Brooklyn. His father, who drives a delivery truck, makes $8,500 a year. His mother adds something to this by doing odd jobs when she gets a chance. He has four brothers and sisters. Neither of his parents finished high school or ever attended college.

Angelo is now a student at a publicly supported junior or community college. He is not quite sure what he wants, except that he doesn't want what his parents have. Chances are, he'll drop out of college and wind up living ten blocks from his parents. (Up to 75 percent of students entering community colleges leave and never return.) If he's lucky, he will complete two years of college and get a job that enables him to live in a neighborhood, as he sees it, one step above the one he

*This first appeared in the *Community College Review* in slightly different form as "Curriculum Comprehensiveness and Tracking" and was coauthored by Dabney Park, Jr. (Spring 1974, pp. 10–20).

comes from. (Fewer than 25 percent of students in community or two-year colleges ever graduate; the average annual income of these graduates is about $9,500.) If he is exceptionally lucky, he will get through four years of college and move up into the middle of the middle class. (Fewer than 12 percent of students in community colleges complete four years of higher education.) The professions (law, medicine, college teaching) and the higher-paying positions in society (executive management, entrepreneurial business) hover just inside the edge of impossibility for Angelo. (Fewer than 5 percent of community college students graduate from professional and graduate schools or ever attain an income in excess of $20,000.)

Angelo is a victim of an educational and social process which has made it virtually certain that he will not succeed enough in school to break into the more prestigious and lucrative careers available in American society. School functions in such a way that it limits the possibilities of Angelo's social mobility. It tells him that he has always been second best, and that the chances are he will never be anything more.

The process which delivers the message to Angelo started early, before experience in the community college, before high school, before elementary school. It started with Angelo's parents, and particularly with the levels of their income, educational background, and aspirations for him. If we know anything at all for sure about the educational experience in this country, it is that a student's chance of educational success is more dependent upon parental income and parental educational level than on any other factors, that the amount of money that Angelo's father and mother make and the level of their educational achievement have more to say than anything else about whether Angelo will be a teacher, a machine shop foreman, or a janitor.

These environmental factors, the crucial determinants of educational success, are clearly tied to social class. Yet we know that human intelligence is *not* tied to social class. We have no reason to believe that, from the moment of conception, Angelo is inherently incapable of practicing law on Wall Street, but the democracy of testing ensures that he will *not* have access to the best parts of the system. The environment of his pre-school years insures that by the time he reaches elementary school his IQ will test out at, say, 95—just about average. The IQ test operates like a two-edged scalpel on Angelo. The belief is that the test gives him an equal chance, in spite of his background: the democracy of testing offers everyone access to the best parts of the educational system. The fact is that Angelo is likely to score low. So as a result, he is placed in an academic track that is supposed to help him fulfill his academic potential—or lack of it. He is put with the Sparrows (he's in a public school, but a "modern" one) rather than with the Blue Jays or the Robins. From first grade on, the kids know that this is a ruse, that the Sparrows are the "dumb" kids and that the Blue Jays are average kids, while the Robins are the "smart" class.

Right away, the psychology of varying levels of expectation begins to work on Angelo and on his teachers. Angelo might aspire to be a Blue Jay or a Robin, but the metamorphosis from species to species is a rare phenomenon, and the more he begins to get used to the idea of being a Sparrow, the more he acts like one. The more he acts like one, the more convinced his teachers are that he belongs where he is. By the time he reaches the end of elementary school, his aspirations have been severely curtailed.[1]

At this point, Angelo gets another chance. High school seems to be a new start, and for some it is. But for most, it becomes a process of specifying what kind of Sparrow Angelo is going to be. High-school counselors gently urge their students toward what they consider to be realizable educational goals. In New York City, until very recently, this was standardized into a rigid tracking system culminating in five different high school diplomas: Academic, Commercial, Technical, Vocational, and General.[2]

What happens outside of class pulls Angelo even more inevitably toward the lower tracks. With few exceptions, Sparrows and Blue Jays and Robins don't mix in high school any better than they did in elementary school. Angelo is likely to be more concerned about his status in a peer group than about anything else in life, and his peer group—especially if they are Sparrows—will undoubtedly be more interested in the immediate pleasures of sex, drugs, and hanging out than in the educational experiences which will eventually lead them to careers and jobs.

Coming off one of the lower high-school tracks, Angelo will get yet another second chance, the opportunity to enter a community college—the final opportunity offered by the democracy of testing and schooling.

Community colleges have been multiplying and growing at an incredible rate—until recently new ones were opening at the rate of nearly one a week—offering second chances in higher education to virtually anyone who wants to take advantage of them. They are commonly believed to be among the great equalizers in a society which professes to be democratic and egalitarian.

The social effect of the community college, however, tends to be just the opposite. Instead of blunting the pyramid of the American social and economic structure, the community college plays an essential role in maintaining it. It has become just one more barrier put between the poor and the disenfranchised and the decent and respectable stake in the social system which they seek. Few Angelos will gain access to the most rewarding and prestigious places in society.

Ten years ago, it was generally agreed that you needed a high-school diploma to get a good job; now it is becoming widely accepted that you need at least a degree from a two-year college or even one from a four-year school to avoid getting a bad one. But while Angelo now needs two more years of school, more and more of the children of the middle and upper middle classes now need—and get, at enormous public expense—at least a baccalaureate degree. Consequently, Angelo and his peers *must* go to a community college in order to remain in relatively the same position in the social hierarchy.

Angelo, to be sure, has a realistic idea of his chances. Just ask him why he is in college in the first place. We arc prone to assume that he is there to take his shot at achieving the American dream of upward mobility. But when asked, he will most likely give you three reasons: "I can't think of anything better to do; college offers a more desirable social life; and besides, I'll get a better job when I get out."

Even at this third level of motivation, most community college students' aspirations are pitifully low. The hope of getting a "better job" turns up far more regularly than the hope of becoming, say, a professional. K. Patricia Cross points out, for example, that some 60 percent of male community college students aspire to be automobile mechanics, while some 78 percent of female community college students aspire to become secretaries.[3]

So Angelo arrives at community college with atrophied aspirations. What happens to him while he is there? Chances are, he'll flunk out. Statistics indicate that, nationwide, community colleges are flunking kids out (or encouraging them to drop out) at an alarming rate—some 75 percent never complete all the requirements for the associate's degree. Community colleges have become "revolving doors," letting students in and sending them right back out again, rather than the "open doors" they claim to be. When it is revealed how few of the Angelos make it through, we can see that the community college is not a lever of opportunity but a social filter. Like any filter, it not only lets certain people in, it keeps certain people out.

Even if Angelo stays in school, the community college performs this function. At the heart of the process of selective sifting lies what is most unique to the community college as an educational institution: a heavy emphasis on academic and career counseling. Traditional four-year colleges usually assume that their students either know what they want and can get it or are capable of figuring it out for themselves—they are left pretty much on their own. Community colleges, however, usually have large counseling staffs who are prepared from orientation day on to lead Angelo by the hand, to help him discover where he is and what he is going to do with his life.

The problem is that only rarely do community college counseling staffs lead Angelo toward stretching his mind to the full limits of his potential. Instead, he is carefully guided toward a decision to select a low-level career or to drop out. "Be realistic" is the message ceaselessly repeated: "You started elementary school as a Sparrow; your high-school average was not good and as a result you are now in a community college. What makes you think you will ever be an engineer or a teacher? Be realistic—try something you are capable of, like mechanical technology or educational assistant." Like gardeners, the counselors tenderly prune Angelo's hopes.

This counseling process is known as the "cooling-out" function.[4] Since we know that Angelo's native ability—what he was born with—is comparable to anyone else's, cooling-out becomes a political and social problem: who gets cooled-out and who doesn't. Students in community colleges come primarily from working-class and lower-middle-class families. Consequently, most of those who are so carefully cooled-out by the community college counseling system are found in the lower strata of the social structure. Not only is maintaining the social hierarchy a primary function of the community college, but the community college is also remarkably effective at the job. It takes students whose parents are characterized primarily by low income and educational achievement and slots them into the lower ranks of the industrial and commercial hierarchy. The community college is in fact a social defense mechanism that resists basic changes in the social structure.

Offering the first two years of college for transfer students, providing training leading to specific but limited employment opportunities, educating people for middle- and lower-level careers, and cooling-out the "misdirected" student—these are the functions community colleges are most comfortable with. All of them speak to secondary and tertiary levels of human aspiration. When community colleges seek their goals and identities exclusively in these areas, they admit that they owe their existence to Angelo's severed hopes, if not to his outright failure.

But of course, like Angelo, the community college must be "realistic." There are significant parallels between the limited goals of community college students and the goals of the faculty and of the institution itself. While going to a two-year college is second best for the students, teaching in one is second best for the faculty, and being one is second best for the college. The functions that these colleges perform, from technical and career training to lower-level transfer programs for students who want to enter four-year colleges, are generally regarded as second- and third-rate educational functions when compared to the functions of four-year colleges and universities. The attitude of second best which results from this permeates the entire institution.

For the college, the two-year barrier is a special problem. It severely limits what the community college can aspire to accomplish and is an explicit statement of inferiority in the educational caste system. The two-year structure tells community colleges that they, as institutions, can do only so much and no more, that they can train kids for jobs or send them on to "real" colleges but they cannot go beyond twenty-four months' worth of education or half a normal baccalaureate degree.

The fact that it is felt that both the college and its students are second best is communicated to Angelo through many varied silent messages. He reads it in the eyes of his high-school counselors, he hears it from the college faculty, and he smells it in the cafeteria. In one of the stalls of one of the men's rooms at a community college in the City University of New York, there is a graffito just above the toilet paper dispenser which reads

Pull For Your Diploma.

How does Angelo feel about this? He is the one who scratched it into the paint! He knows what his associate's degree is worth in the eyes of those with power in the society. Worse, he tends to accept their judgment and to believe that it is only right that his diploma should be written on toilet paper rather than parchment.

If you ask Angelo why things are as they are, why he wrote that graffito, why he is dropping out, why he has selected a two-year career program, or why he seems so little interested in the courses that comprise his transfer program, he will invariably blame the situation on himself. Indeed, ensuring that the student blames his failure on his own incapacity is seen by some to be an essential component of the cooling-out role of the community college. Angelo comes to feel that the institution has done everything humanly possible to help him. Consequently, his lack of success can be attributed only to his own laziness or stupidity.

Accepting the blame for his own relative failure in the educational process has the effect of paralyzing Angelo's motivation. Precisely because he sees it as *his* fault and not the system's, he finds it increasingly difficult to believe in his own self-worth. When a student has a severely diminished sense of self-confidence, even the most elementary verbal and mathematical transactions can seem incomprehensible to him. The system, in other words, not only keeps certain people out, it also tells them that they never had what it takes to get in.

0-07-073090-3

"I learned something in school today.
I signed up for folk guitar, computer programming, stained
glass, art, shoe making, and a natural foods workshop.
I got Spelling, History, Arithmetic and two study periods."
"So what did you learn?"
"I learned that what you sign up for and what you get are two
different things."

—Charles Schulz
Peanuts

ONE
THE HIDDEN FUNCTIONS OF SCHOOLING

At 9:00 A.M. a group of three hundred to four hundred high-school seniors are gathered in our auditorium at Staten Island Community College to have their introduction to the college they will be entering in a few months. If our student demographic surveys mean anything, it's clear that the majority of these incoming students are the first of their families ever to enter a college. I try to imagine the emotions, the thoughts that must be with them, the anticipation of what will surely be new and special experience mixed with a measure of anxiety concerning the unfamiliar experiences ahead. And certainly some pride at having made it this far, often in the face of having been told by teachers and guidance counselors that they weren't "college material." The college promises so much: it is an open door institution; forty-eight dollars per semester is all it charges in tuition and fees and even with that, financial aid is available; counselors are to be found everywhere eager to guide students through a bewildering array of curricula choices. That's what the school offers, but what is hidden within today's first orientation experience communicates very different and powerful messages.

The first words these incoming students hear, poorly amplified through an inadequate podium speaker system, are from the counselor in charge telling them to move closer to the front so they can hear better. "And make sure you take a lap board to write on because you'll be taking placement tests in a few minutes." No official of the school is there to greet them. Not the president or a dean or a student government official. Only a perfunctory welcome from the counselor and then in that slow, patronizing, evenly articulated voice they are all familiar with from elementary- and high-school teachers and principals, they hear how the tests will not affect their admission but instead will be used to "help you make choices about which courses you should take."

Then the financial aid director is introduced. He begins by telling them that it's unlikely they will receive any aid: money is very short. But they should fill out this form anyway which they received in the mail. He unfolds the multipaged form like an accordion and begins to detail what they must do in order to apply for the money that doesn't exist. "Your parents must sign here and attach a copy of their last year's tax statement there. And don't forget, the deadline for applying is December tenth (today is December seventh) so you must get it in by then. Otherwise you will be ineligible for financial aid this year." I am mystified by the complexity of the form myself, and it is clear that the students are likewise confounded. It appears to me that not one student has a copy of the Parent's Confidential Statement form with him; no one even seems to be taking notes. But the financial aid director has done his thing, and if by Monday no one has submitted a P.C.S. form who is to blame but the students themselves?

Then it is time for the placement tests. And whereas a half-hour earlier the counselor was beseeching the students to move closer *together* to facilitate the beginning of a feeling of community (we are, after all, a *community* college), now a half-hour later, in spite of these fine intentions, they are told to spread themselves out once again for the purposes of testing—leaving at least one seat between them. Although they are told this will give them more elbow room and thus make them more comfortable and although it is reiterated that no one's admission to the college will be jeopardized by the test results, the skip-a-seat arrangement delivers quite another message: in this college just as in high school you are not only considered untrustworthy but will also continue in competition with each other, and you will continue to work under the authority and vigilance of the teacher and counselor proctors.

I feel in a rush that I have to get out, if not in body at least then in mind. It is suddenly twenty years earlier and I see myself once more at my own orientation at ivy-covered Columbia College. I connect in an instant of memory to my own excitement and nervousness. And although I would like to recount some exalted recollection of an encounter with a great mind, to be truthful the first thing I remember of that day after Labor Day in 1956 was running around among the sitting rooms of Hartley Hall looking for a men's room to relieve some of that excitement and nervousness. I finally discovered one and in the midst of my relief was struck by something written on the wall:

Nietzsche Is Peachy,
But Sartre Is Smarter.

I knew then that this was indeed a place of higher
learning, even though at the time I didn't know enough
to realize that "Sartre" and "smarter" didn't rhyme very
well.

Emerging from this time warp for a moment, returning to the fluorescent-lit silence of Staten Island's
auditorium, I wonder what today's Angelos must have
thought when, seeking the same relief, they encountered something of quite a different sort in one of our
community college men's rooms:

All Niggers Are Apes!

And what will they be thinking six months from now
when some other bathroom scribbler has added:

So Are The Jews!

Rather despairing, I allow myself to slip back again to
my Columbia orientation and next remember being
brought together with other beanie-wearing freshmen
that first night to learn the college lore—most particularly the school songs, both the sacred and profane. There
was of course the alma mater "Sans Souci" as well as the
less pretentious "We Are From Barnard" with its unfor-
gettably obscene images, and "Roar Lion Roar." But the
college's true alma mater, so essential, I was to learn,
for pep rallies, football games, and tenth reunions, was
"Who Owns New York?" Before coming to college, I had
heard stories, untrue I had thought, that Columbia
owned the land under Rockefeller Center and at least

half of lower Manhattan, but now, in this song, *it was true*, we did own New York! (And to this day when I walk among the buildings of Rockefeller Center I seek out the brass line embedded in the sidewalk and the little plaques every ten yards or so that proclaim the land on the building side of the line to belong to dear old Columbia with permission to walk thereon, revocable at will!) What a sense of power that night surged through those still-narrow class-of-'sixty shoulders! No mere counselor or placement test would get to us that day or the next for that matter. We were being readied for four years of lion meat!

Angelo, back again at Staten Island, seems ready for a much less hearty diet, hunched nervously over the last few minutes of the Nelson-Denny Reading Test, affirming one more time that he still alas reads at only the ninth-grade level. No beanie, no class of anything, just Angelo, first-semester student.

I remember reading a newspaper account of an orientation at Yale. The article quoted the master of Pierson College as observing that incoming freshmen who had been at Yale only two or three *hours* were already asking about the best strategies for getting into medical school.[1] I can't help but assume Angelo's strategic thinking at the moment probably involves working out a way to get his father's car for the night so he can ride around with his girlfriend, get stoned, and try to forget the whole day.

I escape from Angelo's orientation to return to my office for a meeting some teachers have called with one of our students and her parents. Elise is just about to finish her third of four semesters at Staten Island Community College. She came to us because she didn't have the money to go any place else and also because the advice her high-school guidance counselor gave her was based upon his analysis of her *in*ability to do *real* college-level work.

But although she had surprised her high-school advisers by doing excellent work at Staten Island during her first three semesters, earning a 3.50+ grade point average and the respect *and* friendship of many of her teachers, her parents were still reading the messages they had received from Elise's elementary- and high-school experiences and were attempting, as a result, to convince her not to go on beyond two years of college. Elise and her teachers, on the other hand, were eager for her to continue. In fact, Elise had picked out a number of out-of-town colleges to which she wanted to apply.

At the meeting we talk about the kinds of scholarships and loans and work/study programs that might be available to Elise and also about what her parents would have to contribute. This of course is their primary concern because of their limited finances. But the longer we talk the clearer it becomes that more than money is involved. And also more than traditional notions of what is an appropriate life for a working-class girl or traditional parental anxieties about a child's going away to college. The parents simply *refuse to believe what we are saying about Elise's ability* because they have spent so many years listening to her high-school teachers tell them how little to expect of their daughter.*

What I will argue here and elsewhere in this book is that the process through which Elise and her parents came to distrust their own experience, the way in which my college oriented me to higher learning, the messages

---

*As of now Elise has finished one very successful year at Johnson College at the University of Redlands in California. She received a substantial financial aid package, and her parents have come to feel very good about her accomplishments.

delivered to our entering freshmen, are all part of the hidden functions of schooling. Additionally, I will try to show these functions to be intentional: certain schools are, in fact, structured to assure the failure of the majority of their students. The failure, then, of students should *not* be seen to be the result of the failures of schooling. Quite the contrary. Too often when we see failure occurring in schools we misperceive it to be the result of imperfections in the system and thus misapply our remedies. It should be no surprise then that most attempts at reform have failed. I contend that *we must begin by seeing our schools' "failures" to be the successful fulfillment of their hidden social functions.* Only then will real change be possible.

These hidden processes of schooling might usefully be seen to consist of two interrelated categories of functions: (1) the *socialization* function and (2) the role of the school in contributing to the *reproduction of the social order.* The first of these functions can be discovered, among other places, by reading through the many speeches and essays of the early and current proponents of public education—both the philosophers and the politicians—and by taking a clear look at what actually goes on in classrooms—at what gets taught in addition to Reading, 'Riting, and 'Rithmetic. The second major function, more difficult to perceive, can be understood by examining the results—particularly the apparent "failures"—of more than one hundred years of universal public schooling. Thus, the socialization function might more accurately be called an *obscured* function of schooling because it is relatively easy to see—much having been written about it in recent years. The latter, not surprisingly, is truly *hidden*—it is rather unpleasant to contemplate that the schools have been in the business of facilitating and certifying inequality whereas all along they have claimed to be fostering upward mobility for the intellectually able children of the lower class.

It is now almost a commonplace to assert that a lot more is going on in classrooms than the Three R's.[2] Some see the lessons learned by being required to line up in size-places in the schoolyard at the sound of the teacher's whistle to be about as important as learning the seven-times table. That schoolyard whistle is seen to be analogous to the factory whistle or the click of the time clock. In this context, Philip Jackson, a pioneer in analyzing what actually goes on in schools, writes that "the teacher, although he may disclaim the title, is the students' first 'Boss.'"[3] School also is the first place in which children must learn to exist for sustained periods of time apart from their families. The early grades provide a formal and continuous process of separating children from their families.

When I ask students to talk about their first memories of school, they usually recall their reactions to their parents leaving them alone and unprotected the first day of school. It is a wrenching experience, but it is essential that children learn to break family ties if they are to become successful workers in an industrial, technological society. In an earlier agrarian culture, with the majority of workers involved with family farms and cottage industries, these unstated lessons were unnecessary and universal schooling did not exist.[4] Schools additionally prepare children to deal with publicly administered rewards and punishments—most often in an openly competitive environment. In the family setting, punishments—though often severe—at least are suffered in private and rewards (hopefully) have a private and not a public value. To work in an office, a school, a factory, however, one has to be able to take a licking in public; and thus one of school's socializing functions is to help us learn how to handle punitive experiences. It is in school also where the often all-powerful teacher is less subject than the parent to those subtle techniques a child may employ to countervail adult power, and where the line is clearly drawn for the first time between the weak and powerful.

The classroom experience, too, helps one learn how to live in a crowd while simultaneously learning how to be alone—important things to know prior to entering the world of work. Even growing up in a large family doesn't provide one with the opportunity to master these skills. Nor does family life prepare one to understand what Robert Dreeben calls the "norm of universalism," the ability to come to accept being treated by others as a member of a category rather than solely as an individual. The categorical distinction between being a "third-grader" in the "smart" class as opposed to being a "second-grader" in an "average" class prepares one for a future in which one will think of oneself as a "riveter" or "installer" or "lawyer" within an adult system of divided labor.[5]

Another important obscured or hidden function of schooling is to continue the process of teaching children to delay their gratifications, a skill critical for successful adult work. For example, one must keep working even when bored, frustrated, hungry, depressed. If you can remember waving your hand to get the teacher's attention, ready to jump out of your seat with the excitement of having the right answer, if you can remember being told to wait your turn and not call out the answer, or the feeling of being passed over by the teacher and having someone else come up with the answer before you got a chance to be recognized, you may realize how schools help all of us learn to separate our desires from our actions.

And lest one think that the ability to delay gratification results from a rather benign process experienced equally by all children, let me hasten to add that there is precisely the same kind of inequality in the way these hidden functions of schooling are administered as there is in the way skills such as reading are taught.

It has often been asserted that the ability to delay gratification is directly correlated to a person's socio-economic status. In fact, it is almost a cliché in the literature on the "disadvantaged" to point out how the poor, the black, etc., have particular difficulty in delaying gratification sufficiently to do well in school or to chart out careers for themselves that require many years of education.[6] Classroom observers have frequently noted how teachers and school administrators often seem to give up trying to discipline "disruptive" children in inner-city schools, whereas they tend to work doubly hard with children with "behavior problems" in more affluent districts. A quick look at what goes on in the hallways and toilets during classes in a ghetto school as compared with what happens in a suburban school eloquently makes the point. And by *not* helping children develop the capacity for self-control, these schools not only deny their students the skills required to plan for the kind of education that might change the fundamental conditions of their lives, but they also leave these children defenseless against various social snares that are waiting to entrap them within the circumstances of their current unequal condition. Thus, the inequality in the learning process becomes a mechanism for social control.

Jules Henry writes brilliantly about how our consumer society continually encourages us to suspend our hard-won ability to delay seeking immediate gratification through advertising and other methods which create in us desires for ever-changing lifestyles.[7] We're all susceptible to these urgings, but ironically the more affluent who can afford more consumption have also been better taught to control these urges than the poor. The affluent have even created educational institutions to protect those of their young who have, at least by college-age, *not* learned to control their need for instant fulfillment and who would thereby be in danger of not making it through college, thus jeopardizing their chances to assume at least the same social niche their parents occupy. Places such as Goddard College or Franconia College, for a price, protect the affluent young from the dangers of downward mobility by providing a nonpressured haven for them of four more years to "get it together." The equivalent poor who also haven't learned to delay gratification obviously have no such shelters, they must begin to pay *their* price, almost immediately, by dropping out of school to begin work—or worse.

Ivan Illich, in his own examination of the hidden functions of schooling (he calls it the "hidden curriculum"), points out that a student is schooled to confuse process with substance and as a result comes "to confuse teaching with learning, grade advancement with education, a diploma with competence, and fluency with the ability to say something new. His imagination is 'schooled' to accept service in place of value. Medical treatment is mistaken for health care, social work for the improvement of community life, police protection for safety, military poise for national security, the rat race for productive work."[8] Illich claims that once we learn to need school, all our activities take the form of client relationships and as a result all nonprofessional activities and relationships are both discredited and distrusted.[9] We learn to overvalue professional services and insist on upgrading so many forms of work and service to professional or paraprofessional status that we create both an inflation in education and a reduction in the intensity of human relationships because one thing that defines all professional activity is a presumed objectivity and a detachment of feeling from function.[10]

More explicitly, schools have historically claimed that their socializing functions include preparing the young to be good workers and citizens by instructing them in proper moral or ethical behavior. Michael Katz and others see the early advocates of universal public education claiming a parental role for the schools. *In loco parentis*, schools came to attempt to supply their charges with instruction in social behavior required in a society moving from agrarianism to industrialization, from a rural to an urban base. Faced with the decline of the old family structure and the disintegration of traditional social forms, New England schoolmen proclaimed that the state must assert itself and emphasize its character as a parent who should guard its family of children.[11] Secretary Boutwell of the Massachusetts Board of Education put it this way in 1859: "[School] inculcates habits of regularity, punctuality, constancy, and industry . . . and by moral and religious instruction daily given, some preparation is made for the duties and temptations of the world."[12] Along this line, the control of the passions was a major goal; the school was to teach the young to sublimate their energies to "higher" pleasures. Indeed, its immense task was to supply individuals with a set of inner restraints.[13]

Joel Spring, commenting on the same historical process, also sees the schools assuming a greater and greater role in teaching social discipline. He sees the underlying school ideology of the late nineteenth century as antiurban (crime, vice, illiteracy were frequently seen to be indigenous to the cities and their newly arrived immigrants) with school proponents looking to the schools to preserve the best features of an idealized rural past in the midst of a society turning more and more to industry and manufacturing. He claims that a new idea in American society was to replace the use of force with education as a means of maintaining social order: "There was a strong feeling that some method had to be used to assure good character otherwise a Republican government would result in social chaos."[14]

The nineteenth-century school reformers wanted to remove the children of the poor from the negative influence of both their parents and the city to the positive influence of the schools. For these children, it was argued, Moral Education or "the formation of right attitudes was more important than learning any skill or subject. . . . Education, morality, and docility were all equated; they formed a trinity marking a properly schooled man."[15]

But all of this was difficult if not impossible to accomplish because there were internal contradictions in the hidden curricula of the schools. Although it was generally felt that urbanization and industrialization caused social disintegration, it was also felt that these processes were good for the society and thus cities and factories should be encouraged. The schools, then, were to play the double role of fostering urbanization and industrialization by training skilled workers while *simultaneously,* through Moral Education, solving the social problems that were the result of rapid industrial expansion. Much of the present conflict between the schools' overt and hidden functions may be traced back to this historical irony.[16]

Michael Katz quotes a nineteenth-century manufacturer praising the "diligence and . . . willing acquiescence" of the educated who, working their way into the confidence of their colleagues, exerted "a conservative influence" in times of labor trouble, an influence "of great value pecuniarily and morally."[17] A little less sinister perhaps was a 1965 *Wall Street Journal* story that quoted a Safeway supermarket recruiter comparing two- and four-year-college graduates: "'The nice thing about these kids is that they're not as sophisticated and demanding as four-year graduates, who don't bother to tell you whether they can do anything for the company. [Four-year graduates] want to find out what the company can do for them—period.'"[18]

Just as the early public elementary and high schools were supposed to instill in the children of factory workers those traits felt to be essential for good citizenship and upright moral behavior, so was the curriculum of the two-year college set up to do the same thing for its blue-collar clientele.[19] This was all clearly set forth at the beginning by junior-college founding fathers such as Alexis Lange. As early as 1915 he wrote of junior-college graduates: "Their studies and other activities must be expected to have greatly quickened their communal sympathies and deepened their sense of oneness with their fellows. . . . Each junior college graduate should carry with him not merely ideas of intelligent social and political behavior, but also the corresponding ideals, as mainsprings of action. . . . [They] must be expected to have formed the habits that characterize good citizenship on a high level."[20] Carl Seashore's 1940 classic *The Junior College Movement* is a compendium of the hidden—or obscured—socializing function of the two-year college. He quotes the 1931 *Carnegie Report on California Junior Colleges* which recommends a "curriculum for social intelligence . . . [which] aims to train for social citizenship in American civilization." The core of this curriculum "will tend to organize knowledge and intelligence for effective social behavior."[21] He quotes founding father Robert Sproul who in 1930 wrote: "The objective of the junior college is the preparation of young men and women for effective citizenship, for a more disciplined attitude toward the job of life, for a more thorough understanding of the world they live in and for a greater tolerance for each other as they strive together for self-expression and a better ordering of society."[22] Jesse Parker Boque, long-time executive director of the American Association of Junior Colleges, in his influential book in 1950 sets the foundation for the junior colleges' obscured function rather succinctly: "Democratic cooperation means more than topflight leadership. So to speak, *it also means intelligent followership*" (my italics). An important function for two-year colleges then has always been the development of followers, since their "greatest service is in educating and training persons for the semiprofessional fields of employment."[23]

At a New York City community college that I know well, even the half-joking definition of community colleges as high schools with ashtrays is barely accurate—smoking is "prohibited" in most places and thus the cafeteria and bathrooms continue to provide a high-school-like sanctuary. Other things are forbidden as well. A neatly printed sign on prominent display in the men's locker room reads: "Only locks issued by the physical education department *will* be used on those [*sic*—it should read "these"] lockers. All others will be removed." Everything communicates hurry-up-and-let's-get-it-over-with. Learning is divided into meticulously sliced forty-eight-minute periods separated by seven-minute breaks (to squeeze an eleventh period out of the previous ten-period day in order to accommodate additional new students in the same number of classrooms). To satisfy the computer, which has taken over the scheduling of student programs, the eighth period runs from 14:25 to 15:13—in civilian time from 2:25 to 3:13 P.M. No one has yet been able to master the "new" schedule though it's now nearly five years old.

And no one has yet become comfortable with the designation of *R* to stand for Thursday in order to distinguish it from *T* for Tuesday—again to satisfy the computer rather than the people. And without doubt neither faculty nor students have ever been able to remember the numerous conversions of Wednesdays' to Mondays' schedules or Fridays' to Tuesdays'—all in order to make up the time lost due to holidays, snow days, etc. What happens on those metaphysical Wednesdays-that-are-Mondays is that hardly anyone shows up for anything, and those that do remember the conversions wander around, seeking out more than the usual amount of solace in the form of "ups" or "downs" or "joints" readily available in the lounge. What does get accomplished is that the state comptroller, who counts the Mondays and Tuesdays when he distributes tax money to the colleges, and the school administration are satisfied that time and money and study are all in proper order.

That "less is actually more" was also at one point not

so subtly communicated to students at this two-year college via a school-initiated advertising campaign designed to soft-sell students on the advantages of leaving the rather pleasant, almost suburban main campus for a new satellite facility to be set up downtown in a renovated office building. It was unlikely that many on their own initiative would have elected to go there, so one morning the walls of the college were papered with posters proclaiming the virtues of the new place. Most prominently on display was one that seemed to be most persuasive: "At the 'Annex' classes will be scheduled *for only 4 day's,* [*sic*]—and it is possible to schedule for EVEN *FEWER DAY'S* [*sic*]. Find out what's going on." It is apparent that to the administration, at least, the college is more appealing to students the less often they have to be there.

This appears to be the case for faculty and deans as well. On a recent visit, I found virtually all administrative offices deserted between 12 and 2:30 (executive lunches), and rarely were instructors to be found in their offices—in spite of the fact that most are granted dispensations from the usual Ph.D. requirement and the publish-or-perish rule so they can be available to meet with students outside of class. One hard-working dean told me that more than 50 percent of the faculty were on three-day teaching schedules (most between 10 A.M. and 2 P.M.—to avoid rush-hour traffic), earning average salaries of more than $20,000 per year. He facetiously told me how many teachers leave their car engines running while they teach their classes.

Thomas Corcoran has written a piece called "Community Colleges: The Coming Slums of Higher Education." But as my friend and colleague, Ivan Kronenfeld points out, the slums are already here. Stand in

the quadrangle of the place I've been describing, sur-
rounded on three sides by architecturally innocuous
ten-year-old buildings spread out rather generously in
space and let your eyes sweep from the administration
building (officially named the A Building) past the main
classroom and faculty office building (B) to the student
center (appropriately last and least, the C Building). It's a
nice day and Frisbees lace the air. Other less active
students loll on benches, and the faint aroma of grass cut
for the first time this year mixes with the more pungent
aroma of a very different kind of grass.

Moving across the quadrangle the architectural simi-
larities of the three clusters of buildings begin to dissolve
in the small details of day-to-day life at the college. It is
these details that tell one more about what goes on here
than the glass and preformed concrete of the buildings.
Whereas the walkways surrounding the administration
building are as immaculate as can be expected of anything set in New York City, more slumlike conditions
prevail on the sidewalks around the C Building. Empty
Yoo-Hoo cans cluster by the benches, and a breeze tosses
styrofoam coffee cups and discarded student newspapers. The venetian blinds now visible inside the dirt-
streaked windows are in a tangled disarray. A glance back
across to the A Building reveals windows glinting in the
sun like jewels and blinds hung straight and even in
every window.

Music so loud it stops one's breath blasts out from the
student lounge. Pinball machines ring and flash. The
linoleum tiled floors haven't been stripped of chewing-
gum blotches in months. A group of students have set up
some red-painted shelves for a free clothing exchange,
and it is now unattended with shirts and trousers pouring
out onto the floor. There are a few scattered benches in

niches along one corridor; the upholstery fabric has been torn loose and only the underframes now remain. Students are packed together on them nonetheless. Three telephone booths have had their doors removed and the students in them have to cover their ears to hear and to shout to be heard. There is no place for privacy, except in an alcove formed by an auditorium exit. In there four or five students sit on the floor, backs against the wall, passing a joint from hand to hand while listening to one of their friends play his guitar.

Directly across from them is the college bookstore. It is all glass along the length of the hallway and one can easily see into every part of it. The only person inside is the cash register lady, staring blankly into space. It looks as if she hasn't had a customer all day. There are a few school sweatshirts to be seen, and only a few paperback books. I later learn it is bookstore policy to stock only required texts. I also hear from a faculty member that the store manager once refused to order the ten books she assigned for her course because, in his words, "Community college students won't read ten books for a course." I learn as well that though the store is supposed to be nonprofit, the only discounts are for teachers (10 percent), not for students. I can't help thinking about the Harvard Coop.

Kronenfeld points out that in this slum that is the student center one finds virtually all of the same sociopathological "illnesses" one finds in big-city slums: it is here that the college's version of crime and mugging occur— the elected student government president decides to establish a private contract with a pinball machine distributor with profits to be split between them. The president's share goes into a personal bank account although the machines are "sold" to the student body as providing additional funds for student activities. Concessions for a price are sold by other student officials to various vendors who set up booths in the hallways offering plants, incense, tie-dyed T-shirts, and jewelry to student shoppers. Most physical assaults take place here in the C Building—the rate of such crime is much higher here than in the other parts of the college. And virtually no one has ever gotten punished for any of these illegal activities—either by the school or off-campus authorities. An authoritative source told me that in the past seven years—with illicit activities increasing nearly geometrically—only two students have been suspended. The implicit message here, obviously, is that it is all right to rip-off and mug as long as it's confined to the students' ghetto.

In this slum—as in others—a very substantial portion of the population is on welfare, in this case on financial aid or other forms of stipend (well over 40 percent of the full-time student body). Obviously, most need it to survive; many, however, are tacitly encouraged to become passive victims of a system that mocks any notion of academic progress or achievement. I've been told of students who remained on the dole for four or five years at this two-year college by cleverly registering term after term for just the correct number of credits needed to maintain their financial aid package and then during the semester strategically dropping courses one by one so that they can complete the minimum number required to enroll again the next term. Officials at the college are concerned about this, but do little to either stop it or get these students to see what effect this behavior is having on their own lives. Indeed, many of the people I've talked to about this problem take pleasure in recounting amusing little stories about this student "who's been here longer than I have, and I've been here nearly five years."

The checks are given out every two weeks on what the recipients have dubbed Las Vegas Day. They are distributed at the ticket booth near the theater right in the main corridor of the student center. All day long there are long lines of people winding their way by the lounge (dope is even in more plentiful supply there on Las Vegas Day). Anyone passing through can't help but notice that those in line are disproportionately from the college's minority group populations, and I've overheard much resentment from students *and* faculty about this. Methods for giving out the checks more privately have all been vetoed or declared either unnecessary or impossible by the college's business office.

As in other slums, the various student cultures exist separate from and in tension with each other. A walk down any hallway reveals an Arab Student's Club, an Italo-American Organization, an Irish Freedom Fighters group, the Jewish Defense League, the Gay Club, the Over-Thirty Club, etc. The college melting pot has no more turned these students into an amalgam than America's has assimilated their parents or grandparents. When one group invites a controversial speaker to the campus, more often than not the police have to be called in to keep blacks and whites, for example, from tearing each other apart.

Last year when William Shockley was invited to speak (he contends blacks are genetically inferior to whites) one group launched a well-planned offensive to stop him from appearing ("Stop the Doc" buttons appeared overnight). Another group proclaimed his First Amendment right to speak on any subject—no matter how repulsive or misinformed he might be ("Stop Shockley Through Free Speech" buttons appeared a night later). To foster their cause this group plastered the walls of the student center with quotations from the Constitution. The stop-Shockley forces retaliated by going around with a big rubber stamp stamping "BULLSHIT" on all the posters.

But with all of this, still the main business of the college for the students is the accumulation of credits through attending classes. But classes for slum dwellers are also of a different sort than those one encounters at more privileged places. A student at this two-year college told me about her social psychology course—a story that might be considered to be typical. The instructor it seems was not interested in social but rather in abnormal psychology. And so in spite of the title and course description she taught abnormal from a strictly Freudian perspective. "What about my boyfriend who was in the class and who's a psych major? When is he now going to get the social psychology he needs? You know, you're not allowed to take the same course twice—you lose credit."

And he went on to get a C grade at that, she continued, even though he did everything asked of him—all the reading, a fifteen-to-twenty-page paper, he even kept a journal of his dreams. As she put it, "Only those people who had tragedies in their lives got A's." When I asked what she meant, Mona told me about the A students: Mike whose parents are alcoholics, Sara whose husband is abandoning her and their children, Sue who lost her mother when she was six. If you told the class about your tragedy, she insisted, you got your A. Her boyfriend is quiet, and besides he didn't want to put himself through such public exposure; so he got a C even though he did otherwise excellent work (he has nearly a straight A average). He opened up more about himself in his journal, and though the instructor noted in her written comment: "Well at least I got to know who you are," he still got his C.

One day the teacher brought some cards with drawings on them to class. She explained how they're used by psychologists working with socially immature six-year-olds to help bring them out of their shells. She gave one of these cards to each of the quiet people in the class and made them get up before the group and talk free-associatively about the scenes pictured on them. Mona's boyfriend was terribly embarrassed—in large part because these cards were designed for young children. Now she wonders out loud how he's going to get into graduate school. "He worked so hard and did everything the teacher asked. But he didn't have a tragedy in his life."

Ironically for my analysis of community colleges as the slums of higher education, as with earlier schools, they have also been seen to help society rid itself of crime and vice. William Crosby Eells, for example, one of the first historians of the junior-college movement, asserted in 1941 that though it can't be proven that crimes are prevented by having young people attend two-year colleges, "the presumption is strong that the correlation between junior college attendance and arrests for crime is not high."[24]

And then as recently as 1964, Norman Harris, a nationally known authority on vocational and technical education, wrote:

> When people say society cannot afford to provide higher education for all who can profit from it, tell them we cannot afford not to provide it. Remind them of "Society's Disaster Gap." Call their attention to such costs as these, which society seems to pay without too much anguish: $1,800 a year to keep a juvenile delinquent

in a detention home; $3,500 a year to keep a criminal in a
state prison; $2,500 a year (or more) for an unemployed
worker and his family on relief. . . . The $800 per year per
student for a good junior college technical program
sounds like a bargain basement special in comparison.[25]

And now in order to understand just what one gets
along with that "bargain basement special" called a
community college education, it is necessary to examine
the other major hidden function of schooling, its most
insidious function: the school's contribution to the reproduction of the social order.

Throughout the history of educational research in the
United States, educators and social scientists have tacitly
assumed that the goal of educational systems is the
maximization of every individual's potential. Pervading
this research is the meritocratic ideal that sees the "best,"
the most intelligent, rising to the top, with schools acting
to both facilitate and objectify this process. In a meritocracy, people are assumed to (1) have free will and (2) to
be able to rise as high as their motivation, desire, and
ability can take them. Individuals, thus, have only
themselves to blame if they don't take advantage of the
opportunities available to them.[26]

But there is an alternative to this traditional view. The
revisionist position claims that the real goals of educational systems (this second category of hidden functions)
are to serve the potential of only a few. And it is claimed
that these few come basically from the elite or most
powerful classes. There is, to be sure, the possibility for
upward mobility for an additional few *if* the majority are
held in their social place. The schools facilitate these real
objectives—no matter what their rhetoric claims. Now if
this is true, as I believe it is, the apparent problems and
inefficiencies in the educational system—the low

achievement scores of "disadvantaged" groups, for example—are not in fact problems but rather indicate, as Paul Lauter and Florence Howe contend, that the schools "have been terribly, indeed horrifyingly, successful."[27]

The revisionist historian Colin Greer has rather neatly documented this "Great School Legend"—the claim that the public school system was responsible for building American democracy, that it took the poor, the ragged, the ill-prepared ethnic groups who crowded the urban slums; Americanized and educated them, molding them all the while into the homogeneous and productive middle class that is our strength and pride.[28] Greer demythologizes this legend, carefully showing that "the rate of school failure among the urban poor . . . has been consistently and remarkably high since before 1900. The truth is that the immigrant children dropped out in great numbers. . . . It was in spite of, and *not* because of, compulsory public education that some eventually made their way."[29] He examines U.S. census data from 1910, 1920, and 1930 to document his contention that the children of the poor were ill-served by the schools. Social *immobility* was the rule rather than the exception. And so, he claims, we have accepted the schools' rhetoric of good intentions rather than the historical reality. Thus we perversely persist in holding today's urban poor responsible for failing to make the same effective use of the schools as their predecessors.[30]

I should note briefly that this kind of revisionist analysis of the public schools is not all that new. In 1925, to cite one example, Harry Kelly, the chairman of the first board of management of the Modern School at Stelton, New Jersey wrote: ". . . the public school system is a powerful instrument for the perpetuation of the

present social order. . . . From the moment the child
enters the public school he is trained to submit to
authority, to do the will of others as a matter of course,
with the result that habits of mind are formed which in
adult life are all to the advantage of the ruling class."[31]

Returning to more recent revisionist historians, Michael Katz's careful study of why the citizens of Beverly,
Massachusetts, voted in 1860 to *dis*establish their two-
year-old public high school is a model study, particularly
for those of us who wish to probe behind institutional
rhetoric. Those who advocated the continuance of the
high school cited a long list of social objectives. These
included the belief that the school would provide the
necessary social and moral discipline in a society where
this function was not adequately fulfilled by parents and
the church. The high school was to save the town from
disintegrating into an immoral and degenerate chaos. It
was to serve as an agent of community civilization.
Cultural and social unity would prevail and upwardly
mobile youths would be prepared both intellectually and
socially for their new status.[32] What was new in the
rhetoric of support for the Beverly high school was
implicit in the last sentence: *the school was also to serve
as a vehicle for upward mobility.* The high school, in
theory, was to cater to the poor as well as to the rich as
an antidote to the stratification, and the resulting strife,
educators saw around them. Katz quotes Joseph White,
eminent early secretary to the Massachusetts Board of
Education, on the potential of the high school to equalize social differences:

> The children of the rich and the poor, of the honored
> and the unknown, meet together on common ground.
> Their pursuits, their aims and aspirations are one. No
> distinctions find place, but such as talent and industry

and good conduct create. . . . No foundation will be laid
in our social life for the brazen walls of caste; and our
political life, which is but the outgrowth of the social, will
pulsate in harmony with it, and so be kept true to the
grand ideals of the fathers and founders of the republic.[33]

The children of workers would be able to afford to
attend, it was claimed, because the high school was to be
supported via a broad-based tax. This was seen to be real
progress since the forerunner of the public high school
was the private *academy*, which was attended almost
exclusively by the children of the affluent because of its
tuition charges.

But in fact very few poor children attended Beverly
High School; indeed, only a very small minority of the
town's children even entered it and most of them left
before graduation. So the very people the school was
allegedly intended to benefit rarely went; and as an
obvious result it did little to promote their upward
mobility. Economic conditions were so difficult that
most children were forced to begin work just when they
reached high-school age.[34]

Katz is of course correct when he speculates that
promoters of the high school could not really have
expected many children of laborers or factory workers to
attend. They knew very well both the economic reasons
these children couldn't go as well as the apathy of their
parents toward education. What they really were trying
to do was spread the costs of educating a small minority
among the community as a whole.[35] For middle-class
boys, then, the high school served as a means of status
maintenance and as entree into the business world—all
at public expense.[36] And so for at least these reasons,
when the people of Beverly were given the rare opportunity to conduct a referendum on whether to continue

an institution, supported mainly by the votes of factory workers and laborers, the high school was abolished.[37]

Precisely the same kind of analysis can be applied to our public higher educational system. Precisely the same kind of rhetoric sustains it. Precisely the same kind of reality belies the rhetoric. So that now more than ever a major hidden function of higher education is also the reproduction of social standing. Because as Samuel Bowles has written: "Whatever determined the occupational success of the older generation of the corporate elite—inherited wealth, nepotism, ability, theft, political power, or ambition—it is clear that in order to reproduce this success, the next generation is virtually required to obtain a college degree."[38]

At an earlier time, obviously very few people obtained that degree. Today, many more do. But in spite of the claim that mass higher education leads to marked upward mobility and thus results in a more equal society, there is massive evidence that this is not true because what has accompanied mass public higher education is an almost geometrically expanding *educational inflation* and a remarkably stable unequal distribution of wealth and power in America. Educational inflation has occurred because there has been a staggering overemphasis placed on educational credentials; jobs have been "upgraded" to require more schooling in order to give them more status even in the face of abundant evidence that "better-educated" workers are often more poorly trained for their specific jobs, less productive, and more dissatisfied with their work than their less well educated counterparts.[39]

Before we ask how much social mobility there has been in America, particularly during the years that access to higher education has increased; and how much these expanding higher educational opportunities have contributed to whatever mobility we discover, we must remember as Murray Milner has advised that it is essential not to confuse definitions of *mobility* (up or down) with those of equality, since our popular ideology frequently implies that economic growth itself automatically reduces inequality and thus increases social justice.[40] There can of course be economic growth accompanied by an increase in inequality—a situation in which the rich get richer and the poor get poorer. Inequality then is generally considered to deal with *relative* differences. Inequality refers to the overall shape of the socioeconomic pyramid and has nothing to do with the overall, absolute resources of a society. Consequently, the degree of inequality in a society that has a per capita income of $1,000 can be the same as in a society with a $10,000 per capita income. Mobility, on the other hand, is generally agreed to measure *absolute* upward or downward changes in the status of individuals or families. Now in a society that is dramatically unequal to begin with, there must be considerable upward *as well as* significant downward mobility in order to reduce inequality. It is not enough, therefore, just to have everyone experiencing upward mobility.[41] In fact, it is Milner's conclusion that though there has been a marked increase in the income level of all people and in the level of educational attainment through the years for all classes, the way income has been distributed has remained essentially unchanged. In other words, inequality has remained rather constant in the face of educational expansion because the basic structure of the social pyramid has not changed profoundly.[42]

Gabriel Kolko's well known *Wealth and Power in America: An Analysis of Social Class and Income Distri-*

bution[43] supports Milner's contention that there has
been little reduction in inequality despite general prosperity. He sees the distribution of income and wealth as
essentially unchanged since 1939 or even 1910: Though
low-income groups live better, their percentage of the
national income has remained much the same.[44] For
example, in 1910 the richest tenth of the population
received 33.9 percent of the national personal income
and the poorest tenth 3.4 percent. By 1959, the richest
tenth received 28.9 percent (plus considerable additional
"hidden income") while the poorest tenth earned only
1.1 percent.[45] Peter Blau and Otis Duncan, reviewing
1962 census data, see more basic change in the distribution of income through the years than does Kolko
(incidentally, largely the result of changes in the occupational structure itself—the shrinkage in the number of
low-level farm jobs plus the expansion of middle- and
upper-level white-collar jobs).[46] But they, too, assert that
during the last twenty years, during those years when
college enrollments increased most dramatically, the
rate of upward mobility increased only slightly.[47]

Christopher Jencks and David Riesman too, in their
now classic *Academic Revolution,* found little evidence
of any basic redistribution of wealth and power during
the course of this century. Primarily because the "elite,"
while paying lip-service to the idea of equalizing opportunities, take care to ensure that the opportunities
available to their children are in fact more than equal to
those available to everyone else.[48] They have taken great
pains, particularly through the construction of complex
and unequal systems of higher education, to protect
themselves against the perils of downward mobility. All
of this appears to be helped by a tacit agreement among
all classes that the misery of downward mobility is

greater than the frustration of upward aspirations. And in all of this, the expansion of community colleges has played a major role in the larger process of controlling mobility in both directions.[49]

If, as I claim, a principal hidden function of community colleges is to assist in channeling young people to essentially the same relative positions in the social structure that their parents already occupy, one would expect that community college students will come primarily from the lowest socioeconomic classes of college attenders, that the dropout rate among community college students will be the highest of any college population, and that these dropouts—or two-year-college graduates for that matter—will enter lower level occupations than equivalent students who attend higher status colleges. Indeed, what one expects to find is in every instance what one discovers after even a cursory examination of the community college experience.

The reality is that despite the rhetoric about "people's colleges" helping the lower classes to fulfill their aspirations, these "people's colleges" do not serve the "people." Claiming to offer opportunities for the children of workers, they have in fact served more middle-class, more high-ability groups of students than they would like to admit—and of course all the while, just as with the nineteenth-century high school, demanding for themselves financial support from broad-based state and local taxes. As Christopher Jencks shows us conclusively, upper-income youths are more likely to enter four-year colleges, *regardless of ability,* than even the most able lower-income students. But if they fail to go to a four-year college, those upper-income students in the lowest category of ability are almost as likely to attend a two-year college as the lowest-income students who score in the highest-ability category. A chart drawing on 1961 data makes all of this rather clear:

Proportion of Eligible Students Attending Two-Year Colleges[50]

Socioeconomic Quartile	Ability Quartile	
Men	Lower	Upper
Lower	.04	.25
Lower-Middle	.05	.23
Upper-Middle	.09	.30
Upper	.16	.38

More recent data from the Carnegie Commission on Higher Education also points to the same conclusions. Their study, *The Open-Door Colleges: Policies for Community Colleges* reveals that nearly 60 percent of community college students in 1966 came from families earning more than $7,500 per year.[51]

None of this should imply that either in terms of socioeconomic status or ability two-year-college students are *just like* four-year-college students; community college students tend to be both somewhat poorer and academically less able than senior-college students. The point is, though, that junior colleges are no more serving the needs of the poor than the high school in Beverly, Massachusetts, in 1860.[52] And it should be no wonder then that their most enthusiastic community-based boosters, as in Beverly, continue to be the most affluent citizens who obviously have the most to gain.[53]

And if the analysis is correct that the major hidden function of community colleges is to support the social status quo, one should also be not at all surprised that their dropout rate, particularly among their economically poorest students, is dramatically higher than at other colleges. Attrition then turns out *not* to be a problem, as just about everyone claims, but *to be one of the two-year colleges' primary social functions.*

Charles Monroe, author of an important new volume on community colleges, proclaims that a two-year college is *doing well* if 50 percent of its students return for a second year.[54] National dropout rates for junior-college students are generally agreed to range up to 75 percent during the course of the two years. There is authoritative evidence that at the City University of New York, open-admissions students (the poorest students of presumably lowest academic ability) are dropping out at an 80 percent rate during their first two college years.[55] Whereas the national rate of dropping out of four-year colleges during the course of four years is "only" about 50 percent.[56]

But this class-based dropout rate at community colleges is related to a rather deliberate process of channeling students to positions in the social order that are deemed appropriate for them; it also takes the pressure off four-year colleges and universities which would be inundated by applicants or transfer students if two-year schools didn't siphon away so many students or encourage so many to drop out. As is usual in these matters, one need only turn to such establishment spokesmen as James Bryant Conant or Amitai Etzioni or Spiro Agnew to discover the truth. Conant, as early as 1950, sees two-year colleges as functioning basically for social channeling: ". . . no young man or woman should be encouraged or enticed into taking the kinds of advanced educational training which are going to lead to a frustrated economic life." Two-year college programs are the

answer to "the possibility of having too many boys and
girls rush down one long professional road."[57] Twenty
years later, when the push for admission to college is at
its peak, Agnew quotes Etzioni: "'If we can no longer
keep the floodgates closed at the admissions office, it at
least seems wise to channel the general flow away from
four-year colleges and toward two-year *extensions of
high school* in the junior and community colleges'" (my
italics). And then chimes in: "And, of course, that is
what should be done."[58]

Another indication of how well community colleges
function to facilitate attrition is the body of evidence
which reveals that *the sheer fact of attending a two-year
college*—controlling for all other variables such as academic ability, family income, etc.—seems to increase
the likelihood of a student's dropping out. Alexander
Astin, the nation's foremost authority on the demo-
graphics of higher education, has come to this conclusion in a number of studies.[59] It seems that the more
selective a college, the less likely it is for a student to drop
out. And conversely "a student attending a college in the
low selectivity group . . . is about *two or three times*
more likely to drop out after his freshman year than is a
student of comparable ability attending a highly selective
college."[60] Specifically, the most selective colleges "lose"
only 10 percent of their freshmen who earn A—
averages while the least selective (community colleges)
"lose" 31 percent.[61] These findings make it clear that
the correlation between selectivity and dropping out is
not the result of the fact that highly selective colleges
recruit more able students than less selective colleges.
The truth is that the most selective colleges are committed to the success of their students whereas the least

selective open-door colleges are committed to their failure.[62]

As I've indicated, I went to a highly selective college. One of my roommates was a delightful but not brilliant chap from an elite Connecticut family. During our freshman year, the first any of us had been away from home, most of us sowed a few wild oats. Franklin, however, made a career of it, first pledging and later joining one of our fraternities—one that specialized in beer and swallowing goldfish. At the end of the year, he was called into the dean's office to explain all his D's and F's. The dean of course understood and gave him a second chance, particularly since he was a fine athlete and promised to join the track team as part of his rehabilitation. And with the same dedication with which he pursued drinking, he pursued the 440-yard dash—and with the same academic results. At his annual meeting with the dean he explained how track and swimming left him with little time for study. The dean understood again but put him on probation. During his junior year, Franklin settled down and earned his gentlemanly C's, bring his overall average all the way up to D+/C−. What to do with Franklin? Well, the dean conceded he might have been better advised to have recommended Franklin's dismissal a year or two earlier. But now, as he was about to enter his senior year, it would be heartless to take such drastic action. So Franklin went on to graduate. But there's more to the story. He wanted to go on to a graduate school. Which one would accept him with his disastrous academic record? As it turned out, no one would. But alma mater came to his rescue. Schools of this caliber pride themselves on their record of placing their graduates in professional schools; without that record they are doomed to sink to second-rate status. After all, anyone can give out B.A.'s. So they covered themselves by accepting Franklin into their master's program in business. Needless to add, he received his M.B.A. two years later and after a sojourn in the navy returned to Connecticut and his family's business. Obviously, equivalent community college students rarely encounter such institutional largess, especially since one of the roles of two-year colleges is to control the number of people who get B.A.'s.

The final thing to examine here is what happens to those young people who manage to graduate from two-year colleges or who go for a while and drop out. Do they in fact experience the meaningful social mobility that is promised them? Remarkable as it may seem, *the vast majority of these students might very well be better off if they never attended a two-year college.* With the exception of the few who eventually go on to get B.A.'s, (variously estimated at about 10–15 percent of those who aspire to), there is much evidence that, on average, both graduates and dropouts may actually experience *downward* mobility. At the very least there are many who believe that a community college education, in dollars and cents, is a poor investment. Two years of college is not worth the cost of tuition and delayed and lost earnings.[63] (See chapter 4 here for a full discussion of this last point.)

What a two-year education actually succeeds in doing is to provide *an illusion of upward mobility.* The substitution of one generation's white collar for the older generation's blue collar reflects changes in the occupational structure more than changes in the social hierarchy, if the relative position of the one who wears it remains constant. Going to a junior college *appears* to help fulfill the American dream, but it certainly is different from going to Princeton. John Gardner says that to call the two community college years the equivalent of Princeton's is like trying to market the front half of a Cadillac.[64] That's the reality. And that reality is the hidden function of community colleges.

High school graduates were not inclined to regard them as "real colleges," and many preferred to wait in the hope of attending a larger institution rather than become identified with the unappreciated junior college which seemed to them a mere appendage on the high school, even lacking the high school life and attractiveness.

—F. W. Thomas
1926

TWO

A HISTORY OF TWO-YEAR COLLEGES*

Standard histories of the two-year college invariably begin with numbers because numbers have come to be both the blessing and the curse of public higher education in America. We have been blessed, we are told, because it has come to pass that so many of us have been able to enroll in colleges and universities; never before in the history of the world has such a large percentage of a population participated in some form of higher education. But numbers have historically been a curse as well: What to do with so many people seeking forms of education traditionally reserved for a nation's social elite, and thus threatening to destroy the intellectual sanctity of the university?

At the beginning of this century just eight junior colleges existed, all of them "private," enrolling all of 300

*This first appeared in a modified version as "Second-Class Education at the Community College" in *From Class to Mass Learning* (San Francisco: Jossey-Bass, 1974) pp. 23–37.

students.[1] By 1975 more than 1,100 existed, most of them "public," enrolling more than 2,500,000 students. And the prospects are for continued growth in spite of evidence that *total* college enrollments are leveling off. A recent Carnegie Commission on Higher Education report, for example, calls for the establishment of between 230 and 280 new community colleges by 1980 for a total of about 1,400 enrolling up to 4,500,000.[2] The current recession, however, has slowed the construction of these new colleges (nothing much is being built these days), but it has not in the least curtailed the growth of student enrollments. The Office of Education forecasts nearly a half-million student increase for the 1975–76 academic year. Though the stock market has faltered, it is still a bull market for two-year colleges.

But as important as it is to point out this remarkable growth, it is equally essential to examine its pattern. Perhaps as interesting as understanding how we moved from three hundred students in 1900 to more than two and a half million in 1974 is attempting to understand how we moved from about one-half million students in 1950 to five times that many in less than twenty-five years because that is when the modern community college emerged. Also important to notice is how this geometric growth in two-year-college enrollments followed a similar growth in senior-college and university enrollments—because the growth of two-year colleges, as we will see, is intimately linked to the expansion of four-year colleges. In 1830 only one person in 3,200 was a college graduate. Forty years later, there were fifty-two thousand students attending colleges or 1.7 percent of the 18–21 age group. By 1890, 3 percent were enrolled and by 1900 4 percent of the college-age population, two hundred and thirty-eight thousand, were attending college.

Twenty years later, 1920, the percentage had doubled to 8 percent. College attendance then rose to 12 percent by 1930 and to 18 percent of the 18–21 age group at the outbreak of World War II. By 1964, over four million students or 40 percent of the 18–21 age group were in college. More recently we have shot by the 50 percent level with all of this incredible expansion in college enrollments proceeding much more rapidly than the rise in the total population.[3]

Even more interesting is to superimpose these two growth patterns: the parallel expansion of both senior- and junior-college enrollments. It becomes immediately apparent that the percentage of students beginning their college experience at two-year colleges (a new statistic) has also been increasing at a phenomenal rate. Some have estimated, for example, that two-year enrollments will increase from 29 percent of all undergraduates in 1968 to 41 percent by 1980. What this means is that by the year 2000, if current projected trends are realized (and in the community college business such estimates are usually conservative), up to 70 percent of all college freshmen will first enroll in college at a public community college.[4]

But it is essential to add that the history of two-year colleges has as much to do with "diverting" more and more students *away* from the university into some kind of other, *nonuniversity* postsecondary institution as it does with anything else. Even the most theoretical of the founding fathers of junior colleges foresaw and worried about the numbers.

Those theoretical fathers were not concerned with what came to be called junior colleges, quite the contrary; they were concerned about the university—the *real* university. Most of them had been to Europe, either having studied at or visited the great German universities of the mid-nineteenth century. And what they saw they liked. Enough, in fact, to want the same for their own country. When they returned home, they called for the establishment of American versions of the German model. Incidentally related but critical to the Germanization of the American university was the establishment of an American version of the German *gymnasium* or preuniversity preparatory school—the prototype of what was to become our own junior college. For the founding fathers, purging the university of the first two years of "college" work had nothing at all to do with extending higher educational opportunities to a wider public. What they were after was something they called the "pure" university for an intellectual elite interested in professions such as law and medicine or in a life of scholarship and research. In order to accomplish this, the university had to be freed from the burden of having to offer what they considered to be secondary-level instruction. To them it was more appropriate that this take place in a reconstituted high school. Only the most able would pass through the American *gymnasium* into the new university.

There is some dispute as to who was first to propose such a restructuring of American education, but it is generally agreed that it was Henry P. Tappan, president of the University of Michigan, who was most successful in articulating these new ideas. His *University Education* published in 1851, his inaugural address of 1852, his *Progress of Educational Development* in 1855, all extolled the German university and called for its establishment in America. In Germany he found "renewed, the freedom, the spirit, the ideal conceptions of the Greek schools; we find preserved in full energy the organization of the scholastic Universities; but in addition to this, we find the modern University placed in its proper relation as the culmination of a grand system of Education."[5]

Other presidents quickly joined Tappan in an effort to rid the university of its first two years of instruction. W. W. Folwell of the University of Minnesota, Edmund J. James of the University of Illinois, and William Rainey Harper of the University of Chicago (the "father" of the junior college) all believed that the first two years of the university belonged in the high schools where those preparatory subjects best suited to adolescent minds would encounter adolescent students. One of the deans of junior-college development in California, Alexis Lange, expressed this quite forcefully:

> The work of the first two years [of the university] as a matter of history and fact, is all of a piece with secondary education and should, therefore, be relegated as soon and as far as practicable to secondary schools. . . . [This means] the amputation of freshman and sophomore courses . . . and the relegation of these classes to the high school. . . . The result is a truncated and ineffectual, a nonfunctioning education, for most high-school graduates. [The upward extension of the high school would be] in the educational interest of the great mass of high-school graduates, who cannot, will not, should not become university students.[6]

If the truth be told, the idea to restructure higher education along German lines got nowhere. Virtually no university "amputated" its freshman and sophomore years, though a number tried—most noteworthily Stanford and Johns Hopkins. But they had to give up the idea which in virtually all instances had very little to do with academic decisions. Mostly it had to do with economic considerations—during hard times these schools needed the tuition money they collected from their freshman and sophomore students or the subsidies they received from the state for these students if they were public institutions. Athletics also had a good deal to do with ending the restructuring: how could a school compete in intercollegiate sports without two year's worth or half its quota of eligible students?[7]

Many universities, however, did at least grab half a loaf: though they may not have been able to amputate their lower divisions they did manage to make admission requirements more stringent. But essential to their becoming more selective was the creation of a new institution, the junior college. The concept as well as the name "junior college" began *within* the University of Chicago. Its president, William Rainey Harper, was an early advocate of amputation but perhaps saw its impracticality sooner than any of his colleagues. So what he proposed instead *and* implemented was the internal division of the University of Chicago in 1892 into two separate divisions, somewhat awkwardly called the "Academic College" and the "University College." The former offered the last two years of what many considered secondary or preparatory work; the latter offered the real thing as its name indicates. The names didn't stick but the idea did and by 1896 they were redesignated the "Junior College" and the "Senior College."[8] Harper didn't, however, like the new name "Junior College" any better and apologized for using it.[9]

Harper actually preferred the idea of high schools extending their offerings or (and this was a concept unique to him) of some of the smaller, weaker four-year colleges "decapitating" themselves—that is, he called for these schools to lop off their junior and senior years, thus transforming themselves into junior colleges.[10] But he was a practical man and thus worked simultaneously on all fronts to improve the intellectual environment of his *university*. Among other things, he got the University of Chicago's "Junior College" to offer its own degree—the nation's first Associate in Arts. Not so much to reward students for work well done but rather to encourage them to *"give up college work* at the end of the sophomore year" (my emphasis).[11] He felt that many students who "would have been served by withdrawal from college" continue on rather than face "the disgrace which may attend an unfinished course." If, therefore, you give them some kind of degree many may give up after two years, leaving only the most gifted to go on to upper-division and graduate work.[12] Thus Harper had an eye on the future.

He also worked very hard to get Chicago-area high schools to take on the responsibility of extending their offerings to include college-level work. If they would do so, the University of Chicago would be favorably disposed to accept such students with advanced standing, perhaps even admit them into the "Senior College." He worked tirelessly at this and his efforts culminated finally in the establishment of what many feel to be the first independent public junior college in Joliet, Illinois in 1902.[13] This college was, in fact, the result of the expansion of the Joliet high school.

The next two-year college was established in Fresno, California in 1910.[14] Just like Illinois, California had its William Rainey Harper; indeed it had *two* such men— Alexis F. Lange, dean of the School of Education at the University of California at Berkeley, and David Starr Jordan, president of Stanford University. For fifteen years prior to the 1907 legislation that allowed California

high schools to offer "post-graduate courses of study
. . . which . . . shall approximate the studies prescribed
in the first two years of university courses,"[15] Berkeley
and Stanford—prodded by Lange and Jordan—had been
trying to reshape themselves by separating their upper
from their lower divisions. The reasoning was the same
as that of those who wanted to create the "pure"
university: the university most appropriately should
begin in the middle of the traditional four-year scheme;
the work of the first two years is more naturally of a piece
with secondary education and should therefore be
relegated to the high school.[16] Unlike Harper, Lange
was unable to create his Joliet and had to settle for
a separation between lower and upper divisions at
Berkeley.

Lange credits President Jordan's articles and addresses
calling for "the amputation of freshman and sophomore
classes to prevent university atrophy and urging the
relegation of these classes to the high school" as what
was needed to make the public "sit up and take notice"
and to prod the schoolmen and the state legislature to
take the necessary initiative: "What had been a Berkeley
idea at the beginning had become a California idea, and
the spectacle of Berkeley and Stanford climbing the
Golden Stairs together, hand in hand, made its appeal
with great persuasiveness."[17] Jordan was, to use Lange's
language, a dynamic propagandist for the movement; he
was also, it would appear, a pioneer in public relations.
While Berkeleyites had been in the habit of speaking of
the "six-year high school" as the institution that was
essential to the purification of the university, Jordan
used and made popular the name "junior college" which
"proved much more potent in suggestible communities."[18]

Again all of this lobbying, which culminated in the 1907 legislation, had nothing at all to do with extending higher educational opportunities to the masses. Quite the contrary: it was all in the cause of making the university more exclusive. The story of the founding of California's first junior college in Fresno makes this all perfectly clear. In the spring of 1910, armed with the legislative sanction which had lain unused on the books for three years, C. L. McLane, superintendent of schools at Fresno, in the heart of the agriculturally rich San Joaquin Valley, began to investigate junior-college possibilities. Establishing a process still followed to this day, he consulted with the community via a circular letter explaining the concept to patrons of the high school. Over two hundred replies were received—not one of them unfavorable to the idea. And so in May of 1910 the Fresno Board of Education adopted a resolution to establish two years of postgraduate work in the high school. Although the 1907 legislation stipulated that such postgraduate work should "approximate the studies prescribed in the first two years of university courses," the Fresno Board slipped into their resolution that "technical work" should also be included in their post-graduate curriculum.[19] This critical addition may have been the result of Lange's influence: he was the earliest advocate of adding vocational education to the junior-college curriculum.

The Fresno resolution is interesting for other reasons as well; it is the first document I know of that stresses anything other than theoretical, structural reasons for the establishment of separate, locally based junior colleges, reasons that are as current as the recent reports of the Carnegie Commission on Higher Education which continue to call for low-tuition community colleges within commuting distance of virtually all Americans. The Fresno Board put it this way:

> There is no institution of higher education within two hundred miles of Fresno where students may continue their studies beyond the regular high school courses. Many of our high school graduates are but seventeen or eighteen years of age and parents are frequently loath to send these young people so far from home. Many who desire to continue their studies cannot afford the expense necessary to college attendance where the items of room and board mean so much.[20]

But if there is any doubt that the establishment of the Fresno junior college didn't also include "pure" university aspirations, the congratulatory notes from Jordan and Lange should make that clear as well. Jordan wrote from Stanford:

> I am looking forward, as you know, to the time when the large high schools of the state . . . will relieve the two great universities from the expense and from the necessity of giving instruction of the first two university years.[21]

Lange added from Berkeley:

> The state university has stood for the junior college plan for more than fifteen years, and its policy is to further the establishment of junior colleges in every way possible. The city of Fresno is to be congratulated on being the first city in the state to establish a junior college.[22]

And so they began, with Frederick Liddeke, a Harvard graduate who had just finished a year of graduate work in Berlin, as the first principal of both the high school and junior college (it was called "junior college" from the very beginning although it wasn't until 1917 that the term was incorporated into California legislation).[23] Three teachers were hired, one designated "Dean of the Junior College"—beginning a long line of such, who taught both within the high school as well as in the junior college. But they were careful not to get the college too mixed up with the high school; they only began with fifteen or so students and tried in every way possible "to impress upon students and the public at large the fact that serious work of distinctive college standard is being undertaken."[24]

There was no tuition, except to nonresidents who had to pay four dollars per month; and from the beginning, first-year courses at Fresno included agricultural studies as well as the ordinary freshman subjects. Right from the beginning, there was some difficulty in finding an appropriate name for vocational education at the two-year college. As early as 1918, for example, Lange wrote: "Probably the greatest and certainly the most original contribution to be made by the junior college is the creation of means of training for the vocations occupying the middle ground between those of the artisan type and the professions."[25] He called such education "culminal," which later somehow metamorphosed into "terminal" education. Nevertheless, this particular form of education didn't have a very difficult time becoming established. By 1917 in California there was the second junior-college act which put into law what had already been in practice. This legislation officially adopted the name "junior college" and provided financial support for junior-college districts on the same basis as the state supported high-school districts.[26] More important is the fact that the 1917 law extended the junior-college course of study to include the "mechanical and industrial arts, household economy, agriculture, civic education, and commerce." With this legislation, the junior college was given a new focus, and the movement entered what James Thornton calls its second period of growth—the period between 1920 and 1945 during which vocational programs expanded.[27]

This expansion was very effectively propagated by the American Association of Junior Colleges which was founded in 1920. The most clearly articulated purpose of this organization was to act as a cohesive force to give the young two-year-college movement the strength and prestige it needed to make an impact on higher education in the United States. It acted as a catalyst for change, in the words of Michael Brick, foremost historian of the AAJC, "prodding, promoting, and creating an image of the junior college as it was and as it could be."[28] But as it grew in size and power with the parallel growth of two-year colleges themselves, the AAJC began to have more and more influence upon the direction and character of the movement itself. It sponsored studies to define appropriate functions for junior colleges; it evaluated current practices; it published a widely read journal beginning in 1930; it lobbied in state legislatures and in Congress for the passage of legislation favorable to the AAJC's vision of what two-year colleges should be— particularly for legislation to support their technical and vocational curricula.

But before getting involved in sponsoring such legislation, it was necessary for the AAJC to resolve questions such as whether it was appropriate to even offer terminal programs in college—this in spite of the fact that such programs were proliferating. After all, leaders of the junior-college movement had expended a great deal of energy trying to convince students and the general public that two-year colleges were more than just extensions of high school—even though in fact that's how they began.[29] Wouldn't stressing vocational education at a time when junior colleges were just gaining public acceptance undermine all this hard work? Questions such as these were raised from the AAJC's very first organizational meeting. When the principal of the Chaffey Union Junior College of Agriculture in California insisted that junior colleges "must prepare young men and women for the most important vocations of their community," a number of battle-scarred veterans from the early days of fighting to establish junior colleges wondered out loud why the high schools couldn't handle this form of education. Why should the junior college touch it?[30]

Such discussions were a part of virtually every AAJC meeting through the 1930s and 40s before a number of ideas and events made it inevitable that the AAJC begin to take the leadership in promoting terminal education programs at junior colleges. A key idea was the concept of the "semiprofession." Somehow it seemed more appropriate for colleges to be training people for "semiprofessions" than for mere "occupations" or "vocations." A key event was the Depression. Not only did it result in many students being forced to attend junior colleges who ordinarily would have gone to more expensive four-year colleges, but many who did attend were attracted to the idea of a more practical education.[31] Still those members of the AAJC who felt that the junior college was basically an institution of higher education looked askance at the idea of their institutions playing such an inappropriate role.

But the movement was not to be thwarted. In 1940,

the AAJC received a $25,000 grant from the government's General Education Board to undertake a year-long "exploratory study of terminal education." The year's work produced a number of publications favorable to a terminal role for junior colleges and also a series of regional conferences, where, among other things, an understanding was promoted "through press releases, by parents and the public of the important nature of terminal education in the junior colleges."[32] The year's study also produced an additional grant—$100,000-plus from the General Education Board for a three-year continuation study. Again, a good deal of the money was spent on workshops designed to convince junior-college faculty and administrators that terminal education is "a legitimate function for the junior colleges."[33]

The Second World War also proved to be a boost for terminal education: formerly transfer-minded students now wanted even more terminal courses and the AAJC was there to encourage colleges to make the necessary adjustments in their curricula. The organization also became more actively involved in helping state legislatures draft appropriate laws that would allow junior colleges to expand their offerings, and as early as 1937, decided to press for revision of the federal Vocational Education Acts to allow federal funding for occupational programs in schools "of less than *senior-college* grade." (Note the revision of the language of the original Smith-Hughes Act of 1917 which allowed subsidies only for schools "of less than *college* grade."[34]) The AAJC had more success in the state legislatures than in the halls of Congress; it was not until the passage of the 1963 Higher Education Act that two-year colleges received any federal money for their vocational programs.

But money or not, the programs were well established.

The only problem was that so few students signed up for them (only perhaps a quarter of the student body). This in spite of all the lobbying, promoting, etc. the AAJC could manage.

Understanding this strange combination of success and simultaneous failure in the effort to shift the focus of the junior college is critical to an understanding of its true history—and for that matter to an understanding of the real meaning of the dramatic expansion of higher educational opportunities during this century. Because as Eells noticed more than forty years ago: "The development of the terminal function is an essential corollary of the success of" the expansion or democratization of higher education.[35] But is vocational, or if you prefer, "semiprofessional" training an actual fulfillment of the promise of upward mobility through postsecondary education, as is commonly claimed? Or is it, as I believe, a mechanism for diverting as many young people as possible away from the more advantageous liberal arts or transfer curricula? It seems to me to be more than a historical coincidence that precisely at those times when there has been a rush of students seeking admission to college (and before that to the high school) that there has also been a concurrent movement to create and promote vocational programs for these students.[36] To see how this has worked for the junior colleges, it is first necessary to go back a bit in time to trace briefly the early history of vocational education in America.

Since so much American educational history represents an expansion or extension of programs from lower to higher institutions one would expect, when working back from encountering vocational education at the college level, to find it first in the high schools. Not quite. In fact, vocational education in America began in the colleges *before* it got to the secondary schools—in the land-grant colleges in 1862, to be specific, following the passage by Congress of the Morrill Act. The legislation set aside thirty thousand acres of public land in each state to be sold in order to endow and maintain state colleges devoted to the agricultural and mechanical arts and to "promote the liberal and practical education of the industrial classes in the several pursuits and professions of life." They were the first in a series of "people's colleges." But before too many "people" arrived, they rather quickly came to resemble the aristocratic colleges to which they were supposed to provide an alternative. Very early in the game they actively sought to change both their image and purpose—and quite successfully. As early as the 1870s, merely a decade after they came into existence, a few stopped calling themselves "agricultural" colleges and rechristened themselves "state college" or "university."[37] As a much longer-range indication of this change in focus, by 1955 while enrolling only 20 percent of all students in degree-granting colleges and universities, they awarded 39.3 percent of all the doctoral degrees—nearly all of them in nonagricultural, nonmechanical subjects.[38]

As the land-grant colleges moved away from their original commitment, the high school moved into the vocational education vacuum. The early high school was decidedly nonterminal. It was clearly an intermediary step in the educational ladder between elementary school and college. In 1870, for example, eight out of ten high-school graduates entered college and six of them went on to receive degrees. At that time there were more than twice as many college graduates as people with high-school diplomas only.[39] An incredible statistic not even approached today at the height of our educational inflation. Of course relatively few in absolute numbers attended either high school or college, but these percentages dramatically indicate the exclusive college-preparatory function of the early secondary school.

But as high-school enrollments began to increase dramatically a second, vocational track came to join the traditional academic track. After 1880, census figures show a doubling of both total high-school enrollments and graduates for every decade that followed up through 1930. During those fifty years high-school enrollments increased from 110,000 to nearly four and a half million students. And by 1940, only 14 percent of high-school graduates went on to get B.A.'s, whereas in 1870, recall, 60 percent of all high-school graduates earned baccalaureates. It was during this boom in high-school enrollments in 1917 that the Smith-Hughes Act was passed and signed into law, the first federal vocational legislation. A number of things are worth noting about the Smith-Hughes Act, things that set precedents for all vocational education legislation to follow. First, it allocated funds only for high-school-level programs; and second, it insisted upon an impenetrable separation—*within* high schools—between academic and vocational tracks.

There was nothing inevitable about the establishment of this first dual-track educational system in America. There were alternatives presented and choices were made. For example, it was at that time that the concept of the comprehensive high school was first discussed—it wasn't discovered in the 1950s by James Bryant Conant or Admiral Hyman Rickover. John Dewey, for one, argued for such a comprehensive or "unit system" in which academic and vocational subjects would be intermingled; he saw this to be the only democratic method of organization.[40] The dual system won out, however, because the concerns of labor and industrial leaders predominated. They didn't trust traditional high schools which, they correctly felt, were not terribly interested in becoming involved in vocational education.[41]

So the Smith-Hughes Act stipulated that vocational programs must be administered separately from academic, or as they were then called, "general education" programs. Not only were funds provided solely for vocational programs, but the act was specifically worded to exclude from funding *any* program designed in whole or in part for credit that might eventually prepare one to begin a baccalaureate program. As Grant Venn points out, although American educators committed to an open educational system had always abhorred European tracking systems, by accepting the provisions of the Smith-Hughes Act they knowingly accepted a comparable tracking system of their own. In Venn's words "the student electing the vocational program after the ninth grade was severely limiting chances for continuing his education beyond the high school."[42] Thus ironically for many nineteenth-century educators who had looked longingly to the European "pure university" as an educational model, the European model of the tracking system was adopted instead.

The educators also got something else from Europe— hordes of immigrants and their children. These children became the largest group of new students during the first decades of the twentieth century and something different had to be done with them: they seemed less able than "native" students[43] and certainly they were less interested in the traditional academic curriculum. Vocational education was the answer. As Martin Trow has written, it was just the thing to "hold, at least fleetingly, the interest of [these] indifferent students whose basic interests lay outside the classroom."[44] The tracking that occurred as the result of the rise of vocational education in the high school, though, was not at all fully based upon those interests of students that allegedly "lay outside the classroom." Corresponding to the implementation of terminal education and the wave of immigration that spurred it on, was the development and increasing use of intelligence and scholastic achievement testing which offered an ostensibly unbiased means of measuring students' ability and the appropriateness of placing them in different tracks. There was also at the time the complementary growth of the counseling profession which allowed much of the channeling that occurred to proceed from students' own well-counseled choices. As Samuel Bowles and Herbert Gintis have pointed out, this added an apparent element of voluntarism to the tracking system.[45]

Later, when enrollments began to increase in the colleges, when it became apparent that waves of new students were threatening to swamp the colleges and universities as they had engulfed the high schools, the reaction at the college level was identical to that of the high schools before them—create a vocational track. But this time a little differently: create a second track *in a second institution*—the junior college. And again, as with the high school, there were alternatives and choices to be made. There was nothing inevitable about encouraging the expansion of junior colleges or the creation of terminal curricula within them. For example, the idea of the comprehensive four-year college was considered. And models existed for such institutions. As late as 1960, more than seventy-five thousand students were enrolled in subbaccalaureate programs in four-year institutions. In fact, at least 403 four-year colleges and universities offered occupational curricula of a subbaccalaureate nature. Indeed, in 1956, 44 percent of all subbaccalaureate students were attending four-year institutions; but by 1960, as community colleges pulled more and more "terminal" students to them, the percentage had shrunk to 30 percent.[46] To take up Dewey's argument for the establishment of comprehensive high schools, it would have been more democratic to have encouraged the expansion of comprehensive four-year colleges than to have shunted vocational programs, more and more, exclusively to the two-year colleges.

The Vocational Education Act of 1963 and the Higher Education Act of 1972 for the first time gave federal support to occupational education at the postsecondary level—more specifically to community colleges. With these acts the die was cast: it was no longer realistic to expect the development of more democratic comprehensive four-year institutions. Too much money was involved. The 1972 act, for example, allocated $850,000,000 over three years for postsecondary occupational education of the sort offered at community colleges as compared with less than one-third as much ($275,000,000) for academic community college programs. The language of the law contains echoes of the Smith-Hughes Act of some fifty-five years ago:

> The term "post-secondary occupational education" means education, training, or retraining . . . designed to prepare individuals for gainful employment as semi-skilled or skilled workers or technicians or sub-professionals . . . *but excluding any program* to prepare individuals for employment in occupations . . . to be generally considered professional or which require a baccalaureate or advanced degree.[47]

Just as the Smith-Hughes Act specifically excluded college preparatory courses and programs from funding, the 1972 act's exclusion of baccalaureate or transfer work reveals the governmental desire to fill manpower shortages in middle-level occupations more than a commitment to an open educational system.[43] Such legislation deepens the division between transfer and terminal education, a division many junior-college spokesmen regard as regrettable. And such funding leads to separate facilities and separate administrations for academic and vocational education and ironically may contribute to the low status currently assigned to vocational programs: separate-but-equal programs are no longer considered by many to be equal.

My contention is that the expansion of vocational education, first in the high schools (after an aborted beginning in the land-grant colleges) and then in the junior colleges, was more an ingenious way of providing large numbers of students with *access* to schooling without disturbing the shape of the social structure than it was an effort to democratize the society. What is important is the kind of education one gets, and vocational education is not the kind that leads to more social mobility.

I will be even so bold as to immodestly assert *Zwerling's law: As the rate of enrollment-increase in any educational system becomes geometric, a second vocational education track emerges.* We've already seen this occur at the high-school and college levels; and if the "law" holds we should soon be able to discover signs of a vocational track appearing at the graduate school level as educational inflation hits there. And indeed the signs are already there as the larger universities now contain graduate schools of journalism, business, hospital administration, social work, pharmacy, optometry, dentistry, etc.[49]

An unwitting witness for Zwerling's law is Phebe Ward, author of a book sponsored in 1947 by the AAJC, *Terminal Education in the Junior College.* She is an enthusiast for the spread of vocational education and most likely would not accept my conclusion that occupational education has unfortunately been used as a mechanism for social control. But she sees clearly the correlation between rapid increases in enrollments and the emergence of vocational education: "By 1939 . . . when the social and economic forces in the United States had succeeded in raising the enrollment in the high schools to seven million . . . American concern for the scope of the high school curriculum had . . . become aroused. So great was this concern that it resulted in the broadening and the enriching of the high school curriculum [read: vocational education was introduced] and the democratization of the high school."[50] Her date is off but her conclusions are correct. Now it is the colleges' turn: "The number of post–high school institutions has grown considerably, and the enrollments have increased proportionately. And along with this continuous growth, the same inquiring attention is now being concentrated upon these institutions and their curricula that was formerly focused upon high school offerings."[51] And so it came to pass.

The growing numbers that Ward in 1947 saw enrolling in postsecondary institutions were not just the result of the effects of the G.I. Bill. They had a great deal to do with the recommendations of another publication of 1947—the so-called Truman Commission Report, *Higher Education for American Democracy.*[52] It has been claimed that their findings were revolutionary, particularly their assertion that "at least 49 percent of our population has the mental ability to complete 14 years of schooling" and "at least 32 percent . . . has the mental ability to complete an advanced liberal or specialized professional education."[53] I consider their recommendation that the college and university enrollments double to 4.6 million students by 1960 hardly revolutionary and scarcely worth the controversy it elicited.[54] But what the commission in fact recommends conforms to Zwerling's law and thus is another example of how at times the more things change the more they stay the same.[55] First of all, the numbers they projected were just that— projections based upon then current trends—and so what they "recommended" was in the process of happening anyway. What they did, basically, was to give direction to this inevitable increase in enrollment. And that direction was to point these students toward the community colleges and more specifically toward their terminal programs: ". . . the Commission recommends that the community college emphasize programs of terminal education" to train students for the semiprofessions.[56]

If the Truman Commission in 1947–48 looked to 1960, the next presidential commission, the so-called Eisenhower Commission in 1960 looked to 1970. And what it saw was not very different. In its report, *Goals for Americans*, there is the recommendation that by 1970 up to 50 percent of the college-age population should be in college—up only 1 percent from the Truman Commission projection. It was also projected that up to 50 percent of these students would enroll in community colleges—with of course most of these students in vocational programs, because now for the first time terminal education was acknowledged by an "official" study to be the two-year college's primary function. Earlier junior-

college boosters such as F. M. McDowell, Leonard
Koos, Eells, even the Truman Commission, had always
listed the transfer function as number one.[57]

John Gardner wrote the chapter on "National Goals
for Education" for the commission. It is interesting to
note the differences in his recommendations for the high
schools and the colleges. By 1960 just about everyone
was attending high school and a goodly percentage were
graduating. The high schools were no longer the primary
institution for sorting and channeling students; that
honor, along with many other things such as trying to
teach students to read and write, had been passed along
to the colleges. So it is not surprising to find Gardner
officially recommending the establishment of comprehensive high schools. It is commensurate with his ideal
that each student "should be enabled to develop to the
full, in his own style and to his own limit." This requires
that there be a diversity of educational experiences to
"take care of the diversity of individuals" and that each of
these "experiences" should be "accorded respect and
stature"[58]—a year later, in a highly acclaimed book
Excellence: Can We Be Equal and Excellent Too?,
Gardner was urging equal respect for plumbers and
philosophers so both our pipes and theories would hold
water.[59] In these comprehensive high schools, students
of every ability level "sit in the same homeroom, play on
the same teams," etc.[60]

But when it comes to higher education, what he
recommends is a sharply stratified, segregated system. At
one extreme are the community colleges which "will
specialize in those educational plans (or potentials)
[which] are least ambitious." "At the other end of the
spectrum" are other institutions which will be for those
students headed for graduate study and professional

work.[61] Opening the college door a crack, then, doesn't seem to amount to very much.

Presidential commissions in the 1960s and 70s didn't have much time for higher education or the community colleges; they were preoccupied with "civil disorders," assassination, and the like. But there has been one commission on higher education in the 1970s in the tradition of the Truman and Eisenhower Commissions that has looked to the 1980s and beyond—the Carnegie Commission on Higher Education. Though not "official," it has probably been the most official unofficial commission in history. It has published more than one hundred reports and documents, many of them finding their way to the front and editorial pages of *The New York Times*—our official newspaper. The officialness of the Carnegie Commission is underscored by the fact that its original members, with one exception, were either major industrialists or highly placed college administrators. If ever a meeting of the power elite was held it was when these men (there was only one woman) sat down at the table together. As Alan Wolfe has written: "When they looked at each other across the table, each commission member saw a reflection of himself."[62]

Their report on community colleges is a slim but powerful document. If it seems strange that a report that in essence calls for more of the same (230 to 280 new community colleges by 1980, enrolling between 35 and 40 percent of all undergraduates), should have such impact, it should be remembered that it came out at a time when, among other things, the City University of New York was about to swing open the doors of its most elite senior colleges because the hallowed City College campus had been seized the summer before by a group of black militants. If this could happen at City College, what next? So for the Carnegie Commission to calmly ignore such demands that the doors to four-year colleges be thrown open and instead insist that open admissions extend *only* to community colleges was both comforting and influential.[63] All of what they recommend protects what already exists. And they know what exists and are explicit about it as they present evidence to show how our three-tiered higher educational system is socioeconomically stratified with upper-middle-class students most frequently attending elite four-year colleges and universities, middle-class students generally attending public four-year colleges, and working-class students— when they go—enrolling in two-year colleges.[64] But the commission does not stress this analysis nor does what they suggest amount to anything more than support for this three-track system. For example, they are totally opposed to community colleges striving to become four-year colleges, thus eliminating one track—the lowest.[65]

What is so special about community colleges that they must be thus protected at all costs? For among other reasons "they appeal to students who are undecided about their future careers and unprepared to choose a field of specialization." They reiterate this often enough to make one believe that if the community colleges are such good places for young adults to discover themselves, then that just about qualifies every eighteen-year-old for admission to a community college. And since at least as many freshmen at Harvard are uncertain about their future (law, business, college teaching, politics?) as two-year-college freshmen (elementary-/high-school teaching, secretarial work, the technologies?), one might conclude that these Harvard freshmen also would be better off at a community college. But the Carnegie Commission, of course, makes no such recommendation. Even by the year 2000 they see "only" 40–45 percent of all undergraduates enrolled in community colleges.[66] This means that the "top" students (even the uncertain ones) will continue to enroll at the prestigious four-year colleges; and since these top students will doubtlessly still come primarily from the most affluent families, higher educational systems will continue to underpin the social status quo. Even as staunch a friend of the commission as Lewis Mayhew feels that the Carnegie report could "have been prepared in the office of the American Association of Junior Colleges."[67]

Writing about earlier commissions as well, Mayhew points to the Truman Commission as perhaps the most influential, for he believes that it envisioned and may have helped produce the junior-college movement of the 1950s and 60s. Its influence was so great, he indicates, that its language has been incorporated into virtually every state master plan for higher education subsequently completed.[68]

Master plans often accurately set out a state's future educational intentions as well as tell in much detail what is actually going on in the schools. In most master plans for higher education, distinct functions for two- and four-year colleges are specified. The two-year institutions are set up to enable the majority of high-school graduates (or those merely over eighteen in some states) to have some form of postsecondary experience. As Arthur Cohen and Florence Brawer point out, the implication and the result is that these public community colleges do the preliminary sorting and screening of the students for the four-year colleges. They function to allow virtually all of the young people in a state to enroll but then pass on to the university only those who have proven themselves able to do college-level work. But in addition, often spelled out in these plans is the expectation that many (most) of the community college students will be shunted into terminal programs.[69]

The California Master Plan for 1960–75 may serve to illustrate this point. Its major recommendations relate to how to maintain and even further stratify their tripartite higher educational system—in which the junior colleges rest at the bottom with the state colleges in the middle topped by the elite units of the University of California. Disturbing symptoms are found to indicate that if current trends continue, by 1975 lower-division enrollments in the state colleges and the university will be increasing faster than enrollments in the junior colleges.[70] Therefore, students have to be "diverted" (their word) to the junior colleges so that by 1975 this trend will be reversed and lower-division enrollments in the colleges and universities will be lower than in the junior colleges.

These enrollment projections all relate to what are considered to be "appropriate" roles for the three types of institutions in the system. They reiterate the findings of an earlier study that defined them thusly: ". . . the junior colleges continue to take particular responsibility for technical curriculums, the state colleges for occupational curriculums, and the University of California for graduate and professional education and research."[71] And their recommendations also relate to how to deal with "The Problem of Numbers" (the subtitle to their chapter 4), or how to distribute students throughout the system. The democratic/meritocratic position is that the students will sort themselves out through the system on the basis of a fair competition based on ability and talent. But their proposal to "divert" fifty thousand students from the state colleges and the university to the junior colleges does not reflect meritocratic ideals; rather it reflects social imperatives which require fiddling with the numbers in order to fit the higher educational division of labor to the nation's economic division of labor. If the meritocratic process doesn't produce the required twenty technicians for each scientist or engineer,[72] then the meritocratic process has to be adjusted.

This proposed "diversion" is to take place according to what might be considered to be a *corollary to Zwerling's law: As the numbers increase and a vocational track is created, higher status institutions must be made even more selective.* In this way, it might be said, you get them coming and going.

This is how it works in California—the most emulated of our higher educational systems. First, decrease the percentage of high-school graduates eligible to enter the upper two tiers of the system: make 33$^{1}/_{3}$ percent rather than 50 percent eligible for the state colleges and 12$^{1}/_{2}$ percent rather than 15 percent eligible for the university.[73] Next, do a better job of "selling" the junior colleges, including telling students about how it's easier *to park* at the two-year institutions.[74] If necessary, set up further admission quotas. Finally, if all else fails and too many students keep seeping into the elite parts of the system, eligible students will have to be persuaded by "coercion" to attend the junior rather than the senior colleges. But divert them in any case, even if it proves to be "difficult and dangerous." And it must be done quickly to avoid "an atmosphere of clamor and controversy."[75]

This is perhaps the most blatant statement of the social-engineering role of education I've ever encountered. Here the system is nakedly adjusted to serve socioeconomic needs, all the while trying to make it appear that what results is natural—in this case the naturalness of the functions of the different kinds of colleges. In the language of double-think: "Achievement of *modified* projections [the "diversion" of students] . . . will place emphasis in the state colleges and the University of California on the divisional levels most appropriate to the defined functional responsibilities."[76]

Things were not much improved in 1973 when a joint committee of the California state legislature published their report. Actually, they perhaps had become worse because this committee *knew better.* They knew, for example, that "the three-tier system [may be] . . . inherently racist because socioeconomic and cultural conditions in the early experience of minority persons leave them unable to measure up to the admissions standards of the four-year segments."[77] They knew about the regressive way in which the system redistributes money among different classes (from, at least, my correspondence with the chairman, John Vasconcellos). They even flirted with proposals that would make the system more equal (establish open admissions to all of the segments), but they were paralyzed both by politics (anything meaningful would be unacceptable) and a case of intellectual relativity which saw the current educational options as at least valid enough to continue. All of this impelled them, at least, to hope for the best: "Hopefully, every institution of higher education in California will strive always to facilitate each student's learning to the very fullest of his or her potential."[78] But hoping was not enough, particularly when they continued to advocate the earlier admissions ratios—12$\frac{1}{2}$ percent, 33$\frac{1}{3}$ percent, etc.—and even, "if circumstances permit," the elimination of the lower divisions of the state colleges and university. Apparently, the vision of the pure university is still alive and well in California.[79]

And things have not been much better in New York

State which has always prided itself on being somewhat different, a little more progressive than California. But just what this difference has been in New York with regard to public higher education is not all that apparent. New York did not get around to establishing a state university until 1948 (largely because of the powerful resistance of the state's great private colleges and universities), but New York's state university has not turned out to be very different from California's. It is equally stratified; and, in its inception, perhaps more consciously so. In California, at least, the junior colleges began pretty much as transfer institutions. But in New York, early legislative documents studying the feasibility of establishing a state university and more recent master plans articulate as emphatic a terminal role as possible for New York's two-year institutions. The 1948 *Report of the Temporary Commission on the Need for a State University*, for example, estimated that by 1960 the state would need additional facilities for ninety-one thousand full-time students "of whom 80,000 would be enrolled in terminal courses"![80] It is only as an afterthought that transfer programs are mentioned: "Although the community college should be designed primarily for students not seeking the usual four-year curriculum, it should provide sufficient general education to enable qualified students to transfer to four-year institutions."[81]

As in California, the 1970s in New York State are not much better than the 1940s. But again what is distressing is that the most powerful educational policy makers *know better*. The 1972 Regents Plan is an unhappy example of this. Cynically, the regents pretend to be upset by the fact that the state's senior colleges and universities have been compelled to limit admissions to a more and more "elite group of students" because of "fiscal restraints and space limitations." One result, the authors sigh, has been that the socioeconomic background of public college and university students has come to "roughly parallel" that of students in the private colleges and universities of the state.[82] They can't seem to understand why the state university is becoming so socially stratified, even though they cite statistics which reveal community college enrollments increasing nearly twice as fast as those of the senior colleges—up 438 percent between 1961 and 1971 as compared to "only" 245 percent in the four-year schools during the same decade.[83] Just as in California they, too, propose that the state's senior institutions should reduce the size of their lower-division enrollments.[84] In fact, they even go so far as to recommend the creation of perverse new kinds of what can only be called *four-year two-year* colleges— "upper-division technical centers"—which would help absorb some of the flood of successful transfer students who will soon be pouring out of the community colleges demanding access to the state's universities.[85] Thus the rhetoric and the reality of state master plans.

A final example of how systems of higher education reflect employment rather than educational concerns is the 1968 master plan of the City University of New York. It was the plan that mapped out CUNY's first version of open admissions. A scenario that had to be rewritten thanks in no small part to the occupation of City College's campus by students in 1969. But it still serves to illustrate how a system plans for *and then rationalizes* the channeling of its students. The plan begins by claiming that by 1975, 21 percent of the jobs in New York City will require a B.A. or graduate degree.[86] Though this is to say the least a somewhat dubious estimate, it curiously corresponds rather too closely to their assertion that 25 percent of high-school graduates "are considered . . . to have the ability to achieve a baccalaureate degree."[87] Thus ability and job requirements exist in a natural harmony. But just to make sure it all turns out that way, it is proposed that the admissions standards be juggled in ways to assure that only 19 percent of the high-school graduates in 1975 will be eligible for the senior colleges (up only 3 percent from 1967) whereas community college enrollments will be allowed to shoot up from 11 percent in 1967 to 26 percent by 1975.[88]

Clearly as CUNY moved toward open admissions, community colleges were to play an increasingly significant role in channeling growing numbers of B.A.-aspirants into middle-level jobs. Channeling works *within* community colleges as well. First by accepting only appropriate percentages of applicants into the various career programs: only 51.5 percent of those who apply for technical curricula, 30.8 percent of the business applicants, 35.1 percent of the health career applicants, etc.[89] And second by guiding or counseling transfer students into vocational programs so that at least a fifty-fifty ratio is maintained between transfer and terminal curricula. Thus the miracle of open admissions.[90]

In summary, then, it could be that a foreign visitor of forty-five years ago saw things much more clearly than most of us when he wrote that America's two-year colleges assured our enjoying the "best half-educated" people in the world.[91]

All institutions cool students out, but the junior college is unique in that it offers these students alternatives to failure. . . . Though it is not listed as an objective in the college catalogue, changing transfer students to terminal students is one of the unique and most important tasks of the junior college.

—Robert Fitch
1969

THREE
COOLING-OUT: THE ROLE OF COUNSELING

This history, these acknowledged and more so these unacknowledged social functions of community colleges have human consequences. I remember Julia who came to Staten Island Community College from one of Manhattan's better public high schools. When she had gone to her guidance counselor during her senior year, he asked her what she wanted to do. She said she wanted to be a doctor. He told her that she should be realistic: "You're black, you're a woman; your IQ isn't too high (though I can't tell you what it is because it would upset you). Why don't you become a medical lab technician? That way you'll be able to work with doctors in hospitals."

So she came to Staten Island—an hour and a half each way from her home in Harlem by subway, ferry, bus, and a long walk—because we have one of the best med tech curricula in the City University. But after part of one semester, taking such things as "The Fundamentals of Blood Banking" (Med Tech 1), she went to see one of our counselors because little of this seemed related to what she still really wanted to study—medicine. He, too, told her she should be realistic: she was black; she was a woman; her placement test scores weren't too high; she should continue in the medical technology curriculum.[1]

When she came to see us about participating in a special program to prepare students for transfer to fine four-year colleges, we asked her what she wanted to do and she told us that although she liked medicine *she had to be realistic*: "After all, I'm black; I'm a woman; I'm not too smart. I guess I want to be a medical lab technician."

If one of the community college's unstated functions is to channel its students away from the high-status professions while simultaneously helping to reconcile them to middle-level jobs because the limited room at the top of the work hierarchy is to be preserved for the graduates of elite four-year colleges and universities, then this was an instance in which Staten Island Community College had been perversely effective. At least to that point; for after another year with us in a special transfer program, Julia went on to Middlebury College and then, after receiving her B.A., to graduate school.*

But this last part of her story is unusual, for there are many more unhappy human consequences of community colleges' history and hidden functions. A couple of summers ago Ivan Kronenfeld and I established another special program to work with a group of students who had been academically dismissed. Our plan was to work with them during the year to help them prepare for reentry to the college and futuré academic success. We

---

*While at Middlebury, Julia changed her major from pre-med. to political science—in part because of her difficulties with the pre-med. sciences, in part because of new interests.

openly acknowledged that among other things we would be trying to demonstrate that the college had failed them, that they were not incapable of succeeding at S.I.C.C. as their academic dismissals asserted. To select the group we interviewed many of the seventy-seven students who were dismissed in June 1971. They were a remarkable group of people. The first thing that was remarkable about them was that there were so few of them. More than 60 percent of the students who had entered S.I.C.C. the previous semester (September, 1970) had either left or were in serious academic difficulty. Over 51 percent of our lower freshmen had, at that time, less than 1.25 grade point averages (D+'s). This 51 percent numbered more than seven hundred students. Obviously, most would never graduate—they needed at least a 2.00 G.P.A. One would imagine that we would be doing a snappy business in academic dismissals. But hundreds of students saved us the trouble by either withdrawing or, much more commonly, by simply disappearing.

We met with more than half of these seventy-seven to tell them about the program and also to get them to tell us the stories not revealed by their computer-printed transcripts, the "whys" behind the D's and F's. For two weeks we sat through a series of horror stories that often left us weeping or quivering in anger. One older student told us how he had either failed or been forced to withdraw from Intermediate Accounting three times while at the same time more than doubling his salary *as an accountant* at Sears, Roebuck (we wondered about how well we were preparing students in our career programs). Another student told us how he had been dismissed because "they" had added his grades to his father's transcripts, also a student at S.I.C.C., and how the combined grades earned them *one* academic dismissal (we wondered about the wonders of our highly-regarded computer system and how it is programmed to free teachers and counselors to have more time to work individually with students). One student told us how she had missed some final exams the year before because of a series of serious operations and how some of her instructors refused to give her make-up tests (we wondered why some of our teachers were earning at that time some of the highest salaries in the history of college teaching—up to $31,500 for full professors). Another student told us he did poorly because he often didn't have the money to get to Staten Island from central Brooklyn—at the current rate, $2.10 per day round trip (we wondered about the way scholarships and financial aid were allocated). One student told us how when he went for personal counseling, before he could get very many words out, he was told remedial reading was what he needed to improve his grades, when in fact the reason he was having difficulty studying was because his father had recently died and he had to take care of his mother who had cancer (we wondered how we had prided ourselves on our unique student-centered counseling programs).

After listening to these stories—even assuming some may have been exaggerated—we asked each of the students to answer the question: "If you had one person, one thing, one series of events to blame for your lack of academic success, who or what would you blame?" Thirty-nine of the forty people we spoke with said it was *their own fault*. Again we at S.I.C.C. had been remarkably effective. If we had failed to teach them accounting or English or psychology we had succeeded in teaching them that we (the institution) had given them every chance, done everything possible to help them, and if they had failed it was either because they were "dumb" or "lazy" (words they frequently used) or they had not taken advantage of the many opportunities available to them.

The basic process by which this reconciliation to disappointment and failure happens has been called "cooling-out." It is most clearly on display within the total higher educational system, particularly at community colleges, and is our society's best mechanism for protecting itself from the consequences of the false promises of one of our fundamental myths—the myth of Horatio Alger. This myth tells us that we can go from a log cabin to the White House; that from a humble beginning selling newspapers on a Chicago street corner we can end up chairman of the board of U.S. Steel; that we can grow up in a tenement on the Lower East Side of New York and still become a full professor at Columbia. And although we all know there is only one president at a time, only a handful of chairmen of boards, and only a few thousand full professors at schools such as Columbia, the myth of course tells us something else. It does stress, though, that the competition for the best places in society is open and fair. Or at least *seems* to be. The appearance of openness and fairness are essential since people who fail must believe that they have had an honest chance. This is crucial, for if they cannot come to accept responsibility for their failure the country will find itself with a lot of social dynamite on its hands which is apt to blow up. We have had such explosions in our society, none fatal to current structures to be sure, but dangerous nonetheless.

The myth of social mobility is paralleled by and intertwined with the myth of schooling. The social myth tells us that in our democracy, unlike other societies, our background (socioeconomic status) does not doom us. If we have ability, we can rise to the top, with school as the arena in which this struggle of competing abilities takes place. Here we are fairly judged by objective criteria: IQ testing, precise grading on a curve that scientifically mirrors the natural distribution of ability—all monitored by professional administrators, teachers, and counselors. But as I have shown in the preceding chapter, if there is only so much room at the top only a very limited number can be allowed to succeed. And in addition, those who are allowed to succeed are by no means the most able (as the myth would have it). As Samuel Bowles and Herbert Gintis have amply demonstrated, success is *in*signifi-cantly related to IQ (or traditionally measured academic ability). Success is more class-related, with schools facili-tating rather than reducing the transmission of privi-lege.[2] All of this means many disappointed people, especially those who have a good sense of their own real ability and still find themselves failing. Particularly for these people, cooling-out is essential. As Burton Clark first described it, cooling-out relates to one of democra-cy's major problems:

> . . . the inconsistency between encouragement to achieve and the realities of limited opportunity. Democ-racy asks individuals to act as if social mobility were universally possible; status is to be won by individual effort, and rewards are to accrue to those who try. But democratic societies also need selective training institu-tions, and hierarchical work organizations permit increas-ingly fewer persons to succeed at ascending levels. Situa-tions of opportunity are also situations of denial and failure. Thus democratic societies need not only to moti-vate achievement but also to mollify those denied it in order to sustain motivation in the face of disappointment and to deflect resentment.[3]

Cooling-out attempts to lower the aspirations of individuals who have made the mistake of aspiring too high. Clark sees cooling-out to be particularly important for community colleges since so many of their students have "unrealistic" aspirations. For example, up to 75 percent say they eventually want to earn B.A.'s, but only one-fourth or one-third of these ever even go on and transfer to a four-year college. Many say they want to be teachers, but they may only read on the eighth-grade level. Cooling-out is the gentle if deceitful process of guiding these "latent terminal" students (Clark's felicitous phrase for transfer students who should be in vocational programs)[4] into programs more in line with their real potential. These students need to be convinced that they are not capable of undertaking a more extended college education. But since community colleges stand for open access and free choice of curriculum, the students *themselves* must make the decision to adjust their levels of aspiration.[5]

How is this to be done? Counselors play the key role here. Low test scores will indicate the need for remedial courses. A counselor will guide students toward these courses, convincing them, if necessary, that remediation is available to help improve their basic skills. But these courses are not actually to help students improve their skills; they are in fact designed to "cast doubt" on the students' feelings that they can do "bona fide" college work. If students are still not convinced, the counselor should continue to work with them to help them accept their limitations in the face of mounting evidence—the inevitable accumulation of poor grades. If students still persist, they should be put on probation—the real meaning of which, he indicates, lies in its killing off the last hope of some of the latent terminal students.[6]

Hopefully, latent terminal students will remain in school long enough to benefit by being cooled-out and switch to terminal or career programs, although the dropout statistics reveal that less than a majority do.[7]

When students finally accept the reality of their limitations and switch to a vocational curriculum (or drop out), they will believe that the system did everything it could for them and whatever difficulty or failure they experienced was their own fault. It is critical that this process "remain reasonably latent," i.e., hidden from both the students and their parents, otherwise it will be difficult to convince either that the cooled-out students have been through a democratic process.[8] But if everything works according to plan, the general result of cooling-out is that society can continue to encourage maximum effort from its student-citizens without major disturbances that might otherwise result from their unfulfilled promises and expectations.[9]

This cooling-out is a very vulgar process much more suited to the late 1950s and early 1960s. Today, it seems, we require more sophisticated versions of the same thing. For example, in a little book designed as an "Orientation for the Junior College Student" the apotheosis of the psychologically mature student who has found independence is "Student A" who has been successfully cooled-out of his desire to become an engineer. With the help of his counselor he escapes from parental manipulation (it is *their* desire that he become an engineer) and decides that his needs and purposes would be better served by studying engineering technology at a junior college.[10] The insidiousness of the book is such that it does not contain one example of a student who underaspires and then, with the help of his/her counselor, finds independence through the release of his/her true potential.

The process that Clark describes for higher education is actually the elaboration of an earlier idea of Erving Goffman's.[11] Goffman wrote about how con men cool out their victims (marks) in order to prevent the victims from turning them in to the police. They do this by trying to reconcile them to their loss of status (money) and self-esteem. One technique they use involves offering the victim "a status which is different from the one he has lost or failed to gain, but which provides at least something for him to become. The alternative thus presented is usually a compromise of some kind, providing him with some of the trappings of his lost status as well as some of its spirit."[12] Student A's cooled-out "choice" of engineering technology has some of the trappings and spirit of engineering but very little of its status—or salary.

Having mentioned Goffman, I feel it is important not to leave the impression that he is advocating the cooling-out of victims of social institutions. Quite the contrary. When he describes the cooling-out of the mark, he tells how the scheme the mark is enticed to join seems to him to be *rigged in his favor*—that's why he joins—whereas it is actually rigged against him. (Note the parallel feeling that students have about the schools—the schools are there to help them achieve all they're capable of achieving.) Cooling-out involves dealing with the problems that follow from the mark's discovery of the truth. It is a means of dealing with *a deceitful, manipulated reality.*

The ideological foundations for cooling-out were established very early in the history of the community college movement by one of the founding fathers we've already encountered, Alexis Lange. Even at a time when community colleges were only offering college-parallel courses, he was advocating the establishment of programs in the applied arts and sciences. In 1915 he wrote that junior colleges should provide vocational education for the "cannot's, will-not's, and should-not's." Vocational programs "might render a great service to the universities and to thousands of young people by diverting these from the universities and thus preventing their becoming 'misfits' for life."[13] This "diverting" inexorably leads Lange to the conclusion that "the junior college will function adequately only if its first concern is with those who will go further, if it meets local needs efficiently, if it turns many away from the university into vocations for which training has not hitherto been afforded by our school system."[14]

Twenty-five years after Lange, Carl E. Seashore, still writing ten and twenty years before Goffman and Clark, adds to Lange's amorphous notions of cooling-out. Seashore's very influential *The Junior College Movement* is laced with assumptions about junior colleges and their students that make it inevitable for a Clark to explicitly define cooling-out twenty years later. At a time when there wasn't the recent push to universalize higher education, Seashore saw the four-year college or university as preparation for "scholarly erudition" or the professions of law, medicine, theology, etc. The junior colleges were for those students interested in a two-year terminal education geared to a "practical life." But there was a problem: although he saw the junior college as a terminal institution, students saw it differently. Even at that time, up to 80 percent of them enrolled in transfer curricula while only 20 percent seemed to choose the practical terminal curricula. Seashore advocated a reversal of this ratio, with the unstated implication that this new ratio would reflect both the way intellectual ability is actually distributed among people and the way work— from the professions down to unskilled labor—is naturally represented in our society.

It was not a very big step to Seashore's version of cooling-out: "The junior organization . . . becomes a clearing house for the . . . [university] as a whole. Very important in this procedure is the early and *sympathetic elimination* of those who soon show that they cannot profit by any form of college education offered" (my italics). Students are eliminated for their own good "because there are countless areas of training in which he can meet with success that he could not get" as a transfer student. This elimination or shift from transfer to terminal program should be done as early as possible in "a kindly spirit and with sympathetic guidance." Professors and counselors should not try "to make gold out of iron"—the impossible alchemy of overaspiration.[15]

Assumptions that underpin cooling-out pervade *This Is the Community College,* a more recent but at least as influential a book as Seashore's, written by Edmund J. Gleazer, President of the American Association of Junior Colleges. In Gleazer's view, the community college's role is to extend educational opportunities through the fourteenth grade. But there is a warning: community colleges should not become hung up on the prestige attached to the college stereotype in our culture; they should not just be places that only offer "courses preparatory to other courses." A section of this book is called "The Two-Thirds Who Will Not Transfer." The problem, as Gleazer sees it, is that community college programs and procedures often are based upon the assumption that most students will transfer, whereas the reality is that although 75–80 percent say they want to transfer, two-thirds do not. Since the assumption is not supported by the facts, neither are the educational structures that are built upon it. Gleazer points out that no one knows in advance whether students will be in the one-third or the two-thirds until after the fact—that is, until they transfer or do not.[16] With the impetus of such a reading of the facts, cooling-out is put into motion— and justified.

The problem, however, is not to find earlier and better ways to distinguish the one-third from the two-thirds; the problem is *the assumption* that this ratio is immutable and inevitable. The chapter title has the power of an imperative: "The Two-Thirds Who *Will Not* Transfer." It's like an old state university orientation exercise I once witnessed: freshmen gathered together for the first time, sitting nervously in the auditorium, were told to look at the student sitting on their left and then at the student sitting on their right. "Take a good look at them because one will be gone by the end of the first year and the other will be gone before you graduate." The problem is, of course, that you were being looked at too and were a part of someone else's ratio of "success." This is the predicament of the current community college student if Gleazer's imperative is to continue to function as a cruel self-fulfilling prophecy. Gleazer is too quick to start looking for jobs for the two-thirds. And jobs of course mean the "new occupations," "semi-professional positions," "the public services,"[17] all relegating these new workers to continued low-status lives.[18]

During the 1950s and 1960s just as the pressure was most intense to admit more students to college, it was not a coincidence that college faculty began to abandon their negative feelings about counseling and counselors.[19] And it is no coincidence either that the federal government at the same time came to officially endorse counseling, declaring it essential for the identification of talent and human resources.[20] In order to maintain academic standards, and of course maintain the privilege and value of the B.A., instructors were forced to fail more and more students. Without a counselor mediating between them and their failed students (employing the techniques of cooling-out), college teaching—always rather gentle and clean-handed—could become rather unpleasant in open-door institutions. Counseling left instructors free to "objectively" apply their academic standards without thinking about the channeling function of higher education and its social implications. They could leave this to the counselors who would follow Clark's guidelines, using the low grades of students to drive home the message of cooling-out.

On occasion, cooling-out has even found itself embodied in various state laws. The Illinois Public Junior College Act, for example, stipulates that students admitted to the transfer curricula of state two-year colleges are supposed to have "ability and competence similar to that possessed by students admitted to state universities."[21] To be sure, the public community colleges of Illinois consider themselves to be open-door institutions; but the act states only that students be admitted to college, not to the transfer program. Once at the college, the act requires counselors to cool students into appropriate programs: "After entry, the college shall counsel and distribute the students among its programs according to their interests and abilities."[22]

It is often claimed that the role and techniques of counseling have undergone considerable metamorphosis since the early days. It is asserted that Clark's concept of cooling-out has been both soundly criticized and even abandoned. But has it? In fact, most of the new forms of counseling are the old cooling-out decked out in a new wardrobe.

While it is a rare counselor who finds his/her way directly to Goffman or Clark for guidance, most belong to the American Personnel and Guidance Association and along with membership they get *The Personnel and Guidance Journal.* In 1967 Lora Simon distilled Goffman and Clark for community college counselors so they could learn techniques for cooling-out that were at least implicit in the earlier works I've examined. Her article, "The Cooling-Out Function of the Junior College," summarizes Goffman and Clark and is, in fact, a how-to manual for overworked counselors. Things are dressed up a little: in place of what Clark calls "latent terminals" we have "'would-be' transfer students";[23] but she, too, accepts the inevitability of massive failure as expressed in the familiar statistics that show how few transfers actually transfer and how few late-bloomers actually bloom— "these cases are few and far between."[24] The counselor must get students to begin "thinking-along-new-lines" since they are apparently too paralyzed by their own failures to motivate themselves. The goals or results of effective cooling-out might include helping "the girl who fails to gain entry into a school of nursing . . . find her way into a medical secretarial program" (remember the importance of retaining "some of the trappings"). It might also include helping failed students who continue to insist that they remain in college find their way to an "academic Siberia" where they can be successful. Perhaps effective cooling-out might also involve the counselor and the failed students entering into a face-saving (for whom?) "tacit understanding" that the students are leaving of their own accord.[25]

And lest anyone assume that cooling-out merely exists in the literature of community colleges, I can testify that the practice is alive and well, literally throughout America. I have witnessed many of its forms at dozens of different places. Only occasionally is it as blatant as the example I cited at the beginning of the chapter—Julia learning to be "realistic" about her aspiration to become a doctor. Subtler methods are the rule.

It's obviously not easy to sit in on and observe an actual counseling session: a third party tends to violate the intimacy and trust of the encounter. But two years ago I had the opportunity to spend a day with the counselors of an Illinois community college, reviewing with them videotapes they had prepared of some of their sessions. They had taped frequently enough so that in what we saw both counselors and clients seemed relaxed and natural.

One tape (of course condensed here) showed a student coming into the rather stark counseling cubicle, somewhat bemused, holding on to a handful of papers. The counselor half rose out of his chair and motioned to the student to sit down opposite him; a small table separated them.

"Hello, I'm Professor Schorr. What can I do for you?"

The student fiddled with his papers, appearing a little nervous about the whole thing. "Well, my faculty adviser told me to take this aptitude test because I don't know what I want to major in." He passed the results of the Kuder Occupational Interest Survey across to Professor Schorr.

"Oh, you're Ralph Paldino. Fine. Let me see what's doing here. You're in the liberal acts curriculum, I see. How long have you been here?"

"I'll have completed twenty-seven credits by June."

Not looking up from the Kuder profile. "I see. That's good. I see you're strong in Personnel Manager, whatever that is, and Social Case Worker. How are you doing academically?"

"Well, I figure I'll have about a two-point-five average by June."

"That's not bad. Wait, let me get a copy of your transcript." Shaking his head, "I don't suppose you brought one with you? No? Okay, I'll ring Mrs. Fitzgerald and ask her to bring a copy."

He does and while waiting for it they talk about how cold it's been this spring. Ralph mentions he's on the baseball team and they haven't yet been able to practice outdoors. "Oh, yeah, what position do you play?"

"Third base."

"That's great, great." Professor Schorr appears to be about thirty-five, hair modishly long, nearly covering his ears. He's wearing a light-weight turtleneck shirt and a plaid jacket. The student is in sweatshirt, jeans, and sneakers. "Did you play in high school? By the way, where'd you go?"

While the student is filling him in, there's a tap at the door; it's the secretary with the file. The counselor flips through it. "Oh I see you went to Central. A lot of our students come from there. Did you ever have Mrs. Bennett for math? I hear she's quite something." Still looking at the folder, "I see you're taking psychology this semester; you got a C at midterm. But you're not doing *that* badly. How do you like it?"

"Well you see that's one of the things I'm thinking

about, psychology. I really like the course and the teacher and I'm thinking about maybe being a psych major—after I transfer that is—because it doesn't look like we have that many psych courses here. But I don't know." He's looking down at his hands which have remained in his lap.

"I don't know either. The Kuder, which by the way is not the gospel or anything like that—it merely gives one an indication of possible interests and aptitudes, the Kuder though doesn't have you too strong in any of the Psychologist scales. And I can tell you there aren't all that many places in graduate school in psychology. I can tell you that from personal experience. You need, by the way, at least an M.S.W. or a Ph.D. to do anything in psychology." From the tape it was not clear if Ralph knew what an M.S.W. is.

"Well, I think I'd really like working with people. I don't really want to be stuck in an office or something like that for the rest of my life. You know?" He looks up across the table for the first time.

Professor Schorr glances quickly at his watch. "Pretty nearly everyone who comes through here these days seems to want to work with people. I just don't know what we're going to do with all of them. There just aren't that many kind of jobs any more. Teaching you can pretty much forget, except maybe for special ed. And even that . . . . " Looking again at the results of the Kuder and apparently at Ralph's transcript. "Ralph, it seems to me that you might try to get some tutoring because what you're talking about is going to require better than a two-point-five."

"Well you see, I work at McDonald's four days a week after school and all day Saturday and I just can't find enough time to do my best."

"But I think they can help you at the tutoring center. They're your fellow students, you know, who've done well in school and help people who aren't doing that well. I'd give it a try." He buzzes Mrs. Fitzgerald again, "Is my ten-thirty there yet? Okay. Tell her to wait; I'll be done in a few more minutes." Turning back to Ralph, "Now where were we. Oh, yes, you're going to think about getting some tutoring. Also, you know we just began a new curriculum here for people who want to work in mental health centers, nursing homes, things like that. The money's not bad, and there are plenty of jobs. It sounds to me it might interest you from what you tell me. Why don't you think about seeing Doctor Baliff who's the head of it. She's someplace in the A building." He looks through the school directory. "Yes, A-three-o-three. Tell her you talked with me. She's very nice. What do you think?"

"Well, I don't know. I'm really confused. I thought taking the test would straighten me out a little. But I'm still confused. I don't really know about that curriculum you're talking about. It sounds okay, but I'm just not sure it's what I want."

"You never know until you check it out. And by the way, it's quite natural for someone in your position to not know what they want to do. But I will tell you, it's very important that you begin to make plans for your future. It's rough out there in the real world." The counselor smiles. "And the sooner you get started the better for you. I'll tell you what, why don't you come back and see me next week. I've got someone waiting. In the meantime you'll check out the tutoring center and think about seeing Doctor Baliff. Right?"

He stands up and reaches across the table to shake hands. Ralph rises slowly. Professor Schorr walks him to the door, touching Ralph lightly on the back, "Okay?" As Ralph leaves, not looking up again, the counselor asks Mrs. Fitzgerald to send in the next student when he buzzes. Professor Schorr goes back to his seat, for the first time acknowledges the camera, and shrugs his shoulders.

With such techniques at their disposal it is a wonder that counselors at two-year colleges aren't more successful at cooling-out. Just how unsuccessful was revealed, in 1965, when the American Association of Junior Colleges published the so-called Raines Report of a Carnegie Foundation sponsored study of junior-college student personnel programs.[26] It was the judgment of the report that current programs, though ambitious and highly touted, were "woefully inadequate." Two years later in a condensed and popularized version of the report put out by the AAJC the earlier conclusions were reiterated—this time with a suggestion for "new directions" that largely define current practices. The author was Charles Collins, one of the most respected and prolific writers on the subject, and his ideas are well worth examining since they contain, in my opinion, the intellectual underpinning for our newer, hipper versions of cooling-out.[27]

The report is introduced with a preface by T. R. McConnell who is very clear about just where these "new" directions point—now the community college is seen as "the great distributive agency in American education," where the vocational and educational plans of the student can be brought "more nearly in line with his reasonable expectations." Note that now the older terms "sorting" and "channeling" have become "distributing" and "realistic" has become "reasonable." Before Collins himself actually gets to how this distribution will occur, he expresses some hope that it will be more egalitarian than older versions because he apparently sees through the class-biased IQ-ism that sustains much of the ideology of public schooling. Collins sees, for example, that it may not be as unrealistic as others have thought for two-year-college students to aspire to the highest professions since by virtue of sheer numbers "the greatest repository of the high mental ability required for the professions is in the lower-middle and lower classes—the classes from which the junior college students are drawn."[28] But in the next sentence he is on all too familiar ground: a realistic note must be struck—the professions demand at least a baccalaureate and since only a small percentage of junior-college students are ever going to attain even this degree "good sense would advise close scrutiny of the middle-level positions in technology," etc.[29]

Collins is, then, concerned that junior colleges have not responded to the "phenomenal need" for highly trained technicians. Like Seashore he feels that the present ratio of 75 to 80 percent of junior-college students designated as transfer students versus 20 to 25 percent designated as "terminal" students should be reversed to fit the fact that only 20 to 25 percent of junior-college students actually transfer to baccalaureate programs.[30] The *fact* that so few transfer would seem to indicate that community colleges somehow interfere with their "repository" of talent fulfilling itself, that two-year colleges thwart ability rather than encourage it.[31] If this is true then junior colleges are antimeritocratic. For Collins cooling-out is rationalized *not* by readjusting students' aspirations to their real potential (as it is for Seashore and Clark), but by adjusting people to what in fact happens to them *in spite of* their real potential. Ethically, the new rationale seems more perverse than the old—at least earlier writers acknowledged their elitist notions of the relationship between class and ability.

When Collins turns to cooling-out itself (called here: a "new look at the making of career decisions"), there is again something new masking something old. One reason why so many students declare themselves transfers is because of the promise of mobility that will result from acquiring an associate or baccalaureate degree. But career mobility, Collins claims, is overplayed, for the evidence points to most junior-college graduates "only inching up to the skilled or semiprofessional and small-business level." Thus the junior-college curriculum and its vocational counseling must focus on the majority who will not transfer. It is necessary that the student who will not transfer be made aware that he, not the institution or circumstances, made the choice. For his own mental health and for the political support of two-year colleges, it is important when he finds his career mobility isn't a jump from semiskilled to professional, that "he not consider himself a failure nor make the junior college into his scapegoat."[32]

And then again Collins skips to something new as the cooled-out condition is placed in an interesting existential context. Usually community college students apparently destined for middle-level work must face the future-shock possibility of having to retrain themselves for new careers at least once, and maybe several times, during their lifetimes. They will, therefore, have the very slightest hope of finding psychological identity in some lifelong job. As a result, what is necessary to adjust to this reality is a "posture of tentativeness"—hip insecurity. But to be a good worker one has to be devoted or committed to one's job. How is this possible? There is an existential answer: Collins calls for workers to establish a series of short-term job commitments within a long-term, lifelong posture of tentativeness. And then in order to prepare people to remain sane while living with this commitment-tentativeness contradiction it is imperative, in his view, for two-year colleges to clearly place the responsibility for choice with each of their students. To do otherwise denies them "the excitement, if not joy," of facing up to significant choice and also gives them the easy but unhealthy escape of considering themselves victims of "the system."[33] Thus Collins's intellectual claptrap is actually antiexistential in suggesting that there is no real room for self-definition or responsibility—just psychological and social manipulation.

Subtler than Collins is Arthur M. Cohen, one of the leading figures on the current community college scene. In his vision of the two-year college of the future, counseling is eliminated altogether since the students would be given such varied modes of instruction and a curriculum so flexible that they would be able to find their places quickly within the variegated and clearly defined structures of the institution.[34] But Cohen is one who is aware of the clash between community colleges' unstated functions and their overt ideology. In fact, he assails their sorting and certifying functions. He also sees cooling-out as so entrenched in the structure of two-year colleges that it is difficult for staff members to perceive how many of their practices are based on it—placement tests, counseling, the competitive grading system, etc. He recognizes that if community colleges did not fail half of their entrants, universities would be overrun.[35]

Within this context of sophisticated insight, one may

wonder what logic leads Cohen in the end to just another version of cooling-out. His unstated biases become clear when he presents us with a collective portrait of two-year-college students based heavily on the studies of K. Patricia Cross. Although he deplores the use of statistics, his conclusions are nonetheless based upon her statistical data. For him two-year-college students are of low ability, they have negative self-images, etc. It is all just stated. There is no analysis, for example, of how these characteristics often emerge within working-class culture. What he calls for is more information on how community colleges affect their students so plans can be made regarding new educational forms.[36] In discussing these new forms he challenges traditional concepts in education *only when these concepts are applied to community colleges.*

In the traditional, "classical" definition of curriculum, the total college experience is seen by its graduates as coherent, cumulative and unified. Unfortunately, Cohen laments, community colleges have very few graduates to see the whole, beautiful thing: community college students drop in and mostly out, taking courses "at their own whim."[37] Cohen feels we even have to find a new word to describe two-year-college students' learning experiences because "curriculum" at its root means going from one place to another, and it's clear that the majority of community college students are going nowhere. So since they can't make it the traditional way he in effect says, "Let's see if we can come up with a new way for them to at least have the *semblance* of making it." Thus we have essentially a separate but unequal mode of higher education. It is unequal because if Cohen's new ways of structuring curricula (no matter how interesting) are *just for community college stu-*

dents, then what they will get will always remain second best. The distance, then, between what happens at, say, Mercer Community College and Harvard will grow even vaster.[38] What Cohen proposes for two-year colleges is an educational experience in which everything is second best, with students enjoying only the trappings of the real thing. In this new world of cooled-out reality, counseling and even cooling-out itself are obviously not necessary.

At another staff meeting I attended, this time in 1974 at a California junior college, the counselors there also proved to be quite inventive in suggesting new forms for cooling-out. The agenda called for a discussion of plans for the upcoming job fair. In the past, representatives of the major local employers had come, making themselves and their literature available at booths assigned to them by the college. At the time, the five largest employers of graduates and less-than-graduates were: the telephone company, a large chemical manufacturer, the West Coast headquarters of a national insurance company, the local hospitals, and the gas and electric company.

One of the counselors launched into a scathing critique of the previous year's fair. He was assigned to the college's special division designed to provide academic and counseling assistance to many of the college's black and Spanish-speaking students, and he was particularly upset that past job fairs did not relate to the interests and needs of these students. He argued passionately that a wider diversity of careers be represented. It was not enough, in his opinion, merely to have people from Pacific Gas and Electric or Metropolitan Life passing out brochures describing job opportunities. In addition to beefing up the contingent from the health and service industries (the main interest, he claimed, of his black students), he argued for a better way of reaching his students more directly.

He paused for a moment to scan our faces, looking, it seemed to me, for some appropriate expression of either support or guilt from his colleagues. Most appeared to avoid his searching eyes. "Well," he continued, "I prepared something that I think will be helpful in this regard." He passed around copies of a memo he had written for the dean who was coordinating the fair. As the papers were circulating, he began to lay out his plan to diversify career-planning opportunities for his inner-city "counselees": "To reach these students in a more direct way I propose we set up a panel of pimps and prostitutes at the job fair. They're people the students I work with encounter every day in their neighborhoods and are certainly relevant to their lives."

I waited for the reaction. The copies of his plan were now in everybody's hands, and they all were reading intently. I looked at my copy: there was a student whom he knew who had volunteered to help secure the suggested panel members—three prostitutes and their pimp; it would be necessary to work out a way to protect them from the police (he had a suggestion for that too); he didn't think it would be necessary to arrange for an honorarium for their appearance; etc.

Finally, there was a response to his plan: "Are you sure we'd be able to provide them with protection from the police?" The question was raised by Professor Erwin Glatt, one of the senior members of the staff. "It certainly wouldn't be fair to bring them here and then have them arrested." A couple of people chuckled and others started talking privately to each other.

"Wait, wait. Just a minute." It was one of the newest

counselors; someone I learned later who was hired because he would hopefully be able to establish close rapport with the students since he was nearly their age and had himself graduated from the college. "Wait. I'm not sure it would work. I really doubt if they would talk honestly or openly. You know, they'd be sort of like freaks at a circus side show."

"I don't agree with you," someone from the student activities office interjected. Her job was to represent the college's interests in student clubs and extracurricular cultural events. "I think it's a marvelous idea; just the sort of thing to motivate students. Everyone's so apathetic these days."

"I think it's the worst idea I've ever heard," someone new to the discussion blurted out. All the counselors turned to look toward him. "It's even worse than just having the same old people that we've always had in the past. Just think of what it will say to our kids to tell them, in effect, that if working for the gas company turns you off and if you're looking for something more relevant—in quotes—to do with your life, why don't you check out being a pimp or a prostitute."

"That's not what I have in mind." It was the original proposer of the idea. "I'm not suggesting they become pimps or prostitutes. I merely want us to be more relevant to their lives in general. We have to relate to them better if we want to help them."

"I agree." It was Professor Glatt again, "Let's face it, half the students who arrive here are D.O.A." A couple of people were nodding. "And the kinds of options we've been offering them are frankly just inadequate."

"Wait a minute, what's this 'D.O.A.'?"

"You know, dead-on-arrival."

"What?"

"Dead-on-arrival. Let's be honest with ourselves for a moment, it happens to be true."

"Just listen to yourself Erwin. Do you know what you're saying? Can you imagine a similar conversation at Stanford? How can you work with people if you assume they're dead before you begin?"

"Come on, you know I'm not speaking literally. I was just trying to make a point." Professor Glatt had recently completed his Ph.D. in clinical psychology, I learned, and was in the process of dramatically expanding his evening and weekend private practice.

"I don't know. I don't know."

From that point the meeting drifted rather aimlessly toward irresolution and a number of people left for other appointments. Someone finally said, "I guess that's it."

After the meeting, I had a chance to be alone with Dr. Glatt. We talked about what had gone on and his D.O.A. speech. He confessed that the president of the college and some of the deans were dissatisfied with the counselors' performance; they felt the counselors were ineffective in either reducing the academic probation and dropout rate or effectively helping students make more strategically sound plans for their lives. "One thing the president doesn't understand, though," (he is a nationally known figure in the world of two-year colleges and higher education in general). "He doesn't understand that we counselors are *sheep*. He can hit us, so to speak, and we'll cower. But he can't make us move."

Whether he can make them move is not yet clear (more than 75 percent have tenure), but at least no pimps or prostitutes were invited to the job fair that year. But West Coast sources inform me that the counselors there continue to help cool-out students at an undiminished if less inventive rate.

But what finally has been the effect of the rapid expansion of counseling programs, vocational programs, and new learning structures? Have these programs been effective? In a twisted and unstated sense, yes—in that so very few transfer students actually go on to transfer or get B.A.'s. On the other hand, attempts at cooling-out can also be deemed a failure since so few "latent terminals" are in fact ever cooled into vocational curricula—the stated purpose of cooling-out.

An interesting study by Leonard L. Baird, "Cooling Out and Warming Up in the Junior College," attempts to evaluate the effectiveness of counseling programs designed to cool-out students. If there are more overaspirers ("latent terminals") than underaspirers ("latent transfers") in community colleges (everyone's assumption) and if counseling is at all effective, one would expect to find much more cooling-out than warming-up going on. Baird, however, found just the opposite.[39] In addition, he found that students who were cooled-out were not, as predicted, lower in aptitude. Also, as one might *not* expect, those who got warmed-up (raised their levels of aspiration) came from lower socioeconomic families. From all this he concludes that junior colleges are not doing very well in their efforts to discourage those lacking in ability.[40] Another study of the effectiveness of cooling-out by Robert Fitch reveals similar perplexing patterns: although placing students on probation is supposed to facilitate cooling-out, he found that students on probation were as unlikely to lower their aspiration levels as were students off probation; transfers to more difficult majors were as common among students on probation as off; and over a period of time students seeking terminal degrees actually declined. As he puts it: "Apparently students would rather 'fail than switch.'"[41]

Neither Fitch nor Baird is able to come up with much to explain these paradoxes. They fail even to spell out adequately just what they mean when they speculate that perhaps transfer students and terminal students are simply different personality types: it may go against transfer students' basic personality structure to be cooled-out.[42] The actual reason why so few students allow themselves to be cooled-out may turn out to be much simpler: though community college students all too often accept full responsibility for their failure, they may still retain the strength to resist the school system's final effort to deceive and manipulate them.[43]

We have damaged the cause of civilization and culture by trying to convince people that they are 'good business,' and that education has a yield as good as that of a jam factory.

—C. F. Carter
1972

FOUR

THE ECONOMICS OF SECOND BEST*

There's an old expression which claims that "money talks," and what money says about our systems of public higher education eloquently reveals another fundamental way in which the schools are structured to help support and maintain our current social and economic order. The major assertion of this chapter is that these systems of higher education serve, in a variety of ways, to redistribute money from low-income people to high-income families. Another way of putting this is that poor people—through regressive state and local tax structures, the primary source of support for public higher education—are paying a disproportionate share of more affluent people's college costs.

The idea of "human capital," that *people* as well as

*This first appeared in a modified version in my essay-review of Douglas Windham's *Education, Equality, and Income Redistribution* and W. Lee Hansen's and Burton Weisbrod's *Benefits, Costs, and Finance of Public Higher Education: School Review*, 81, 4(August, 1973), pp. 643–649.

property form part of the wealth of nations, was first stated by Adam Smith.[1] He also set the ideological basis for a human calculus by which the value of education to individuals and to society could be measured:

> When any expensive machine is erected, the extraordinary work to be performed by it before it is worn out, it must be expected, will replace the capital laid out upon it, with at least the ordinary profits. A man educated at the expense of much labour and time to any of those employments which require extraordinary dexterity and skill, may be compared to one of these expensive machines. The work which he learns to perform, it must be expected, over and above the usual wages of common labour, will replace to him the whole expense of his education, with at least the ordinary profits of an equally valuable capital. . . . The difference between the wages of skilled labour and those of common labour is founded upon this principle.[2]

With such a promising start nearly two hundred years ago, it seems remarkable that the economics of education had to wait until very recent days, the 1960s, to emerge from neglect as a subject of scholarly interest. But there has long been a certain repugnance to the very idea of human capital—the equation of people with property and machines. The literature of education is full of expressions defining the value of education in social rather than economic terms—with the expressions themselves full of distaste for human capitalism. In 1890, Alfred Marshall, in his *Principles of Economics,* rejected the notion of "human capital" as unrealistic. He preferred the more conventional definition of his day which did not count the skills of the population as forming part of the capital stock or wealth of an economy. In our own time, C. F. Carter in "Costs and Benefits of Mass Higher

Education" claims: "We have damaged the cause of civilization and culture by trying to convince people that they are 'good business,' and that education has a yield as good as that of a jam factory. . . . Perhaps the greatest harm which has been done by the jam factory approach is to rob that part of education which is concerned with the summits of human achievement, and with the awe and wonder which surround it."[3] Another educator, Howard Bowen, echoes the summit-of-human-achievements view of the value of education. For him the purpose of higher education is to raise the quality of civic and business life. Higher education contributes to the "refinement of conduct," the generation of aesthetic appreciation, and the addition of graciousness and variety to life. It also, he goes on to point out, teaches many to eschew material strivings: it produces millions of persons who go on to enter professions such as teaching and preaching which have compensation rates below what is paid for work requiring less education.[4]

Nonetheless, in the last ten years there has been something of a revival of Adam Smith's economics of education. Although the noneconomic social values of education are undisputed, it is now also generally agreed that there are individual and collective *economic* values as well. For example, the amount of education that an individual possesses is positively correlated with personal lifetime earnings. This correlation is far from perfect, but in all modern economies of which we have knowledge, it is true for the average person and indeed for most people.* Obviously other factors beside education-

*As this book was about to go to press a widely publicized article appeared in *Change* magazine (September 1975) citing the declining value of college attendance. In a sentence, the authors note that since college graduates have increased much more rapidly than professional-level job opportunities, the

al attainment contribute to one's earning capacity—age, sex, race, ability, social class background, occupation, quality of on-the-job training, etc.—but apart from age, none of them are as powerful in their influence on earnings as the number of years of schooling completed.[5]

A question that follows from this involves concern about who should pay for education if its economic benefits are derived primarily by individuals rather than society. In one view it is felt that the individual should pay the costs of education either through parental support, summer or part-time work, student loans, etc. But if it is agreed that society's benefits from higher education are substantial, then society should subsidize the costs through free or near-free tuition, scholarships, tuition grants, etc. But as a Carnegie Commission on Higher Education study states, we all pay—directly or indirectly—for *everything*. It is an obvious, but often obscured, fact that *people* pay the total bill for higher education. The current cost is shared among users and nonusers, the well-to-do and the less well-to-do, older and younger generations.[6] How actually do the people pay the bill? Most obviously via tuition payments. Less obviously via federal, state, and local taxes (estimated variously to cover between 60 and 70 percent of the total costs of higher education).[7] And least obviously via

---

ratio defining the difference between the incomes of high-school and college graduates has shrunk significantly: college grads earned 53 percent more in 1969 but only 40 percent more by 1973.

But a college education is not of declining value for *all* young people. Black graduates, for example, seem to benefit handsomely: their incomes are now for the first time on a par with whites'. What the article then actually reveals is that college may be of declining value for some (the affluent) while at the same time coming to be of real economic value to many others. (Richard Freeman and J. Herbert Holloman, "The Declining Value of College Going," pp. 24–31, 62.)

tax-exempt gifts of money and property to colleges and universities.

These gifts, because they are tax exempt, contain hidden public subsidies and begin to give an insight into the most complex and most crucial issue in the economics of higher education: *How does higher education contribute, if at all, to a redistribution of money within the society?* In the case of "gifts" to colleges the Carnegie Report is quick to point out that these publicly subsidized gifts go predominantly to relatively selective colleges and universities and that this increases the share of public subsidies benefiting the middle and upper-income families who send their children to such places.[8] When you add this to the fact that richer students get the most costly and most protracted schooling, one finds, with Christopher Jencks et al. in *Inequality: A Reassessment of the Effect of Family and Schooling in America,* that America spends about twice as much on the education of the children of the rich as on the children of the poor and that an extra year of schooling also seems to do about twice as much economic good for students from a middle-class background as for students from a working-class background.[9] When all of this is calculated, one might correctly imagine there is a *negative* redistribution of money through higher education from the poor to the rich.

One way to calculate this redistribution is to establish *a human investment calculus.* On one side of the equation one puts the direct and indirect costs of education (tuition, tax revenues, *and* foregone earnings* that result from college attendance rather than full-time

---

*The concept of "foregone earnings" assumes young people can find jobs if they choose not to go to college. Obviously, a rather shaky assumption.

employment, etc.).[10] On the other side of the equation one calculates the additional average income that is expected as the result of the education obtained. Then by comparing the average earnings associated with various levels of education in relation to the additional cost of obtaining that education, one can estimate the rate of return of various amounts of higher education. Additionally, if one were to do these calculations *by income group* (that is to say, see how the lowest income group—for example—fares in comparison to the highest income group), then one would produce a rather good picture of how higher education serves to redistribute money within the society.

One of the first system-wide studies of this kind is Douglas Windham's analysis of Florida's public higher educational system: *Education, Equality and Income Redistribution.*[11] He begins with certain questions of social policy, delineating the fundamental differences between the egalitarian and elitist versions of higher education and the social-political consequences thereof: the egalitarian view has it that higher education should be a force for reducing income inequality by providing a means for social mobility for all qualified applicants, rich or poor.[12] The elitist version is that there are certain social revenues inherent in higher education (the well educated will increase society's body of knowledge, be more productive and thereby create more jobs and tax revenues, etc.) and therefore the cost of educating this intellectual elite should be borne by the population at large. The rhetoric supporting public higher education is of the egalitarian kind (the motto of the State University of New York, for example, is "Let Each Become All He Is Capable of Being"); whereas, as Windham points out, the way the higher educational system is financed and the way it redistributes income reveals that it is *operationally* structured on elitist principles. As with so much else, the reality belies the rhetoric. He concludes, in fact, that while certain members of the lower income classes are able to get a subsidy "as a whole, the lower income classes would be better off without a public system of *higher education*." [13]

In dollars and cents, how does this work? As I have indicated, people pay for their public higher educational system primarily through state and local taxes. Windham calculates the *costs* of this education by distributing the total taxes collected to support higher education among the various income groups to indicate each group's share of the costs. He then calculates the *benefits*, also by income groups, on first the short-term basis (how much the state spends per student for higher education) and second on the "long-run investment opportunities" derived from higher education (how much more one earns over a lifetime as the result of having gone to college).

Finally, again by income group, he calculates whether the benefits outweigh the costs (a *positive* redistribution of money) or the costs exceed the benefits (a *negative* redistribution). The answer he comes to is that for *families earning more than $10,000 per year with students in college, there is a positive redistribution; while for families earning less than $10,000 the redistribution is negative.* In the four income groups he distinguishes, the precise redistributional effects for 1967–68 were as follows:

	Income Class			
	$0–2,000	$3,000–4,999	$5,000–9,999	$10,000–above
Net Gain/Loss (for *all* students in the system)	−$7,122,590	−$12,900,160	−$6,037,480	+$26,119,540

This means that Florida's system of higher education, in effect, is one in which the "poor" are sending the "rich" through college.

If we look at Florida's system of community colleges—which has received substantial popular support because of its supposed ability to provide greater opportunity to a wider range of students, one finds that because the state provides a larger share of the total cost—financed from more regressive taxes than those forming the basis of federal support—the effect of the way two-year colleges are financed is more regressive than the way the universities are financed.[14]

In the face of these startling findings, Windham's suggestions for developing a more egalitarian system of higher education are merely cosmetic. Because he does not perceive that public education has historically been devoted to certifying rather than attacking inequality, his suggestions for revised public policy are more economic than structural: there should be more federal and less state money for higher education since federal taxes are less regressive than state taxes, we should change the admission policies of public universities; we should alter the fees and other costs incurred by students; etc.

A second major study by W. Lee Hansen and Burton Weisbrod of California's system—America's largest—*Benefits, Costs, and Finance of Public Higher Education* reaches similar conclusions. California's system, too, is structured along elitist lines in spite of its egalitarian charter. It is also the most thoroughly hierarchical system as well as the most class-serving. For example, the 1964 median income of the families of junior-college students was $8,800; the median income of families of state college students was $10,000; and the median annual income of families of students attending the elite university colleges was $12,000. Completing this hierarchical picture is the fact that the median income for all California families in 1964 was $8,000.[15] The fact that even the junior-college figure was $800 per year *above* the state median means that a full picture of California's higher educational system includes a substantial number, 41 percent, of college-age, college-eligible students who are not in any direct way served by California's colleges and universities. And the majority of these young people are from the lowest income groups.[16]

When Hansen and Weisbrod examine the effect of this system—which is unequal to begin with—on the redistribution of money within that system, their discoveries are more startling than Windham's. A number of things stand out in addition to the perception that high-school average (which solely determines the level at which a student enters the California system) is directly correlated with family income and that the three tiers in the system are thus class-related.[17] First, since the state distributes its tax money to the various levels of the higher educational system in an unequal way that parallels the economic hierarchy operational within the system's admissions policy, the colleges themselves substantially contribute to maintaining the state's social structure. For example, the state spends at least $1,000 less on the two years of a junior-college education than it does on the first two years of either a state or university college education.[18] Another way of looking at this negative redistribution of money is that after subtracting the regressive state and local taxes paid by families with children in the three tiers of the system from the amount of subsidy received by these families as the result of state aid to higher education, one finds that the "net transfer" is $40 per year for junior-college students, $630 per year

for state college students, and $790 per year for universi-
ty college students. In other words, students going to
university colleges (those from the "richest" families)
receive nearly twenty times more annual subsidy from
the state than junior-college students (those from the
"poorest").[19] You add to this the fact that there is also a
correlation between the type of college a student attends
and the average number of years he or she remains there
(1.2 years for junior-college students, 2.6 for state college, and 2.8 for university college students) and the
negative effects of higher education for the lowest socioeconomic group are further multiplied.[20]

If the picture could be worse, there is the fact that the
attrition rate within the tiers of the system parallels the
students' socioeconomic background (while 55 percent
of university college students finish their B.A.'s and 50
percent of state college students complete theirs, only 30
percent of junior-college students complete *even two
years* and only 8 percent ever go on for B.A.'s).[21]
Therefore, the amount of added lifetime earning capacity derived from either having attended "some college" or
having earned a B.A. is also class-related and class-
serving. In California in 1959—according to the figures
cited by Hansen and Weisbrod—the median annual
income for high-school graduates was $6,039, for
"persons with some college education," $6,399 (an in-
crease of 4 percent over the high-school graduates'
earnings), and $8,108 for persons with "4 or more years
of college" (an increase of 34 percent over the high-
school graduates' earnings).[22] The fact that the advantage to persons with only "some college" is so little
indicates the *lack* of economic value of a junior-college
education—even if students there were to complete the
full two years. Jerome Karabel cites more recent census

data (1967, 1968, 1969) to indicate that the recipient of five to seven terms of college is closer in income to a high-school graduate than to a college graduate—121 percent of a high-school graduate's income as compared to a college graduate who earns 150 percent of a high-school graduate's average income.[23] This is particularly serious because junior college is proclaimed to be the place where the children of the lower classes have a real chance to achieve social and economic mobility through higher education.

But if the "richest" students get the highest high-school averages and are therefore admitted to the "best" colleges in the system and while there receive both the highest subsidies and have the best chance of getting B.A.'s which help assure them substantial advantages for lifetime earning,[24] then the California public higher education system is structured to serve its socioeconomic elite by helping them maintain their privileged position.

Hansen and Weisbrod come close to saying this explicitly a number of times: in their conclusion for example, they note how some low-income persons have benefited handsomely from the availability of publicly subsidized higher education. "But on the whole, the effect of these subsidies is to promote greater rather than less inequality among people of various social and economic backgrounds."[25] Then, as if reluctant to draw the full implications of their findings, they at other times step back to say that any strong conclusions about the class-serving nature of the entire system of higher education in California cannot be drawn.[26] So their book is flawed, particularly—as is Windham's—in their suggestions for future public policy. They, too, suggest changes only in the way schools should be financed, taxes should be collected (less regressively), and how subsidies should be distributed (not just through schooling but perhaps through direct grants to young people for them to spend in any way they feel would expand their earning power[27]—Hansen's and Weisbrod's most interesting idea).

The controversy surrounding the publication of their work, considering its rather obscure beginnings as an essay in *The Journal of Human Resources*[28] indicates that they hit a more sensitive nerve than they had suspected by calling into question an important part of the folklore about higher education's role in income redistribution. Joseph Pechman, for example, claims that a reanalysis of Hansen's and Weisbrod's 1959 data indicates that California's system of public higher education is actually progressive rather than regressive as they had asserted.[29] He points out that only a small portion of the state and local taxes collected from low-income families is applied toward subsidizing higher education, and thus the taxes *actually* paid by the lowest income classes for public higher education in California are smaller than the benefits received by families in these income classes.[30]

But more recent studies indicate that not only were Windham and Hansen-Weisbrod correct; but in spite of dramatic increases in college enrollments, in spite of the rapid expansion in the size and number of community colleges, the regressive economic structure of public higher educational systems remains remarkably stable.

In *Inequality*, Christopher Jencks describes the impervious nature of inequality. For example, he sees it as not entirely accidental that 87 percent of high-school graduates whose parents earned $15,000 or more entered college in 1967 compared to only 20 percent of those whose families earned less than $3,000. Or that public subsidies are more inequitably concentrated now on middle-class students in college than on middle-class students in high school. Or that the most extensively educated fifth of the population received about 75 percent more than their share of the nation's educational resources whereas the least educated fifth received only about half their share. Or that the eventual disparity between the most and least favored students comes out to favor the best educated by at least four to one.[31]

Inequality further corroborates Windham and Hansen-Weisbrod when dealing with the correlation between numbers of years of schooling and lifetime earning capacity (incidentally, the former is the *one* significant educational correlate Jencks identifies as predictive of economic success): The table reproduced

From Table 7-4[34]
Incomes of Full-Time, Year-Round Workers
Over 25 With Different Amounts of Schooling, as
a Percentage of the 1968 Average

Amount of schooling	Males	Females	Total	[% of increase]
Didn't finish elementary school	70%	40%	64%	
Finished elementary school, no high school	85%	47%	76%	[19%]
Entered high school, didn't finish	96%	51%	84%	[11%]
Finished high school, no college	111%	61%	95%	[13%]
Entered college, didn't finish	129%	71%	115%	[21%]
Finished college, no graduate school	170%	84%	150%	[31%]
At least 1 year of graduate work	188%	106%	171%	[14%]
All individuals	114%	62%	100%	

below indicates that each extra year of elementary and secondary school is associated with a 6 percent lifetime income increase. Each year of college is associated with a 12 percent increase. A year of graduate school is associated with a 7 percent increase. But the chart also indicates, as did Hansen-Weisbrod, that *some* years of college are "worth" more than others, particularly that *the community college years aren't "worth" very much more than high-school years.* The largest percentage of increase in earnings is between the classifications "Entered College, Didn't Finish" and "Finished College, No Graduate School" (see dotted line on table). The figures Jencks gives us for 1968, if compared with Hansen's and Weisbrod's 1959 figures, indicate that having some college education was more valuable in 1968 than in 1959 but that the *relative* value of a B.A. when compared with only some college remained notably consistent (34 percent more valuable in 1959; 31 percent more valuable in 1968).[32] This may in fact mean that a B.A. is becoming *absolutely* more valuable (or at least its value is being preserved in spite of open-admissions programs) *as the result of* more and more students being induced to attend community colleges. A rather neat sleight-of-hand.[33]

A summary of the major themes of this chapter can be distilled from the Carnegie Commission report *Higher Education: Who Pays? Who Benefits? Who Should Pay? First*, their data concerning fall 1971 college attenders (the most current figures available as of this writing) indicates the continuing relationship between family income and the college attendance of their children; obviously, the richer the family the more likely it is that their children will go to college:

From Table 3[35]

Family Income	College attenders as percentage of 18–24 age group
Under $ 3,000	23.0%
$ 3,000–$ 5,000	26.7%
$ 5,000–$ 7,500	28.3%
$ 7,500–$10,000	38.0%
$10,000–$15,000	40.6%
Over $15,000	66.1%

Second, other data both update and confirm Hansen's and Weisbrod's delineation of the economic stratification of California's multitiered system of higher education—the dominant national pattern. The richer you are the more likely you are to attend the elite, *highly subsidized* state universities and colleges and the less likely you are to go to low-status, poorly subsidized two-year colleges. The Carnegie Commission cites 1971–72 data for the California system which reveal that the mean family income for students in the University of California was $15,150; in the California state colleges $12,330; and in the community colleges $11,420.[36]

Then *third*, since state systems are still primarily supported by state and local taxes (approximately 68 percent of their tax support comes from state and local taxes with 32 percent from federal sources—primarily for vocational programs) and since these taxes are still basically regressive, for these reasons money continues to be distributed regressively through public higher educational systems. The commission says: "the lowest income groups have a larger share of . . . [college-age] dependents (8.4%) than the share of the higher educational benefits they receive (4.9%), while the over

$15,000 group receives an estimated 27.6% of subsidy benefits for its 16.4% of the 18- to 24-year-old group."[37] This is their way of indicating how the "poor" are footing the higher education bill for the affluent.

But as with the other educational economists we have seen, it is in their policy recommendations—particularly those that apply to community colleges—that one can perceive the limitations of their analysis: they, too, fail to deal with the way systems of higher education *are structured* to frustrate the expectations of low-income students. For example, if as the Carnegie Commission claims, community college (and lower-division) students pay a higher proportion of their total educational costs than do upper-division or graduate students and as a result are actually subsidizing the more advanced students, how can the commission then go on to assert that the lower subsidy per student in the two-year college should not be a matter of major concern since this low subsidy is a means of "conserving scarce resources to maximize the educational benefits to society"?[38] Is there any logic or justice in spreading the money thinnest among the poorest and "least able" students and among the institutions (community colleges) with the highest rates of failure? Perhaps, they seem to be conceding, this failure is inevitable. After all, why send good money after bad?[39]

Since the Carnegie Commission has been able to perceive the limited economic benefits to individuals of "some college" education, how can they justify recommendations that would, in effect, *drive* low-income students into inferior two-year colleges? The commission reiterates their earlier recommendation (in *The Capital and the Campus*) of free or nominal tuition for the first two college years, particularly for short-term technical and vocational education programs, with tuition charges increasing after the first two years when a student or his family can be expected to make a larger contribution toward college costs.[40] This economic policy, if implemented, would clearly drive poor students into community colleges, especially into the vocational programs, and would stimulate the creation of a new mercenary class of workers and technicians—drawn from the lowest income groups, drawn to the community colleges because of their low or free tuition. The parallels are disturbing between this projected future for higher education and our new "voluntary" armed forces which are more and more composed of predominantly black, predominantly low-income mercenaries.

One way to cope with this mass of literature on students is to look at people as pebbles—how they appear on the surface and then how they look under close scrutiny. To talk about characteristics of either pebbles or people and to come up with an approximate picture of the average are not at all difficult tasks. It is infinitely more difficult, however—and vastly more interesting—to describe unique traits of a single pebble or an individual and, eventually, to arrive at the conclusion that no pebble—and no person—is exactly like any other.

—Arthur M. Cohen and Associates
1971

FIVE

THE
STUDENTS

The formal data on two-year-college students has undergone the same historical metamorphoses as has the data on students in general. Students' ability, most often measured and represented as IQ, was until recently considered to be the key to understanding children in schools and was seen to be the proper basis on which to predict their success, divide them into various kinds of homogeneous groupings, admit them to special programs, and even to sort them out among schools of differing quality and status.

But gradually different emphases arose. Intelligence continued to be measured in a variety of standardized ways, and researchers and admissions officers still considered it to be an essential academic quantity; but attempts were also made to measure and value noncognitive personal qualities such as motivation and goal orientation. Later it came to be seen that emotions and values were important as well, and should be considered (if they could be described and quantified) when assessing students' characteristics and potential. For some educators the noncognitive characteristics became the ultimate expression of what it is to be a student (or person); while for others cognitive ability still seemed to be most critical for predicting academic as well as economic success. The most recent position involves the notion that neither affect nor cognition is most important—they are coequal—and that when attempting to describe students, predict their success, develop programs for them, we cannot separate one from the other. Most of the more current studies of students I will be describing attempt to encompass this complexity. On the surface at least, these descriptions of college-age students may seem to be a long way from Carl Seashore's impression of the junior-college students of 1940: "good citizens who crave and deserve higher education beyond the high school but are not interested in or preparing for a learned career, . . . [instead they] are looking forward to leadership in vastly varied fields of arts and crafts through intelligent and competent living."[1]

There have been literally hundreds of studies since 1940 that have attempted to substitute the "precision" of social science for Seashore's intuition. Remarkably, with regard to their findings concerning two-year college students' academic ability, career potential, and aspirations, these have come to support Seashore's conclusions. Indeed, there seems to be a virtual unanimity of opinion concerning the academic and personal *inferiority* of community college students.

These studies also help shape the popular view of community college students since they often are set in and researched at individual two-year colleges throughout the country. I distinctly remember sitting in on a faculty meeting at a nameless New Jersey community college where the dean of students read off a collective student portrait culled from the latest institutional administration of the highly-touted Comparative Guidance and Placement Test. It was not a promising picture. But rather than creating either a mood of depression ("Look what we're up against.") or provoking a call to action ("How are we going to really help these students learn?"), a certain calm filled the auditorium. When I checked out my reaction to the dean's report with a couple of faculty members after the meeting, they told me the staff probably felt good about the report because its picture of their students' *inabilities* helped reconcile them to the fact that most students weren't showing up for classes or doing much of the assigned work. One administrator told me when I asked about the college's high attrition rate that they were actually doing quite well considering the kind of students they were up against.

If one surveys these small-scale studies of college students, one learns that although various investigators' concerns have become more diverse over the years, with more and more of them attempting to include measurements of the noncognitive characteristics of community college students, their main focus remains the same— the comparative academic abilities of two- and four-year-college students.

Whether they employ graphs or not, the findings of these studies could still be represented by a graph similar to the one drawn by Leonard Koss (see figure 1 on page 126) back in 1929 in his study of California secondary school graduates.[2] It shows two overlapping bell curves (curves that portray a "normal" distribution of scores) that represent the distribution of scores of freshmen on the Thorndike College Aptitude Test administered at four

Figure 1

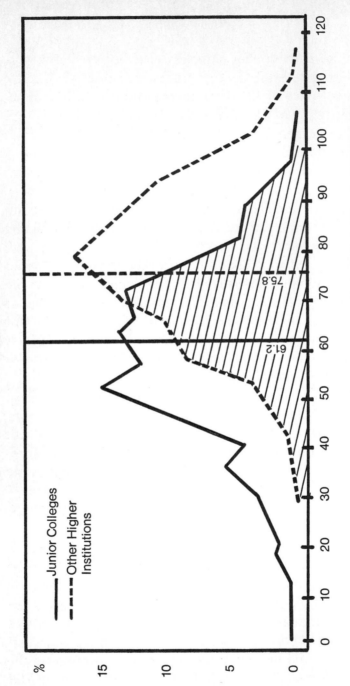

Comparison of the Distribution of Freshmen on the Thorndike Aptitude Test at Four Junior Colleges and Three Other Higher Institutions in California.

junior colleges and three senior colleges. Among other things the curves reveal a lower mean score for the junior-college students (61.2 as compared to 75.8 for the four-year-college students). The intersection of the curves also shows a considerable overlap (the shaded section). This indicates that although the "average" two-year-college student is not as bright as the "average" four-year student, *many* junior-college students are just as smart as *many* senior-college students. And it is within this shaded area of overlap that most community college staff find some measure of solace, for even though they have to deal with a great many not-so-bright students, there are enough that are really college material to keep them going.[3]

Beginning in about 1965, paralleling the almost geometric expansion of community college enrollments, there was a corresponding expansion in the studies of the academic abilities of the students who made up these enrollments. But there was no significant deviation from the earlier findings. Dean Seibel, for example, used Practice Scholastic Aptitude Test scores (PSAT's) to compare the abilities of two- and four-year students. The mean verbal scores were 38.4 for community college students and 45.9 for four-year students; mean math scores were 41.3 and 49.9. There was the now familiar overlap but Seibel also found community college students to be more like noncollege students than senior-college students—a new theme to be orchestrated in ensuing years.[4]

Leland Medsker and James Trent studied ten thousand June 1959 high-school graduates. They divided these students into three groups: those who went on to private colleges and universities, those who entered public colleges and universities, and those who enrolled in public two-year colleges. They then measured how these students had done in high school (what were their averages?) and how they scored on national aptitude tests. Not surprisingly they found that of *private* university students 84 percent had graduated in the top two-fifths (quintiles I and II) of their high-school class as compared to only 42 percent of the two-year-college students (74 percent of the *public* university students had been in the top two quintiles). And only 3 percent of the *private* university students had graduates in the lowest two quintiles (IV and V) as compared to 26 percent of the two-year-college students (11 percent of the *public* university students had graduated in the lowest two-fifths of their high-school classes). The scores on the aptitude tests followed virtually an identical pattern. More evidence of community college students' academic inferiority.[5]

Things get a little stickier when these findings of community college students' academic inferiority begin to suggest regressive social policies. Donald Hoyt and Leo Munday's study reveals these dangers.[6] They, too, found two-year students to be of lower ability: In overall academic potential, junior-college students in this study averaged about one-half a standard deviation below four-year-college freshmen. The danger lies in the conclusions drawn from these allegedly "empirical" findings: Hoyt and Munday claim that their study supports the "common contention" that junior colleges should not try to imitate four-year colleges since the two kinds of colleges have different kinds of students and therefore appropriately different institutional objectives. And those objectives for students of four-year colleges are not "necessarily suitable for students of junior colleges."[7]

Though the tests that lead to such regressive suggestions have more and more been revealed to be biased in favor of white children from socially and economically favored families, it is rarely pointed out that whatever these tests of ability measure—*it is not something absolute.* Ability is always measured in a competitive or comparative manner. There is a tyranny in the assumption that ability or intellectual potential is comparatively distributed in a natural pattern best represented by a bell curve:

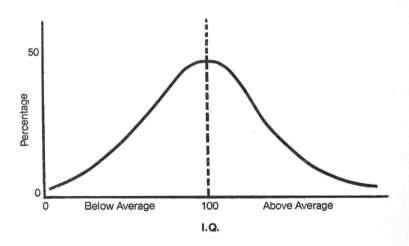

The bell curve's assumptions about human normalcy are based on the concept that for every "above-average" student there MUST BE another student equally "below average." Thus individual scores, the fates of children, the evaluation of schools, and finally the expectations teachers have for their students are all victims of this statistical tyranny—because this method of scoring always dooms one-half of whatever is being measured to exist *below the norm.* Though this may be a perverse version of what constitutes normalcy, it is a perfect method of measurement for a hierarchical society that makes the same assumptions about the way people are "naturally" distributed among the various classes and categories of work. It is the theoretical underpinning for the laissez faire of "benign neglect."

In addition, rarely have socioeconomic factors been perceived to be critical in understanding the supposed intellectual inferiority of two-year students. Even less often has IQ-ism itself been seen to function to rationalize or legitimatize social and economic inequality among Americans. In a most perceptive article on the subject, "IQ in the U.S. Class Structure," Samuel Bowles and Herbert Gintis discuss these interrelated themes in new ways.[8] What they do is to *reject* totally the traditional assumptions of IQ-ism which claim that ours is a meritocratic society in which those with the highest IQ's, with the help of the schools, achieve the most success. They observe instead that it is basically one's socioeconomic background that predetermines one's future success or failure. In order, though, to justify and thus make acceptable in a democracy this intergenerational transmission of privilege it must be *believed,* even if not true, that success and failure are based on an open, objective, and equal competition among people of unequal ability. Thus, if Bowles and Gintis are correct (and they examine a mass of data to reach their conclusions), *all* of the current debate about IQ (or for that matter, the academic ability of two-year-college students) is largely irrelevant to an understanding of inequality in the United States. And what then becomes critically important here is to understand the actual socioeconomic status (S.E.S.) of community college students—since it is so significantly related to their future success or failure— *and* the relationship between S.E.S. and success in school since that, too, significantly correlates with future success or failure.[9]

The key question, then, that must be dealt with regarding the potential of two-year-college students is complex: If as Bowles and Gintis claim (accurately, I feel) that intelligence or traditionally measured academic ability is not as significantly correlated with success in life as is one's socioeconomic status or the number of years of school completed,[10] what does correlate with success and how does the mechanism work? For example, how does S.E.S. contribute to how long one remains in school (in addition to the obvious point that having money makes it easier for one to stay in school) and what is it about S.E.S. itself that contributes to either success or failure?

The answers, I believe, lie in the realm of noncognitive personality traits. Success in the world of work, for example, has more to do with one's motivation and ability to compete, with how one asserts authority, with one's ability to accept the work norms of society than with one's cognitive skills (one's ability to read, write, cipher, etc.). Perhaps the reason such success is correlated with the number of years one spends in school is the fact that schooling powerfully affects the acquisition of these noncognitive traits and rewards students who possess them by allowing them to remain in school longer than those young people who lack them.[11]

And these noncognitive personality traits that contribute so much to one's potential success or failure are also class related.[12] Bowles and Gintis point to how one's personal "modes of presentation" are in important ways correlated to one's eventual place in the social hierarchy.

Social class lines connecting generation to generation are in part the result of reproducing these modes of self-presentation: successful parents teach their children how to behave, dress, and speak in ways that tend to help guarantee their future success.[13] S.E.S. also affects child-rearing practices which in turn affect children's noncognitive personalities and hence their chances for future success. For example, some claim that lower-class parents tend to emphasize conformity to external authority more than middle-class parents who in their patterns of child rearing stress curiosity, self-control, and happiness as valuable personal characteristics or life goals.

These are the kinds of personality traits that families from different S.E.S. strata pass along to their children, traits that contribute to the reproduction of their social differences. Thus the IQ ideology which *pretends* that intellectual ability *causes* the critical differences in life's outcomes but which in fact works to get people to accept their eventual positions in society. This is all well served by the seeming objectivity and meritocratic orientation of the schools.

Studies of these traits of personality of students and their families began to appear in the mid-1960s just as IQ testing came under its heaviest attack. And in some sense, these new studies have come to replace IQ tests as the primary means of sorting and tracking students while at the same time helping to reconcile them to their "destined" slots in school and society. If in the past IQ testing separated the "smart" from the "dumb," personality testing is more and more being used to make the same divisions along the same biased lines. This time, however, "smart" equals "academically oriented," "motivated," and "adaptable"; whereas "dumb" has become "vocationally oriented," "impulsive," and "less autonomous."

Such tests of values and personality, when applied to college students, continue to reveal how two-year-college students have all the less desirable noncognitive traits. Whereas "traditional" college students in these new studies are found to be eager to study and sport in the groves of academe, "new" two-year-college students seem to be longing to discover the mysteries of auto mechanics or stenography. Whereas "traditional" students seem to come to the halls of ivy with open, flexible, inquiring minds, "new" students show up at their concrete computer campuses trailing their parents' depressingly traditional values and morality—the youth culture, the sexual revolution appear to have passed them by.[14]

Actually many of these studies of college students' personalities date from 1963, the year Paul Heist and colleagues at the Berkeley Center for Research and Development in Higher Education "perfected" their extremely influential Omnibus Personality Inventory (the O.P.I.). It purports to measure, among other things, students' liking (or dislike) for abstract, reflective thought on its "Thinking Introversion" scale. Its "Autonomy" scale claims to measure students' inclinations for "liberal," "nonauthoritarian" thinking and the degree of their desire for independence. Low scorers on this Autonomy scale, for example, think their parents are right about the world in general and believe in the established order of things. The "Practical Orientation" scale measures, it claims, just that—one's practical orientation. High scorers believe that the best theories are those that lead to direct application; they prefer factual questions on tests rather than those requiring the analysis and synthesis of data and believe in the need for intelligent leadership to maintain the established order. High scorers on another scale, the "Impulse Expression" scale, presumably tend to act on the spur of the moment without stopping to think and also are inclined to seek immediate gratification. All together, there are fourteen separate scales that have proven to be most helpful to researchers and to college counselors who wish to profile their student "clients."

Studies employing the O.P.I. to compare two- and four-year-college students have come to a number of not-so-startling conclusions. Dale Tillery, for example, concludes that junior-college students show greater interest than university students in "applied learning" as demonstrated by their higher scores on the Practical Orientation scale. University students are socially mature and flexible in ideas and values, whereas two-year students are less respons've to new experiences.[15] When using the O.P.I. exclusively on the upper 14.8 percent of California's high-school graduates—all of whom were eligible to enter the University of California but who instead sorted themselves out among the various tiers in the state system—he found that on the scales that measure "intellectuality," 31 percent of university entrants scored high, whereas only 18 percent of the junior-college students had high scores. Also, 40 percent of the university students but only 20 percent of the junior-college students had high "social maturity" scores.[16] This pattern of findings is either echoed or extended by others with scarcely a murmur of dissent.[17]

Seemingly carried away by the results of the O.P.I. studies, even inveterate investigators such as Arthur M. Cohen and Forence Brawer come to regressive, indeed absurd conclusions: The O.P.I. suggests a "relatively low intellectual disposition" among two-year students and therefore, they state, "a new pedagogy may be required to deal adequately with young people who are not intellectually oriented."[18] The "Adaptive-Flexibility" inventory of the O.P.I. reveals community college students' tendencies toward vivid imagery and creativity—enviable traits. But what kind of educational programs do Cohen and Brawer suggest to develop and release these talents? They wonder: "Can fantasy be given free rein, school made more fun? If so, can the sudents *then* acquire the basic concepts and disciplines so necessary to achievement in higher education?"[19] I can't help wondering why school must be made "fun" for the creative community college student while at many fine four-year colleges student creativity is expected to result in so much more.

In line with making two-year colleges more fun, Armand Mauss—when he attempts to apply Martin Trow's typology of college student subcultures ("collegiate," "academic," "nonconformist," etc.) to community colleges—comes up with a felicitous new category that he claims describes the largest single group of two-year-college students: the "perpetual teenager." Perpetual teenagers compose 44 percent of the junior-college population; 24 percent are "vocational"; only 9.5 percent are "academics."[20] But unlike other teenagers who at least seem to have some fun in life, community college perpetual teenagers—according to at least one faculty member's account—do not even have much of a sense of humor. After thirteen years at Berkshire Community College but now safely ensconced at the University of Connecticut, Marjorie Fallows reports that her Berkshire students were not "secure enough" even to laugh: barely one-fourth (compared to three-fourths at the University of Connecticut) were able to laugh while learning.[21]

Fun aside, *not one of these writers* who draw so many of their conclusions about the personalities, values, and motivations of students from the O.P.I., ever questions its validity, particularly its validity as a measure of two-year-college students' personalities.[22] Even the designers of the test indicate in the O.P.I.'s manual that the test was "standardized," its norms, means, and standard deviations were established, by administering the test to groups of *above-average* college freshmen. Only a couple of two-year colleges participated in the standardization, with only one enrolling a decent number of big-city students.[23] Furthermore, among other biases, the O.P.I. was structured according to a limited psychological assumption that is worth pointing out. The scales that purport to measure intellectual inclination and potential are based on the assumption that little or no significant change in attitude toward intellectual pursuits occurs after age seventeen. It is in fact considered "unlikely that a strong 'quest' for knowledge would be demonstrated thereafter."[24] In other words, if you don't have it by the time you enter college, forget it. These expectations, of course, relegate community college students to a nonintellectual college education.

Not one of the researchers I've encountered who employs the O.P.I. ever looks into the biases implicit in individual test questions, biases that are particularly discriminatory against community college students. All investigators, for example, claim that these students score particularly low on the Autonomy scale (and thus reveal their authoritarian personalities) and high on the Practical Orientation scale (and thus reveal their inclination for auto mechanics). But a look at some of the specific questions that comprise these scales shows a socioeconomic class bias of a kind that would especially penalize the lower-class students who are so prevalent at two-year colleges. The O.P.I. is composed of hundreds of value-laden statements to which students are asked to respond "true" or "false" depending upon their orientation to the values seemingly explicit in the statements. A few examples will show how a working-class background alone might cause students to choose the "wrong" responses often enough to indicate unattractive authoritarian personalities. The "right" answer to one statement requires students to prefer their freedom *from* their family rather than to see value in a lifelong relationship with them—a working-class value that comes from a more fully developed sense of extended family than is found in the middle class. Other "right" answers require students to reject all the hard work and sacrifice that may have helped sustain their families while they were growing up; these "right" answers require that students reject hard work and sacrifice and favor more theoretical or aesthetic values. Some of these statements include: "More than anything else, it is good hard work that makes life worthwhile." (The Autonomous "right" answer is False; the Practical "right" answer is True.) "Every wage-earner should be required to save a certain part of his income each month so that he will be able to support himself and his family in later years." (The Autonomous "right" answer is False.) "Nothing in life is worth the sacrifice of losing contact with your family." (False.) "There is something noble about poverty and suffering." (False.)[25]

The distorted assumptions about student personalities that such tests proclaim are central to the major book-length works on community college students. When looking into them, in light of the above, it is imperative to search for *the missing connections between ethnicity, class, and intelligence* and also for *the unstated social functions of the concept of ability itself*—issues critical to a true understanding of these "new" college students' real strengths and limitations.

The work of K. Patricia Cross comes first. She perhaps more than anyone else has studied and restudied community college students. Her two most fully elaborated studies of more than seventy thousand high-school juniors and seniors and first-semester two-year-college students are regarded as the definitive works on these "new" students and are quoted and requoted frequently.[26] Much of what she writes substantiates older intuitive or social scientific data. But there are a number of new wrinkles, most of them concerning new students' personal characteristics. What is particularly new, and insidious, is that her policy recommendations are not just based on what we can measure on "objective" tests—the usual practice—but more *on what the students tell us about themselves.* "For a change," she in effect says, "let's listen to them." And with not a word about how previous academic failure and the resulting negative self-perceptions might shape one's responses to a questionnaire that asks you what you want and *expect* from school, without a word on the effects of what being poor in this society means to one's view of education and careers, she presents her picture of how community college students see themselves and draws conclusions from this concerning what the community college should offer them.[27]

In their own words, then, the students tell us that they are more inclined than traditional students to watch television than to read books, more apt to party than to study, more likely to want to work with their hands than with their minds, more practical than theoretical, more passive than active, more emotionally disturbed (they ask to see counselors more), and most enthusiastic about vocationally oriented education.[28] Remarkably, on their own initiative, *they channel themselves* to two-year colleges, for when asked to describe their ideal college new students describe a community college whereas traditional students describe something that resembles the Ivy League. And if we listen to what they tell us about their aspirations we would expect to find most of them in terminal programs. When asked to "dream a bit" about what they would *like* to do, without thinking about what the job would pay or whether they have the necessary qualifications, the careers most frequently dreamt about were as follows: 60 percent of the male new students choose "auto mechanic" and 78 percent of female new students choose either "typist" or "secretary," whereas the majority of traditional students dreamt about becoming authors of novels, high-school and college teachers, doctors, U.S. senators, etc.[29]

But as we have seen, in spite of how they respond to Cross's questionnaires, when it comes time to select curricula, up to 75 percent of new students choose transfer programs—and probably more would if institutional policies and counselors would let them. How to explain this paradox of new students acting in opposition to their own aspirations—a rather Dostoevskian idea of people consciously acting to assert their own disadvantage? She barely examines this paradox. Instead, she advocates that community colleges shift their focus away from the more popular—but unsuccessful (look at the dropout rates)—transfer programs to the less popular vocational programs that *seem* to correspond more to the students' self-stated interests. She dreams about a society in which community colleges will free students to realize their, to her, *real* aspirations. In her new society equal status will be assigned to doctors and auto mechanics. And significantly, while waiting for this new society to materialize, community colleges should not try to make too many of their new students into traditional students because even if this were a good idea (which to her is questionable) community colleges cannot expect to be successful considering what the questionnaires reveal they are up against.[30] However, this should not be too upsetting because even the traditional "high-achieving" student has his/her problems: "For example, as he copes with the intricacies of machine repair. In the first place, he discovers that he lacks the vocabulary to know one machine part from another. Furthermore, he may find that while he is trying to use *his* developed skill in reading the repair manual, the instructor is 'moving too fast' in a field that does not depend on verbalization. . . . In other words, a student who has been successful in school finds himself 'educationally disadvantaged.'"[31] The stereotyping is chilling: her new society still seems to be peopled by thin-chested, absent-minded college professors who can't catch a baseball or fix a car and hairy-ape mechanics who can barely read or write. It doesn't help very much to declare them equal in the eyes of God.

Cross though is capable of transcending this, of perceiving how social forces shape self-perception and aspiration. In her chapter "Women as New Students" she writes brilliantly and with feeling about how women have been conditioned to set their aspirations at "realistic" levels for jobs that will be open to them: women have been encouraged to think about elementary-school teaching rather than college teaching, about typing instead of business management, and about becoming nurses rather than doctors.[32] But she seems incapable of applying this same analysis to other new students. There is no equivalent account of how blue-collar students are "encouraged" to dream of becoming auto mechanics. It is not enough to prefer, with John Gardner, excellent plumbers to mediocre philosophers. And so it would seem that what Cross prefers for future community colleges is in fact essentially just more of the same.

Charles Monroe also devotes much of his book, *Profile of the Community College,* to new students, and a large portion of that concerns their personalities and the educational policies he deduces therefrom. As if to substantiate his claim that the book is the most complete ever written on two-year colleges, he takes his analysis of new students' personalities one step beyond Cross's to what might be called *The Psychopathology of Community College Students.* To him the students display a syndrome of characteristics that psychologists have named the "authoritarian personality." Many of the symptoms Cross defined as characteristic of new students are brought together in Monroe's diagnosis: the authoritarian personality is insecure and threat oriented. He has difficulty seeing subtle differences—to him things are either right or wrong, good or bad. He is a conformist and is easily swayed by what he perceives to be authority. The authoritarian personality's thinking is stereotyped, etc., etc.[33]

Another new idea with Monroe is his view that the problems community college students have in an academic setting are in a sense *self-caused.* Although he recognizes that society exerts a great influence on personality development, the best explanation for the origins of the authoritarian personality seems to be found in the faulty psychological development of the individual: it is a malady of incomplete ego formation.[34] Society, they, the schools, the degradations of poverty, the political structures, none of these have anything to do with the kinds of students who come to two-year colleges nor the kinds of failure they encounter there. The institutions are innocent. The individual has only himself or herself to blame. Somehow Monroe doesn't ever manage to reconcile this with his own evidence from Nevitt Sanford that all college freshmen tend to have authoritarian personalities, not just community college students.

And there are other ways too that Monroe finds to affix the blame for their "failure" to the student-victims. It is an ingenious argument that's based on two inter-locking but self-contradictory premises. On the one hand he asks community colleges that have not been all that successful at teaching cognitive skills to consider that maybe it's more important to concentrate on help-ing students make a smooth transition to adulthood by working with them on their "adjustment" problems rather than on their academic problems.[35] In the same breath, however, he cites myriad studies that indicate that the college experience can have little or no impact on these kinds of things either—that families and peers exert the most powerful influence on young people's values and personalities. So, he says, we shouldn't feel badly if we fail in the affective domain as well.[36] Monroe's message appears to be that since it doesn't seem to matter what we do, we should keep on doing what we're doing—accepting failure because we're up against both the powerlessness of institutions to make a difference and the helplessness of community college students to either learn or help themselves. Perhaps the reason his book has been so widely heralded is that it more or less locates the pain and simultaneously supplies the morphine.

In response to all of this, if there is one thing I've learned through years of experience encountering and working with community college students, it's that most of those whom Monroe and others describe as inept and pathological in fact *lack confidence rather than ability.* And it is the consequences of this lack of confidence that are most responsible for their frequently noted academic difficulties.

Lack of confidence in one's abilities and its many academic consequences is neither traceable to a traumatic incident nor is it easily remediable via a pep talk or pat on the back. My best evidence for this does not come from studies or statistics but rather from the lives of the students I have known.

The first thing Ronald remembers of his schooling is being literally tied to his seat by his first-grade teacher because he couldn't or wouldn't sit still during reading. He now feels this may have had more to do with the fact that he already could read than that he was a discipline problem. But "discipline problem" became a part of his permanent record, perhaps because, as he looks back, it was more usual to think of black six-year-olds as disruptive or "hyperactive" than as reading "above grade level."

At home, his mother supported the teacher's assessment: Ronald never seemed to want to do any homework—he always preferred the excitement of the streets to the discipline of his parents. His sister was the family's pride and joy. She was beautiful whereas Ronald was ungainly and awkward; she accepted and excelled at her piano lessons whereas he rejected anything extra his parents scrimped and saved to provide for him. As a result, he was offered less and less, and less and less came to be expected of him. When by the fifth grade he was judged to be nearly a year behind in reading, nobody was surprised. Quite the contrary. No one by then remembered how "strange" it was that he was able to read the words on TV commercials and on the ads on the sides of buses even before he went to school.

He was good with his hands—first fiddling with home-made soapbox racers, later with broken-down toasters and alarm clocks—so by the time he reluctantly entered high school a trade program seemed naturally suited to his interests and abilities. He got into the automotive curriculum but pursued it in a lackluster manner. Though still in the streets he spent endless hours with friends "customizing" junkyard cars they somehow managed to get their hands on. He also spent many hours, quite privately—almost secretly, reading everything he could find by James Baldwin, John Williams, and Richard Wright. His friends would have made fun of him if they knew of this secret pleasure. And when years later I asked him about how he felt about his reading and extremely sophisticated perceptions of both the themes and prose style of Baldwin and Wright, he shrugged it all off with the casual comment that that was all easy for him because after all they were *only* writing about "black folk" which is not all that special or difficult to understand. Even his tenth-grade English teacher who sensed this interest and had a glimpse of Ronald's own writing (rather powerful poems) encouraged him to continue working on cars: "There's good money in it," she advised.

His sister was accepted into Hunter College's nursing

program; and during the family party that brought aunts, uncles, and cousins all the way to Brooklyn from as far away as Massachusetts, Ronald remembers holing up in his bedroom to finish reading John Williams's *Night Song*. No one seemed to miss him; he was only called out to have a piece of cake and to get his picture taken—a stiff family portrait he showed me one time.

He doesn't quite remember how he got to community college. During his last two years in high school he had a weekend job pumping gas and he was offered the chance to work full-time, even doing some repair work, when he graduated. He also recalls his father pushing him to take the job so Ronald could get set to live on his own since his people were preparing to retire and move back to North Carolina. His father kept asking, "How long are we going to have to keep supporting you?" All of this, plus a friend's having applied to Community and the one-page application with its guarantee of admission to any high-school graduate apparently was enough to motivate Ronald.

He worked at the station full-time during the summer after he graduated, and without telling his parents was accepted by and decided *perhaps* to go to college in September. He still didn't know why he was doing any of this. He had no idea what he would study at college, though he was admitted via the mechanical technology curriculum. Maybe it was to be with his best and only friend who was going to major in liberal arts—whatever that was. He finally did have to confront his father when he unalterably decided to go. It was an ugly scene which he vividly remembers but is reluctant to recount. The effect, however, was clear: he was instantly cut loose from any further financial support (his family is now somewhere in North Carolina—he doesn't know quite where; he hasn't heard from them in nearly a year) and as a result was riddled even further with doubts about what he was doing.

The doubts, the struggle to survive economically, the irrelevance to him of most of the courses he was required to take during his first term at Community, almost broke him. He got heavily involved in wine and drugs and came within a breath of dropping out. He managed somehow to make it through the semester only because the vision of what he would be dropping out into frightened him more than the prospect of trying to hang on at school.

I met Ronald as the result of overhearing part of a conversation between him and his English Composition instructor. I was working out one morning by an open window in the college's exercise room when they happened to walk by. It was near the end of the term and they were discussing Ronald's final grade—rather the instructor was talking and Ronald was walking alongside with his head and shoulders hunched forward. What caught my attention was the teacher's attempt to blackmail Ronald into taking a remedial reading course. After expressing some concern about Ronald's reading, the instructor laid out the deal, "I'll tell you what, I'll give you a B if and only if you agree to take reading next term." They passed out of hearing but what continued to strike me was my sense of Ronald's despair, my feeling of his intense though thoroughly internalized anger at what was being proposed to him. Thus I sought to meet him.

It took a while before he would tell me very much about his experiences at the college, much less anything more about himself. But I did come rather quickly to learn about his English class. Though his instructor is widely known to be one of the more liberal faculty members, publicly devoted to the realization of his students' submerged potential, according to Ronald (and others) he is an ill-prepared and totally ineffective teacher. He had spent the semester basically reading directly from the anthology of essays he assigned. When students would try to ask questions, his eyes would become slits as he would break in before they could finish, obviously ignoring them. During the semester Ronald had heard him speak at a Food Day rally before a large audience of colleagues and students. Organic farming is one of the professor's major interests, and to hear Ronald's version of it, he was positively brilliant. He wondered out loud, "Why didn't he speak to *us* that way?" A rare moment of self-assertion for him. Much more typical was his comment later that same day when I asked if he was coming to hear Allen Ginsberg read that evening. He looked at me wide-eyed, incredulously, as if I were a man from Mars, "Why would he be coming *here*?"

He's now vaguely thinking about switching to liberal arts, perhaps because for the first time in his life his interest in reading (in spite of his Composition instructor) and writing is publicly acceptable, perhaps because he feels there aren't any good jobs for mechanical technologists, perhaps because he wants to be more than just "good with his hands." In any case, Ronald has seen a counselor about it who recently told him that before he can get into the liberal arts curriculum he has to prove himself "worthy" of it. "Worthy" involves getting a B average (not at all school policy incidentally) which means it's more than likely Ronald will be taking remedial reading next term. I can't help wondering to myself if it will include any James Baldwin.

Lorraine's parents were divorced when she was seven years old. They are Catholic and the divorce did not sit well with the family. No support was forthcoming from them and so Lorraine's mother was forced to go back to her bookkeeping job to keep herself and her three young children off welfare. Public assistance of any kind was to be avoided at all costs. Self-respect required as much. She hated the work and came to resent it and the children who seemed to be the cause of all her troubles. She was young and attractive then and longed to be able to go out, perhaps meet someone, and eventually remarry. But when anyone became interested in her in more than a casual way the fact that she had three young children drove them away. At least that's the way it seemed to Lorraine's mother. And as a result, Lorraine and her two brothers in a sense paid the price for their very existence.

In spite of this, Lorraine did very well in school. Her teachers adored her. She was very well behaved, read and wrote ahead of schedule, and was class monitor for everything from cleaning the blackboard erasers to collecting milk and cookie money. As early as the first grade she began bringing home an annual armful of awards and certificates of merit—for reading, conduct, good citizenship. Her mother acknowledged none of them though Lorraine's father remained affectionate and supportive at the legally required distance.

One brother left school and began full-time work in a local diner at sixteen. The other finished high school, immediately got married to a non-Catholic, and disappeared from view somewhere in California. The pressure thus began to build on Lorraine to take a secretarial course in high school. One night during her last year in junior high, with the stereo blasting away in her bedroom, she slashed her wrists with the razor she used to shave her legs and underarms. When the music suddenly stopped her mother found her and rushed her to the hospital. Luckily the wounds were superficial and Lorraine was home, heavily bandaged and sedated, in less than three hours. Nothing much, however, changed for her at home.

The following fall she entered high school—and the commercial program. High school was sex and drugs for Lorraine. Lying to her mother became a way of life. "I'm with Vivian" when she was parked with Jimmy; "We're going to the movies" when she was flying high on marijuana; "I'm at a party with Debbie" when she and her friends were stealing cars and joy riding in the Bronx. She loved every minute of it; though now she says she hated the whole thing as well. Whereas she had formerly helped with the housework, she now did nothing but make a shambles of her room. Teachers who knew her in elementary and junior high school barely recognized her. She avoided her father who felt concern but couldn't find the words to tell her so. Her mother kept pressing her to quit school and find a job. She didn't want to work and was having too exciting a time, so she applied to community college.

The party continued there, but something new and inexplicable happened to her: she began to feel guilty. She hated her mother for ample reasons, but more and more frequently she had to admit to herself that her mother had also had a difficult life. Lorraine as well began to think back on her earlier more successful schooling. Not that there was much to inspire her at college. She had a steady diet of required courses taught by instructors, she felt, who would rather like herself be doing something else. She had done miserably during her first year and was on probation—just two one-hundredths of a grade point away from dismissal and the waiting office job or inevitable marriage she desperately wanted to avoid. But at that time she didn't have a very good idea of how to avoid either. She was bored with everything. Her teachers were aloof. To go for counseling or any other kind of help was an admission of personal weakness, an inability to get through life solely by one's own efforts.

During the summer her crowd of friends got involved in helping a young politician mount a primary campaign against a hithertofore perenially reelected state senator. No one was very much interested in politics; it was just that one of the campaign storefronts was reputed to be a good place to party after the day's mailings and phone calls were done, and grass was said to be both plentiful and safe. However, without planning to, Lorraine got involved in more than the partying. The candidate was more than young; he was attractive, even charismatic, and really stood for something important. Lorraine was at first merely attracted to him, but after a short while she became attracted to his ideas as well and began to work harder and harder—canvassing, stapling posters to traffic light poles in the middle of the night to avoid the police, and even having a try at putting together a position paper on health care for the aged.

I met her briefly just before her involvement in the campaign and saw her for the second time when it was at its height. The transformation in her appearance alone was astonishing: her eyes blazed with an intensity that was difficult to return when she talked of the issues in the campaign. And that's all she wanted to talk about up until primary day and the defeat that was unfortunately inevitable. But she bounced back—considerably wiser, it seemed to me, prepared for the first time in quite a while to take on the troubling complexities and contradictions of life—particularly those of her own life.

No miracles occurred at school in the fall. She struggled to get through her courses (no more inspiring or relevant than before) and had a long way to go in order to get off probation. She's not as yet certain why she's doing it all; office work of some kind and/or marriage still loom for her, as inevitable as her candidate's defeat. If you were to ask her today if she thinks she'll make it through Community, wistfully but without hesitation she'll tell you, "Not a chance." I'm not so sure.

When I knew Norman, his family's income was nearly $30,000 per year. Everyone worked, and worked hard. His father was an assessor for the city and earned a little more than $22,000; his mother worked part-time as a salesperson in a department store in the neighborhood; his brother had a newspaper route; and Norman worked twenty-five hours per week after school and on weekends at a hamburger franchise. But in spite of this they never seemed to have any money and they had very little idea how it all disappeared. Norman always talked a lot about leaving school to work more (his employers had offered to make him store manager) to help bring in more money. But college meant more to him (particularly the B.A.) and his going meant a lot to his family: Though his father considered himself to be successful—many of his co-workers were college graduates—no one in their immediate family had ever gone to college.

I got to know them all rather well, and as I perceived them they were a close and loving family. They gave each other the distance to be individuals without sacrificing either the desire or the time to enjoy each other. Norman's mother was a fairly good amateur painter and they all took pleasure in her latest canvas. On those occasions when she would have a picture in a local show they would attend en masse and root for her to get a prize ribbon. Norman's brother was deeply involved in Little League baseball, and though they went to all his games it was never to pressure him to win at all costs; they somehow managed to enjoy his errors as well as his hits. Norman's father loved to fish, and often he would take the boys out with him. They would get up at 4:30 in the morning in order to catch the 6:00 A.M. boat out of Sheepshead Bay. His mother would pack a shopping bag full of the best sandwiches imaginable and they would bring her their catch for dinner that night or to stock the freezer in the basement.

Norman wasn't an outstanding student at any time in his life. And that was all right with all of them, just so long as he was trying to do the best he could. His teachers liked him and some even came to respect him. It's true he had few close friends and had a great deal of difficulty breaking into the world of dating, petting, and going steady. This concerned the whole family and of course Norman as well. It's just about the only thing he can recall from his youth that caused any sustained tension at home—he felt too much pressure to get involved in what his parents considered normal dating practices. But when in his senior year in high school he met and eventually went steady with a girl his parents both approved and enjoyed, that tension disappeared.

His high-school grades were just good enough to entitle him to enter one of the four-year units of the state university. But he chose instead to go to the local two-year college—it would be cheaper (he could commute); and since he wasn't yet confident of his academic ability, he could test and prepare himself for a senior college in the less demanding academic environment of the community college. So he entered as a transfer student, determined to begin his quest for an eventual degree in education. He very much wanted to be either a high-school biology or chemistry teacher.

Norman liked his courses and teachers at the college. He felt sufficiently challenged; his instructors in general seemed to care about their subjects and about his progress. When he sought them out after class in their offices, they made themselves available to him. He got involved in the school newspaper and the weight-lifting club. He became features editor at the end of his first year (having written a first-rate piece on the excesses of some student government officials) and managed once to bench press 220 pounds. Things were obviously going very well for him.

He was a student in a literature class I was teaching. It certainly was not his major interest, but Norman was quite competent in analyzing the stories and poems we dealt with. I respected his hard work (unasked, he would revise his papers two or three times) and I enjoyed his company. We talked quite a lot about the advantages and disadvantages of chemistry and biology (I was an English major and chemistry minor at college). We went through catalogues of four-year schools together; Norman wanted just the right place to go to when he transferred. He asked me to become his adviser and I was delighted to do so.

Then about three-quarters of the way through the semester, he missed two or three class sessions in a row (they were his first absences). Just as I was about to call him at home to see what had happened, he showed up at my office to ask me to sign a form that would enable him to drop all his courses and thus withdraw from the college. He refused to talk about his reasons. I was miserable and frustrated about the whole thing. I pleaded with him to talk about it, but he sullenly refused. When in despair I finally signed the form (I could not refuse), I ruefully noticed that where the form asked the reasons for his withdrawal ("Personal," "Academic," "Health," etc.) Norman had checked the box next to "Financial." I later learned from his father that he had accepted the manager's job at Burger King.

It's been two years since then. I have tried to reach Norman from time to time but without success. I understand he married his high-school girlfriend and that she's expecting a baby.

Hopefully some of this, though hardly "scientific," may help call into question our overreliance upon conventional analyses of the personal and intellectual characteristics of community college students. This is especially important because the kinds of structures we establish for our schools have and always will depend upon who we *think* our students are. One final example will show how this works in day-to-day practice.

The two hundred students entering a special program for "the disadvantaged" at a New York community college were given a multiple-choice reading placement test. It was scored by computer, and the results indicated that *all* two hundred read below the seventh-grade level. So all of them were put in specially designed remedial reading classes. After about a month and an inordinate number of complaints from students that the course was too easy, too watered down, someone in the testing center rechecked the results. He immediately noticed that the distribution of scores looked as if all the students had *randomly* chosen their answers to the questions.

So he asked to have the test rescored. This time there was a distribution of scores indicating that the students read between the sixth- and fifteenth-grade levels. Much more like past results. Further checking revealed they had used the wrong answer form for the first scoring. But further checking didn't reveal why the teachers and counselors in that special program had so easily accepted the "fact" that all their students were reading at the elementary-school level and were blithely proceeding accordingly.

PART TWO
NEW DIRECTIONS

Educators think that when they have made arithmetic or spelling into a game, made it unnecessary for children to "sit up straight"; defined the relation between teacher and children as democratic; and introduced plants, fish, and hamsters into schoolrooms, they have settled the problem of drill. They are mistaken.

—Jules Henry
1965

SIX

AN ACKNOWLEDGED POLITICAL EDUCATION

New directions for community college education must begin by acknowledging the political consequences of education and the class-serving role the schools have been playing. New political lessons must be included in the curriculum. In order to have a chance to become truly equal, students—particularly the kind of students who have traditionally come to community colleges—must come to see how they have been misserved by schools so that they will be able to understand that their previous lack of academic success was not entirely their own fault.

In other words, the old process of cooling-out has to be replaced by a process of *heating-up*. When students learn these new political lessons they become angry. But that anger, if properly focused, can become the motivation for students to define themselves differently, to learn to respect their true abilities, to begin to do well academically—if that is their choice, and even to make an upward adjustment in their aspirational levels.

Michael Katz has pointed out that early efforts at school reform failed because the reformers stressed "only" the need to change human nature—its tendency toward chaos and vice. Nothing was said about the greater need to apply the same kind of reform *to the social systems* themselves. This misapplied emphasis obscured the depth and character of the social problems that needed to be addressed in order to bring about important social reform. And by focusing on human nature rather than on human institutions, reformers wound up compounding the problem they presumably were attacking: they estranged from the schools the very people they said they were concerned about serving— the working-class community. They did this by haranguing them about their own viciousness, immorality, short-sightedness, about how they were inadequate as parents, how their lack of concern for their own children and their education was the cause of their poverty, crime, vice, etc. Only the schools, they proclaimed, could save them from themselves. And not surprisingly the "people" stayed away in droves.[1] The problem, unfortunately, has a contemporary ring to it.

For fundamental reform to occur in the community college the focus has to shift from the students to an examination of the real but unacknowledged political role of education. Otherwise we get a continuous series of reforms that bring no change—Erik Erikson calls this "reformulation," change directed toward maintaining the status quo.[2] A quick example of this is the fact that the inclusion of ever increasing numbers of students in schools and colleges since 1900 has not caused a significant change in the relative condition or number of the poor in relation to their position in the social order.

Colin Greer outlines a process through which schools might come to lead rather than reflect the society in which they exist. First, the harmony that now exists between the schools and society must be broken. Then by stimulating a change in education, one of the major institutions by which society shapes itself, we might be able to provoke a reformation of society. This might occur through making the contradictions between institutional rhetoric and reality apparent.[3] In part, this would mean teaching students the real history of institutions—family, school, etc.—so that they would be able to connect this reality to their own personal histories within these institutions.

This political education is a very powerful *and* a very dangerous process. Paulo Freire calls it "conscientization." Originally it meant that adults could be taught literacy more readily if the teaching were related to the basic concerns of everyday life. But the term has come to mean much more. It now means the entire transformation of the consciousness of people. Through it they can come to understand the political constraints within which they live and the possibilities of changing their situation. People will be able to liberate themselves from political and social control only if they first liberate themselves from the patterns of thought imposed by coercive institutions.[4]

Traditional political education in schools is rather blatant. In Michael Parenti's words, more political socialization goes on in the average public school than in the average political club.[5] The school comes complete with its hymns (the "Star-Spangled Banner"), its sacred symbols (Old Glory), its rituals (the daily drill of the salute to the flag), its scriptures (the Declaration of Independence and the Constitution), its litany and incantations (Pledge of Allegiance), its early church fathers (Washington, Jefferson), its prophets (Paul Revere, Patrick Henry), its martyrs (Nathan Hale, Abraham Lincoln), its Judases (Benedict Arnold, John Wilkes Booth), and its history of divine origin (the *Mayflower*, Plymouth Rock, Constitution Hall).[6] The school, as Ivan Illich points out, is in effect the new church, and political education is the new religion.

But our political education in elementary school had additional personal consequences which—for those who obviously deviated from the acceptable ethnic, Protestant, middle-class, norms—had long-lasting, perhaps permanent effects. If we were taught to "love America," many of us were also taught to hate ourselves, particularly our class origins and our ethnic identities. Our working-class European parents' speech, dress, physical appearance all earned the disapproval of our Americanized teachers. We were taught to be ashamed of them and of the way they behaved. We learned the reserve and proper speech to replace their gusto and accent. For this we were rewarded with gold stars and more. But if we persisted in asserting our "old" ways we were punished with more than demerits—soon finding ourselves with the slow readers, perhaps even in the "dumb class." We quickly became a mass of competitive persons, experiencing less and less self-generated cooperative effort, directed more and more by a centralized authority that monopolized the resources of initiative and command. Thus, the components of our early political education—though it was never called that; and thus our political indoctrination.[7]

Much of what I am proposing in the way of reform involves a process of unlearning that must take place before new learning can occur. This might include having my New York City community college students read something one is unlikely to find on any standard reading list: *The Graduates Restudied: A Comparison of the Follow-Up of New York City High School Graduates of 1970 and 1971*,[8] by Blank, et al. Hardly compelling the same interest as Tolkien's trilogy, but if properly presented more meaningful. It provides an unintentionally clear picture of the vicious cycle within which socioeconomic status is reproduced with the help of the schools. It is a cycle that must be understood if community college students, among others, are to have a chance of escaping its social snares. One can derive, with students, a pictorial representation of this hidden political role of education:

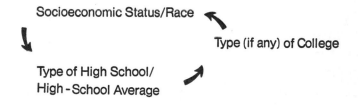

Socioeconomic Status/Race

Type (if any) of College

Type of High School/
High-School Average

They can trace their own movements within this process, and also discover what they *don't know* about how being in a two-year college itself largely determines what is likely to happen to them next. In order for them to understand that perhaps fewer than 10 percent of them will get B.A.'s, that up to three-quarters of them are unlikely to complete even two years of college, that the kinds of jobs that await them even if they finish two

years are not all that different from their parents', or that
the cycle will tend very soon to complete itself in spite of
their intentions and dreams, they first have to understand what they've already been through in the lower
schools.

And unless they are eager to accept the notion that
poor people inherently have less ability or motivation,
they will begin to look for more plausible explanations.
These reasons, as we have seen, are contained in the
history and hidden functions of higher education. It thus
becomes imperative for students to learn and understand
this history—again connecting it to their own educational histories which in brief contain the essential elements
of that larger history. Before they can make their personal plans, they have to understand society's master plans
for them.

We have to be careful, however, that our students do
not just wind up learning *the new-right-answers* to replace the old. I've frequently overheard some of our
experienced students initiating a newcomer into the new
dogma: schools are all messed up; it's because I'm
working class that I'm at this second-rate place, teachers
never expected very much from me so I never did very
well in high school; etc. But I know too that some of
these students with the new answers frequently can't
seem to do more than two hours of reading *a week*, that
they spend most of their time on campus hanging out in
the lounge stoned out of their minds. I also know that
my letting them call me Steve and say "shit" and the like
in my classes doesn't necessarily mean that we're not
playing old games by new rules.

Often for them, and for me, a way out of the trap of
the superficially understood new-right-answers involves

a mutual examination of the political structure of the classroom experience itself—we look at the question of power between teacher and students and between the students of different social and academic skills. Arranging the chairs in a circle, using first names and profanity changes nothing. When students talk to each other they still look at me, seeking nonverbal signs of approval or disapproval: I continue to be a moral switchboard for their classroom communications with each other.[9] Things get quiet when I come into the room, assuming they've been talking to each other before I get there. When things slow down during the class, the same two or three students are there to pick things up. My ideas or opinions—even about last night's New York Knicks game—are definitive. If I have to leave a little early but suggest that if they wish they might keep a lively discussion going until the end of the hour, the class ends when the door closes behind me. Even when we venture into the realm of gut-level feelings and experiences, inequalities exist—they must tell more than I: their emotional lives belong to me for the asking, mine remains hidden in much the same way that my third-grade teacher's first name and marital status remained hidden from me.

Even if we're careful about this we can't avoid this political reality, but we can use it to aid both unlearning and new learning. We can try to stop a class if we notice Peggy riveting her eyes to mine while talking to Norman and make *that* the lesson. Next week we can try to find out why a lively and seemingly important class ended when I said, "I guess that's it for today." But it's hardly enough. The things I've suggested so far are analogous to what early school reformers proposed—and fall short of real achievement in much the same way. We can help

Peggy look at Norman when she's talking to him and I may even be able to tell a class something about my emotional life, but the structures (here, of the classroom) still remain basically untouched.

Can very much be done about questions of power in the classroom within bureaucratic school settings? There are at least ways to begin to deal with these political problems. One is to begin to restructure the assumptions that determine the relationships between the teacher and the taught, between the helper and the helped. I know of teachers and counselors, conducting what might be called freshman orientation courses, who have developed means of group counseling in which there has been a measurable equalization of power between the faculty member and the students. To help demythologize the aura of the professional, the whole group becomes the teacher or counselor. And not in the usual way where everyone is glibly seen as "teachers and learners together," while the teacher remains the sole active source of motivation and knowledge. A committee of students from the class or the class as a whole with the faculty member as an *ex officio* resource person might chart out the curricula directions for the course, develop group projects for the class, present suggestions for modes of evaluation and grading, even decide the extent of the faculty member's participation. They might decide, for example, that rather than continuing with competitive grading arrangements or settling in advance on a single grade for the entire class that they agree to a cooperative grading system in which all individual and group assignments and projects must be successfully completed to predetermined levels of competence before anyone in the class or the class as a whole receives (or gives itself) a grade. Not only does such an arrangement avoid the subtle and not-so-subtle scrambling and hustling for grades, recognition, or acceptance that is a commonplace even in many alternative schools; but it has the benefit also of putting the whole question of the hidden political functions of grading squarely within the curriculum of the course itself—even in a history or a science class that is basically devoted to other matters but in which real learning is often thwarted by grading games.

In such a restructured situation not only must the students develop new cooperative skills and new ways of relating to teachers, but the instructors, too, must examine their needs and their behavior. Is their need to help people learn or is it to *control* the direction and content of that learning? One way to find out is to try to look closely at the hidden content of the counseling and advisement we give to students during office hours— both to those students who come seeking us out and those we summon to us. I have come to feel that much of what students tell me in these sessions and much of what I or the situation cause them to tell me intensifies the hierarchical relationship that exists between us. At times I catch myself more titillated by their stories of problems with parents, boyfriends, and girlfriends, more stirred to liberal guilt by their economic and personal tragedies than motivated to help them understand their existential situation or the things we are reading or studying together. For the slice of real life they offer me I give them understanding and release from both the assignment and the difficulties of facing what we are doing to each other: I deny them the challenge that is necessary to help them to become powerful and they deny me the chance to allow more of my inner self to enter the classroom. In our unacknowledged arrangements we are mutually exploited and together remain separate and powerless. At those times when I've been able to see this and bring it up with the students I'm advising we begin to find release from our roles and become stronger. We may, and probably should, define limits to how much they "must" reveal or I am "allowed" to tell them, but what emerges, hopefully, is a counseling or advisement situation in an acknowledged political and human context that facilitates a clear look at what exists between us and between us and the institution.

With that clear look students can begin to discover how the school *setting* or *environment* also imposes political lessons. A community college dean of administration's memo posted in the school's toilets reveals familiar double meanings:

> It seems to me that simple human consideration calls for treating this bathroom as if it was in your own home, since in effect this is your own home while you are a student here. My attention has been called to the terrible condition of the restrooms by the staff responsible for their upkeep. Our people, your neighbors and friends [the cleaning staff], do try to keep these restrooms clean. However, you must help us with this job . . . .

Students who have unlearned sufficiently so as not to respect such memos just because of their high source can read this with the same interpretive and analytical skill they have learned to apply to a piece of assigned poetry or prose. They can see that the notion of regarding the bathroom as their home (the syntax is ambiguous enough for such an interpretation) is truer than the dean imagines—for many using drugs, for someone seeking privacy, the bathroom in an overcrowded two-year college remains the same kind of sanctuary the high-school or junior-high-school bathroom was for adolescent smokers or class-cutters. They may also notice that the dean got his information about the condition of the rest rooms from "the staff responsible for their upkeep"; it's clear that his high office entitles him to a key to the executive bathroom and keeps him away from casual on-site personal investigation whenever nature calls. Students who have unlearned also can't help noting that the dean thinks he knows who they are or at least has a stereotypical notion of their "neighbors and friends"—the staff responsible for cleaning the toilets; it's unlikely that he would make a similar kind of appeal to the students to get them to respect their teachers (clearly not "neighbors and friends") by, say, asking students to attend class more regularly. It's inconceivable also that students at Harvard would ever encounter such memos in their bathrooms (or anywhere) making such assumptions about them. Someone who had unlearned enough to understand some of this had scrawled "HELP!" across the memo I encountered—and with good reason.

From the bathroom to the cafeteria is a short distance and there the lessons are equally vivid and equally useful to the development of a new, acknowledged political education. And many's the time we've used these environmental lessons for a class on comparative cafeterias. It begins in our own which is typical of those at two-year colleges throughout the country. At best you don't get ill from the food; at worst you sit at uncleared tables assaulted by noise so loud you have to shout to be heard by your friend sitting across from you. For literally more than two years the two electric clocks in our cafeteria have been about an hour fast and a half-hour slow respectively, seemingly impervious to changes from Standard to Daylight Savings. Time, cleanliness, health, conversation, it seems, are not important to our students. But less than a mile from us is Wagner College and its cafeteria. Wagner is a private school charging, by today's standards, modest tuition to its middle-class student clientele. It's not a great school by any measure—except perhaps as judged by its cafeteria. At least to us it's great because of its carpeted floor, comfortable chairs, modern wooden tables, its quiet, and the fact that for $1.25 or so you can eat all the lunch you want: salads, sodas, ice cream, the works. At our place, $1.25 buys you barely a thin hamburger, french fries, and a coke—all on paper dishes with plastic forks.

When the class assembles itself at Wagner (and there are Wagners near almost every two-year college), settling down to its second helping of dessert, we try to figure out the differences. What we immediately come to is that the differences between the cafeterias is the result of the fact that Wagner charges tuition (about sixty dollars per credit) and our place has "free tuition." As we probe this a bit, we quickly discover that there is more truth to be discovered in that oxymoron "free tuition" than was perhaps intended by the City University officials who first used it. For tuition to be tuition it can't be free: "tuition" means "cost." And at the City University, as in *every* system of public education, the free tuition is largely paid by the taxpayers who use (or don't use) the system—though not all that equitably as my chapter The Economics of Second Best indicates. And by a quick calculation we find that it costs us (the students and their families) about sixty dollars a credit to attend a City University community college. The city "spends" about $1,800 per year for each full-time student taking thirty credits per year: thirty into $1,800 equals sixty dollars per credit. So it "costs" about as much to go to our place as it does to go to Wagner. The answer then must lie in the fact that Wagner subsidizes its cafeteria—they obviously can't be making money at $1.25 a head. The answer turns out to be two answers: yes, they do subsidize the cafeteria, but also it does make a profit. The cafeteria is run by a profit-making caterer who receives the subsidy of free rent (like free tuition) for the facilities—precisely the same arrangement enjoyed by our caterer. The reasons behind the differences, as with everything else, lie more in the institutional intentions. Each cafeteria reveals precisely what its school thinks is appropriate for its students: one institution wants and gets quality service for its students; the other doesn't care.

The lesson becomes fully clear during a day-trip visit to the eating places (no longer a cafeteria) of a college such as Princeton. We're now in another world altogether. The food is more varied and frequently quite good. The seating arrangements are more intimate, more like restaurant dining. The food is often served and beer or wine is available. For certain money is very much involved at such places, no denying that. But more is at stake as well. It's quickly very clear to all of us that of the three places, only the students at Princeton are being prepared to be served more than just dinner. And thus at our college and at Wagner people must also be getting prepared for more than just eating. One doesn't learn at our school from plastic forks and soup in a styrofoam coffee cup how to perform in an executive dining suite or at a publisher's lunch in a little French restaurant. Skills, I suggest, as important in their way as those derived from memorizing the periodic table of elements.

One student who went through this kind of learning process discovered some of the contradictory messages of our college's new, liberalized grading system. For example, the transcript calls the D grade "passing" (A is "excellent," B is "very good," etc.); however, if students earn less than C averages they are eventually flunked out of college (in our language, "academically dismissed"). So you can "pass" and "fail" at the same time—a truly existential dilemma. Also, this student revealed to us, we have a couple of grades that seem to contradict a central part of our cherished work ethic: if you work hard all semester long, study, come to all the classes, but are still not successful, you get an F. But if you shirk all your work, never come to class, and don't even take the trouble to withdraw officially, you get an H for "excessive absence" which counts as an F in your grade point average. There is, however, one critical difference between an H and an F: the H, as opposed to the traditional F, is easily changed into a retroactive withdrawal grade upon the simplest appeal to the teacher or to a counselor ("I didn't know until too late that I could drop the course"; "My mother was sick a lot so I couldn't get to class late in the day"; etc.). Embodied, then, in the system is a perversion of the American axiom that you must try and try again if at first you don't succeed. But too often at our school neither trying nor succeeding is encouraged. The catalogue and the convocation speeches notwithstanding, our students are being prepared for passivity or at best success within narrow limits.

A number of people have pointed out that if "the system" is viewed as responsible for one's social condition, it becomes contradictory and perhaps even futile to want to build a sense of individual efficacy. Unless the kind of consciousness raising I've been discussing has an arena in which to find fulfillment, paralysis and cynicism may result because individual efforts may come to seem insignificant given the scope and intractability of the system's power.[10] Excellent point. But what I'm proposing doesn't grant all power and responsibility to the system. I claim that powerless individuals have developed a stake in their own powerlessness, that often they have become more accustomed to their failures than to their potential successes. The system is powerful, but its power is dependent upon such massive individual abdications of responsibility. To change things, people have to learn the skills to reassert their own power.

Sociologist John McDermott points to another potential difficulty: the danger of faculty types such as myself encouraging our students to lay on the culture of the university in place of their own. Most academics, he asserts, take it as an article of faith that students benefit by such an exchange. But what in fact happens, he feels, is that the students we have worked with are pacified and made passive in the process of acquiring the external trappings of the university: "Pacified because they were acculturated away from their own historical values and traditions; passive because they could at best be spectators of a culture whose home [the university] remained an alien institution."[11] These academic missionaries feel that what they bring is good for the new-student natives and will improve them just as earlier missionaries felt confident about the value of what they brought to their

natives. But McDermott feels that in culture, as elsewhere, this is manifestly not so.[12] I believe there is
something dangerously elitist about McDermott's position that it is inevitable that new students will remain
alienated from the best the university has to offer. And
I've also seen those I call radical downwardly-mobile
blue-collar professors taking a similarly elitist position,
unasked, in the name of their students. It's one thing not
to invalidate our students' culture (much of what I
propose in fact attempts to help students respect their
lives and their culture); it's another matter, however, to
trap new students within the limited opportunities these
downwardly-mobile instructors chart for their students
by encouraging them to reject the traditional university.
Hopefully, the political education I'm advocating would
enable students to develop the power to take what they
want from the university (reversing the process in which
the university takes from them) and to learn how to see
through the pressure of those who minister to them to
either take on a new culture in place of their own or
reject it out of hand.

I've tried to indicate how the school has been and is an
instrument of social and political control. It is an institution that quite consciously tries to turn people into
something manageable. Within this framework, the
school must be viewed as an instrument of power.
Whether the established relationships among students
are competitive or cooperative, whether those between
teachers and students are authoritarian or democratic,
whether the relation between students and their work is
alienated or creative, a better measure of what is taught
in school is revealed through an on-site examination of
such questions than by a study of either the texts or the

curricula of the school.[13] In my terms, the new political education is built upon an understanding of this and on an alteration in the affective content of schooling—the values, expectations, and patterns of behavior which schools encourage. It is time to see if such change is possible within individuals and within institutions.

From Peggy's Educational Contract:

I want to do really well in school because it is important to me—maybe for the first time in my life. School is, I guess to me, the place where reality is thrown in my face, but there are people who have been through it and can help you face it . . . .

I want to start writing—because I've just found out that I could write for myself about things that are important to me and not what someone else wants me to write about.

To think a lot about the future, to try and contrive a plan of action for what I would like to do for the rest of my life.

I think sometimes I would want to stay the way I was, in isolation, unaware, because it's scary to think there are so many important decisions I will be faced with, knowing that I will have to follow through with what I decide no matter what the consequences.

—Peggy DeA.
1973

SEVEN
HEATING-UP

It has been claimed by many authorities that college does more to *confirm* the values and attitudes students bring with them than to have any impact on altering them. This is certainly the conclusion of Philip Jacob, whose *Changing Values In College*, published in 1957, is still the best known and most influential study of the impact of college upon students, despite the fact that it draws upon rather unsophisticated social scientific evidence.[1] According to Jacob's observations, college appears to cause students to become more like each other—just the opposite of what is proclaimed in thousands of college catalogues which promise, for a price, individual attention to one's uniqueness. Although many of his findings have subsequently been contradicted, most educators still seem to proceed as if he had discovered the truth. Jacob was intent on showing that the most powerful influences upon students emanate almost entirely from students' peer groups and their extracurricular activities. Relationships with instructors, the structure of the curriculum, the content of courses themselves all appear to produce little significant change.[2] What goes on in the dormitories, as many besides Jacob will testify, is for most people more important in shaping basic lifestyles than what happens in Freshman Composition.

But a good deal of recent, more substantial research has begun to contradict this pessimistic view. For some reason, however, this research has remained rather obscure. I suspect that many educators would rather embrace their own inability to make a difference in the lives of students than risk being held accountable for the lost possibilities of their potential to effect change. That potential, however, is there and important things do happen to students as the result of attending college. Kenneth Feldman and Theodore Newcomb, for example, in their recent major study conclude that there is a trend among students away from conservatism on various kinds of public issues, a decrease in religious interest, and a movement toward independence of thought, originality, and a widening of interests. Seniors tend to be less "authoritarian" than freshmen, less dogmatic, ethnocentric, and prejudiced.[3] They note, interestingly, that colleges have an impact on students even before they arrive on campus as if there is a kind of self-fulfilling prophecy involved. It is as if students say, "If Stanford accepted me, I must be pretty good," and as a result tend to act appropriately.[4] Or, "If only Big-City Community College accepted me, I must not be so hot."

Additionally they point out, certain kinds of colleges look for and attract certain kinds of students. Students likewise look for colleges that suit their interests and aspirations. And a college's ability to attract and keep faculty is to some extent dependent upon the kinds of students a college is able to enroll. So we face a situation in which the nature of the student body itself helps to determine the kind of education these students will encounter. What we get, as a result, is a fit between the selected students and the institutionally provided environment.[5] This may be part of the reason why students at many colleges have often been observed to become more alike in political and social attitudes and behavior.[6] This may also help explain why two-year colleges, structured for the failure of so many of their students, are so perversely successful.

But to accurately isolate the impact of college it is necessary to compare developmental changes that occur among college students with those among equivalent groups who do not attend college. There are few such studies, and actually in strictest terms equivalent groups are impossible to set up: the very act of choosing either to go or not to go to college is a significant enough variable in itself to interfere with the purity of the experimental design.[7] Another longitudinal study by James Trent and Leland Medsker followed ten thousand students beyond high school to discover the differing developmental states of college attenders and nonattenders.[8] The researchers carefully controlled for academic ability and socioeconomic status in order to isolate the effect of the experience of college attendance itself. And they discovered that the college experience, as an independent variable, does lead to important personal changes among young people—even among those who attend for less than a full four years. Predominating among these college-induced changes are those in personal qualities that affect the level of one's aspirations, open-mindedness, and the capacity to find satisfaction in work and with life in general.

But these observations depend upon the assumption that fundamental personality development continues at least through the college years. Traditional developmental theories claim that the personality is formed by a rather early age—say, by age six or thereabouts. The essential outline is drawn by then and all that remains is the filling in of details. Newer theories and evidence, however, call this into question. In fact, there is a growing body of belief that sees personality development proceeding in discreet stages throughout the entire course of one's life.[9] Thus what has been observed by Trent and Medsker may be seen to be part of a progressive and largely irreversible process of growth rather than merely a manifestation of how students put on a surface of new attitudes and values. Knowledge of the structure of such growth is important to an understanding of how collegiate experience can affect and facilitate this process.

There is, however, no universally accepted theory of human development that effectively defines the life cycle from the cradle to the grave. Perhaps the most ambitious and successful attempt at generating such a theory is Erik Erikson's elaboration of the "eight ages of man," eight developmental stages stretching from infancy to old age. At each distinct "age" a series of crises occur that impel that individual forward toward the next stage where a new series of developmental tasks must be mastered. It is a rather dialectical process because at each age there is a fundamental conflict that must be resolved before progress can occur. In Erikson's terms the earliest age is one of struggle between "basic trust" and "basic mistrust"; other ages involve the resolution of "autonomy" and "shame and doubts," "initiative" and "guilt," "industry" and "inferiority," "identity" and "role confusion" (the developmental dialectic that takes place during the college years), "intimacy" and "isolation," "generativity" and "stagnation," and finally "ego integrity" and "despair."[10]

The process of passing from one stage to the next is marked by expansion and greater complexity of personality. The higher stage bears some dynamic relationship to the processes of the prior stage. In order to move from one stage to the next one must be in a state of readiness to move on. Individuals, though, do not automatically unfold. Readiness simply means that a person is open to new kinds of stimuli and is prepared to deal with them in adaptive ways.[11] To illustrate: A youth entering college may be in a state of readiness, in Erikson's terms, to seek "identity." The stimuli to provoke this struggle for self-definition include, among other things as we have seen, the powerfully influential campus student culture, the character of the peer environment in which Erikson's youth finds himself or herself. Thus, with the needed combination of readiness and stimulation, college students progress toward the unfolding of their individual identities.

A number of people have written meaningfully about that which characterizes youth as a distinct period of human development.[12] William Perry, for example, posits a sequence of ethical and intellectual development during the college years which rather closely parallels the quantitative research of Trent and Medsker.[13] In Perry's view the student begins in high school or college from a stage of "dualism"—the belief that all questions have right or wrong, true or false answers (something, we have seen, that others describe as central to the authoritarian personality). If confronted in college by classmates and instructors who hold other, more complex views, the student becomes aware of "multiplicity"—a diversity of opinions, areas of uncertainty, legitimate disagreements about crucial intellectual and moral questions. If this confrontation with multiple points of view exists *and* persists, the student then moves on to a stage of "relativism" where he or she perceives values and knowledge as contextual. Perry goes on to argue that it is possible for college-age youth to move beyond this basically relativistic position to still higher stages of "commitment within relativism" where the student potentially develops the capacity to accept the responsibility for intellectual and ethical commitments within a relativistic universe. This process of intellectual and ethical development corresponds closely to the already observed "liberalizing" impacts of college—the increasing perception that knowledge is relative, the decline in dogmatic or authoritarian thinking, the increase in general open-mindedness, etc.

Lawrence Kohlberg's theory of the development of moral reasoning in early adulthood provides another way of understanding these liberalizing effects of higher education.[14] He theorizes that the child passes from an initial "premoral" stage of thinking about ethical issues to a stage of "conventional" moral reasoning which is characterized by an adherence to conventional social expectations and existing community standards. However, during and after adolescence he or she *may* move to a "postconventional" level of moral reasoning which is characterized by a greater personal responsibility for ethical judgments. These judgments are now made on the basis of thoughts about the long-range good of the community and according to more universalistic principles. Again, the unfolding of moral development coincides with recent empirical findings on the impact of college.

Nevitt Sanford, Joseph Katz, and others in their California-based group have been producing an impressively expanding body of theoretical literature since the early 1960s that stresses the substantial affective or ego development that may occur during the college years.[15] Such personality changes, in their terms, may include the "freeing of impulse," increasing "differentiation and integration of the ego," and the growth of personal "autonomy." Sanford even sees the freshman year in college to be a distinctive period of development which intervenes between adolescence and early adulthood. The freshman student is ready to concentrate upon relations with the external world—to improve his or her understanding of the world and find a place within it. The freshman doesn't know how to define himself or herself and thus tends to look to external sources of definition and measurement. College, then, becomes a good external environment for young people in this stage of development to refine their sense of self-esteem: here they have a continuous opportunity to test themselves in various ways without their "failures being catastrophic and without their successes leading to premature commitments."[16] Thus students in the early college years are allowed to think of themselves as people who will change—while participating fully all the while in whatever it is that changes them. Students at this stage of development need to feel that it is all right for them to be uncertain about their future selves and their future roles. It is easier for them to feel secure about this uncertainty if they are in fact engaged in activities that are calculated to bring out their true potential.

Also, if the potential for continuous, fundamental personal change is a natural state of being, we must reverse our traditional thinking on the subject of the meaning of the college experience: we should come to *expect* significant personality changes to occur *as the result of* college attendance rather than continue to assert the conventional wisdom that very little is possible. Thus, if significant personal change *isn't* occuring in students in colleges, then something must be wrong with the curriculum and learning environment. Also, if the changes that do occur tend to involve everyone becoming more like everyone else, then too something is wrong with the collegiate experience. Jerome Karabel provocatively puts forward the idea that a school's evaluation should depend upon the "value added" to its students. If this were the case, the most highly selective colleges where students earn the highest grades, graduate at the highest rates, etc. may not be the most successful. Like horseracing handicappers, they are more interested in predicting performance than in improving it.[17]

It's unlikely that American higher education will abandon its handicapper ways until and unless it adopts a developmental learning model for itself. And this appears to be at best only a remote possibility since our colleges have traditionally ignored the noncognitive side of human development. The report of the Committee on the Student in Higher Education, profoundly influenced by Eriksonian ideas of personal growth, concludes that the college is a major influence on the development of the student's personality—whether it realizes it or not—and that the college's central task of guiding the intellect cannot be done well unless the school realizes that the acquisition of such knowledge takes place in the context of emergent adulthood.[18] But American higher education has failed to acknowledge explicitly that intellectual development which is integrated into the student's search for identity. It is, for example, generally assumed that students' personal problems are not the province of the college. Professors who take too much interest in such problems are likely to be advised that such an investment of energy might interfere with the progress of *their* academic careers: "Once orientation week is over," the message reads, "it is high time for freshmen to begin to prepare for graduate school."[19]

Even those higher educational objectives that appear to be developmental have frequently been goals for what is actually no more than socialization: the attempts to produce "gentlemen" or "well-rounded" individuals too often consist of attempts to produce reliable and predictable people for business and social purposes.[20] Furthermore, the pervasive emphasis on cognition and its separation from affect or feeling poses a threat to our society in that this separation in our educational institutions produces cold, detached individuals uncommitted to humanitarian goals. To be sure, knowledge can and does generate feeling, but it is usually feeling that generates action.[21] Thus it would appear that a developmental approach to higher education based upon a collateral emphasis on thinking *and* feeling would conform more to the expressed social functions of education in a democracy than the current virtually exclusive focus on cognition. It might even be argued that separating feeling from thinking in the schools is another form of social control since it thwarts social action.

A number of people have suggested that colleges should devise new forms for freshman orientation: it should not merely be the familiar one week (or day) of adjustment to a particular college but rather "a whole year of acculturation to an entirely new and exciting activity—serious and systematic thought—and a year of integrating the pursuit of skill and knowledge with the search for identity and intimacy."[22] Trent and Medsker similarly suggest that a core course in which students are stimulated to think critically about their assumptions, prejudices, and goals be built into the curriculum in acknowledgment of the fact that lower-division students are developmentally in what Erikson calls the "moratorium" of youth, searching for and reality-testing their emerging adult identities. Indeed, a number of colleges, including Staten Island Community College, offer such courses.

Ours is called an Educational Development Seminar (EDS), and I would like to sketch in its objectives and structure before examining some of its constituent parts in more detail. We ask each of our first-semester students to join an EDS. Examining and stimulating aspiration and motivation is one of its major functions. The seminar meets once a week for an extended period of time and includes fifteen to twenty students and a faculty leader or facilitator. The objective of the EDS initially is to help students understand how they got where they are—that their presence in a community college is at least as much the result of class, ethnicity, and the inadequacies of their prior schooling as it is the fault of their own inherent limitations. This helps students build the self-confidence which is essential to their making ambitious but strategically sound plans for their future education and careers. When a student begins to see a new career goal as realizable, the problems of English Composition or Biology 100 or Math 15 become just that—problems to be dealt with. No longer are they insurmountable barriers in themselves. The difficulties of acquiring verbal and mathematical skills are perceived to be important skirmishes in a larger struggle.

The EDS often begins with an exercise designed to help students trace the contours of their educational biographies. "What is your first memory of school?" is frequently the initial question. As the members of the group track down these memories and begin to discover the connections between their early experiences and their current situation they begin to relate to each other in an intense and open manner because what they discover comes from deep within themselves and to share it with others requires both an openness to giving and to listening empathetically. This atmosphere of honesty and sharing is essential to the success of the seminar. Faculty members must demonstrate equal candor. We, too, must explore our educational and career histories; we, too, must check to see if we feel that community colleges are second-rate institutions and that teaching in one makes us second-rate people. It is virtually impossible to try to help people understand their educational histories or to make plans for themselves if we ourselves are not involved in the same process.

If one of the lessons of the EDS is that our dreams and aspirations in part result from the model of society we have internalized, the implication of this lesson is that our future attainments will also be sociologically rather predictable unless we understand and intervene in the process. Therefore, part of what we do is help students shape their own educational and career plans. These plans include components of traditional academic advisement (What courses should I take? To which college should I transfer?), personal counseling (Is smoking dope a problem? What do your parents think of all this?), financial aid advisement (Is applying for financial aid the same as going on welfare? Is it a good idea to take out a loan?) But the approach is holistic, and it also frequently places the interests of the student above those of the institution. This perhaps is the essential difference between the old cooling-out and the new *heating-up.*

It is also important to note that unless the EDS begins with the way we *feel* about our own histories and goes from affective exploration to cognitive and rational understanding, it is no more than a new version of a familiar academic exercise. The new directions proposed here also assume a powerful affective environment in schools that often goes unacknowledged but which must, as with the social and political roles of schools, be made explicit in order to aid the release of our students' potential. If, for example, the college bookstore refuses to stock anything other than required texts and school sweat-shirts, it teaches students something about how the college regards their academic potential. These affective environments must either be changed (unlikely) or, at the least, students must come to be able to perceive their hidden messages and thus learn to protect themselves against their effects.

Another important function of affective learning is to help our students validate their own prior experiences. The academic world reflects upper-middle-class values and values upper-middle-class culture. Lower-class people feel put down or alienated by this kind of exclusive collegiate environment. Validating working-class culture via affective learning in community colleges does not mean a different kind of exclusiveness (although at times I see this happening, encouraged by a misdirected radicalism): it means a cultural balance within which all people can have a chance to feel good about themselves. By validating the experiences and feelings of the students, we tell them in essence that they *do* know something. Probably this is the most important factor in uniting relevant academic content with self-content. Because when an instructor indicates to students that the experiences they bring with them have nothing to do with the "worthwhile" knowledge that is the school's exclusive property, the message, however unintended, is that students are worthless. People are, after all, their experiences.[23]

It has frequently been pointed out how new students of low socioeconomic status have difficulty delaying gratification or projecting themselves realistically into the future.[24] It has also been frequently noticed that various other social forces (the climate of parental expectations, the level of parental educational attainment, racism, etc.) severely restrict the extent and quality of an individual's ability to plan for the future—whether it be for factory work or law school. And all of this functions regardless of either the true ability or real potential of the individual.

With this in mind, we set about devising some way at Staten Island to help students understand these social processes and, if they wished, do something about them. What we came up with emerged a few years ago out of a weekly, informal seminar between open-admissions students and faculty. The purpose at first was for us to talk as equals about things that concerned us—personal and otherwise. Some people wanted an encounter group atmosphere, but in general we avoided that. Others were interested in action—political and otherwise; in general we avoided that too. We wound up doing much more than talking. The students came to do what we called *plans*. It quickly became clear that most of them did not have a conscious plan that they were following: they were drifting through school and life not knowing where they were headed. But it also became clear that they were all in fact following a plan that they had little to do with designing. If they were from a certain background, if their parents had so much schooling and earned so much money, if they had a certain kind of high-school diploma, if they were involved with drugs, etc., they were headed some place, some place they might not like, that they hadn't determined; but they were pretty sure that they were headed there nonetheless.

They discovered that even the institution that was there purportedly to help them get to some desirable future, tended to deliver conflicting messages in this regard. Or at the least the orientation of our college toward its students' future was very different from that of the kind of college I had attended. At Columbia when I first set foot on campus I immediately became a member of the class of 1960 (my beanie and lapel identification tag thus designated me and proclaimed me to the world). With the help of the institution, I was from day one projected four years into the future and was *expected* to complete my work by then. And indeed the vast majority of students at that college did—and still do.[25] At two-year colleges, as we have seen, students are not the class of anything: the computer knows them by two numbers— social security and the number of credits they've completed. Their sense of the future, their projected completion date, consist of the sixty-four credits at the end of the community college rainbow.

To try to do something about this we decided that each person would come up with, indeed assert a plan of his or her own—a plan to do or become whatever he or she decided. No value judgments, just what the students wanted for themselves.

What will sound now like a very cut-and-dried, mechanical process is nearly always full of warmth, caring, humor, and at times tears. The person doing the plan first tells what his goals are—*or* the fact that he has no idea what he wants to do. He is then asked to describe step by step, year by year how he will go about achieving his goal *or* how he will go about discovering a goal for himself. All this is written on the blackboard in outline form. No one passes any judgment on what is said. The group, however, asks questions that help clarify the goals or steps in the plan. After the plan is completed the group is asked to evaluate its chances for success.

The first plans were usually full of problems and the chances for success—acknowledged by the planner too—were slim. It was clear that few were conscious that society's plan tended to have a greater chance of succeeding than their own. Many found that they had to modify their plans if they were serious about succeeding. (Distressingly, we had many students who did not want to succeed, who were in fact so scarred by negative academic expectations that they learned to deal better with failure than with success.) And alter their plans is in fact what most did: I had better cut down on drugs. I should change to a different curriculum. I'd better pull up my marks if I want to transfer to an out-of-town college, etc.

It might be helpful at this point to include a plan we did that first year and the questions raised by the group after it was sketched out on the blackboard. It's John's plan, as it appeared in outline form:

Goals: To be the best high-school history teacher on Staten Island. To be different than my high-school history teachers. To work with all kinds of kids. To bring enlightenment to them like I never had.

Number of Years to Reach Goals: 5

Year 1 (this year)

Education at S,I.C.C. Job at supermarket—30 hours per week. Girlfriend. Living at home. Have own car. Get stoned occasionally: 3–4 times a week. History courses: Western Civilization 1 and 2. Student deferment.

Index—around 2.30.

Summer

Work at supermarket.

Year 2

Continue education at S.I.C.C. Same job—30 hours per week. Living at home. No financial aid. Still with girl. Stoned occasionally. Courses related to teaching history—1 history course as elective plus psychology.

Summer

Work at supermarket.

Year 3

Transfer to Richmond or Brooklyn College to major in history. Living at home. Different girlfriend. Same job. Stoned occasionally—2–3 times a week.

Summer

Work.

Year 4

Do student teaching. Graduate from college.

Summer

Work.

Year 5

Teach in high school.

At this point we raised some of the following questions with John: How can you teach in a New York City high school without the required master's degree? Your plan doesn't include this. It was obvious that the plan had to be modified and it indeed was; an extra year or two had to be added to include graduate study. You say you are interested in teaching "all kinds of kids," but where in your plan do you learn about the "other" people who comprise such a large part of New York City's school population? Your Western Civilization course, for example, is only about Western people. Wouldn't it be good to have some kind of teaching experience before the fourth year of the plan? How do you know you'll like working with kids?

John decided to alter his plan to include at least summer experiences working with children in a camp or playground program. He also revised it to include some travel to broaden the range of his experiences. (In fact, with a group of S.I.C.C. students and faculty he got to travel through Eastern and Western Europe a couple of summers ago.) We asked him why he was working at a supermarket and how that was related to his goal. It turned out that he was working primarily to pay his car expenses. He had no significant financial needs other than that. He decided that he would reevaluate that need in the light of the time and energy he put into working.

John eventually decided to get an apartment of his own; he realized that he used the car as his place to be alone, away from the tensions of his parents' house. He transferred to a senior college, took a semester off to work, read on his own, and reappraised the direction his life was taking. He later returned to school where he changed his major to anthropology. He is currently doing very well, seeming to have his life under his own control—a major objective of the EDS.

The faculty member's role in the EDS doesn't end when the plan has been satisfactorily revised. The group, but particularly the instructor, continues to monitor the

students' progress (or lack of it) toward the goals defined.
At times, indeed frequently, someone may decide that
he or she wants to change goals. Fine. Then the group
helps the student come up with an alternative plan. At
times, actually quite often, someone's plan requires
various resources not readily available at the college or
within the group: reading lists, help in transferring to
another college, in-depth counseling, internships to see
if the career that is being planned is in fact what the
student wants, travel, exposure to experts or practition-
ers, etc. The faculty members especially have a commitment to help students secure these needed resources
during the course of their stay at the college. This is of
course greatly facilitated if the EDS instructor becomes
the assigned academic adviser to the students in the
group; this in fact is our practice.

A major problem that we always encounter among
first-semester students in EDS's is that although they
come to form longer-and-longer-range plans for themselves, all kinds of things in their day-to-day lives seem to
keep cropping up which seriously interfere with the
realization of their objectives. Steve's experience is fairly
typical and can serve to illustrate. He says he wants to be
a serious student, to read not only for his courses but for
himself as well. He also values good writing and thus
wants to improve his own. One day when he hadn't
gotten around to writing a little paper he had promised to
complete the week before, I asked him why not. He told
me he hadn't had the time during the previous week. I
knew he didn't have a job and I would frequently see him
lounging around the campus "wasting" many, many
hours each week. How come, I asked, he didn't have the
time to write a measly two-page paper? I asked him to
keep a log of how he spent his days during the coming

week because I still felt he had more than enough time to do the work he set out for himself. With his permission I'm reproducing a part of his log because I feel that, better than anything I might write, it reveals *how various forces in our students' lives interfere with their doing what they themselves want to do.* This illustration, as well, will show that if students can come to understand this, they can then go on to do something about it.

STEVE'S LOG FOR THE WEEK BEGINNING THURSDAY, FEBRUARY 14 AND ENDING WEDNESDAY, FEBRUARY 20

Thursday

6:15–7:45 A.M.: Woke up, washed, read newspaper, got dressed and ate. Went to school.

8:00–9:00 A.M.: Science class.

9:00–9:50 A.M.: Hung out talking to people.

9:50–12:28 P.M.: Study Skills course and Transfer Seminar.

1:00–1:30 P.M.: Drove home.

1:30–3:00 P.M.: Came home, ate lunch and hung out for a little while expecting to read until. . . .

3:00–4:45 P.M.: Seth and Norman came over and we hung out, got high and had some good laughs pertinent to school and the future.

4:45–5:30 P.M.: Picked up my mother from work.

5:30–8:00 P.M.: Talked on the phone for about 45 minutes, ate, and showered.

8:00–1:45 A.M.: Picked up Joanne, went to see my father and went to bring my skis to the city so I can ski Saturday. Finally, went to the movies.

Friday

1:00–4:00 P.M.: Norman and Ira came over and woke me up. We hung out, got high, and listened to music for about 1/2 hour. I then went to buy pants which I didn't get. Last we went to Henry's where we hung out, got high and listened to music. [Talking with Steve, he indicated that since he doesn't have any classes on Friday, and his house is empty during the day, he had planned to read but couldn't turn down his friends.]

4:00–4:50 P.M.: Came home and read *Ski* magazine and received a phone call.

5:00–6:30 P.M.: Read (1 1/2 hours).

6:30–7:00 P.M.: Ate.

7:00–8:00 P.M.: Watched TV.

8:00–12:00 P.M.: Joel came over. We went to see Norman and Jeff. We then went to the Junction Bar. After a few beers, we went to the movies. Went home.

12:00–1:15 A.M.: Got things together for skiing tomorrow, made an outline for [skiing] instruction and reviewed teaching methods. Sleep! . . .

Sunday

12:00 Noon: Woke up, ate, and read newspaper.

1:15–2:30 P.M.: Read (1 1/4 hours).

2:30–3:00 P.M.: Ate lunch.

3:00–6:15 P.M.: Watched TV.

6:15–6:45 P.M.: Read (30 minutes).

6:45–7:15 P.M.: Received a phone call from Seth. We spoke a while. It was worthwhile, not like a typical conversation. (What's new? What are you doing later? Etc.)

7:30–8:00 P.M.: Read (30 minutes).

8:00–8:30 P.M.: Ate.

8:45–11:00 P.M.: Picked up Joanne and went to David's house with Norman, Seth, and Lee. Hung out, got high, and listened to music.

11:00–2:00 A.M.: Came home with Joanne, hung out.

2:30 A.M.: Went to sleep. . . .

Monday

3:30–6:00 P.M.: Went to Joel's to hang out–did some shit.

6:00–6:30 P.M.: Ate.

8:00–1:00 A.M.: Went with Joel to the city to see a show and drank beers.
1:30 A.M.: Sleep.

Tuesday

6:30–7:00 A.M.: Woke up, washed, ate.
8:30–12:30 P.M.: Classes.
1:00–3:30 P.M.: Went to Richy's (same cycle).

Wednesday

10:00–10:30 A.M.: Woke up, ate, dressed, and went to school.
11:30–1:30 P.M.: Children's Literature course.
1:30–2:00 P.M.: Hung around school.
2:00–2:30 P.M.: Drove home.
3:00–5:00 P.M.: Joanne came over to hang out.
5:00–7:00 P.M.: Hung out by myself.
7:30–10:00 P.M.: Went to school for evening class.
10:00–10:30 P.M.: Drove home.
11:00 P.M.: Sleep.

While we were going over this with Steve a rather important perception came to him: As part of one of our college's special programs, Steve had spent the month of January as a visiting student at Franklin Pierce College in New Hampshire. Only a couple of weeks prior to recording this log he had been going to classes there, studying long hours in the library and dormitory, having meaningful conversations with new friends, barely using drugs at all, getting papers done on time, etc. In a word, for the first time in his academic life it seemed Steve was doing what *he* wanted to do. But then when he came home, it was as if a switch had been thrown—he immediately reverted to the familiar patterns revealed in his log. As important, though, as noticing how environmental forces affected his life, it was equally important for Steve to see that he was not powerless in the face of them: all along the way—at Franklin Pierce and at home—he had confronted choices and selected among options. At Franklin Pierce, for example, when a marijuana joint came around the room to him, he just passed it on; at home when Norman and Ira came by to take him out shopping for pants, he chose to go along with them even though he wanted to read. No claim is made here that these insights have irreversibly changed Steve's life. He has, however, confronted his friends about how he wants to spend his time—and they seem to be leaving him alone; he has been accepted at Franklin Pierce for the fall—with a scholorship; and his study skills instructor tells me he's been working very hard since late February—writing a great deal every week and showing significant signs of improvement.

What I want to emphasize throughout this chapter is that the establishment of a personal version of what Erikson calls "a future within reach" as part of a person's life plan is *normally* expected to occur during the developmental period that spans the first two college years.[26] It would appear that the quality of life experienced by so many community college students, under pressure as we have seen to accept sparse immediate gratifications rather than vaguely possible long-range ones, seriously affects their *planning capacity* itself and thus the kinds of exercises described as part of our EDS's are necessary to revive this important, *natural* skill.[27]

Skill, however, is generally thought to include only various collegiate forms of the three R's. Reading and 'Riting are of course supposed to be a part of virtually all courses but are explicitly taught in different versions of freshman composition or its remedial counterparts. 'Rithmetic for nonscience majors can be discovered in different kinds of math-for-liberal-arts-students courses as well as in numerous modularized forms of remedial math. Certainly it is vital to acquire these skills, particularly for new college students who begin so far behind by all measures. But traditional compensatory education programs, by the admission even of their most ardent advocates, have failed.[28] Projected dropout and failure rates for the City University of New York's community college open-admissions students, for example, run as high as 80 percent during their first two college years.[29] There is even evidence that students who take remedial courses are more likely to earn *lower* grade point averages than equivalent students who didn't take such courses.[30] To close the large gaps in reading, math, and writing (often at least four or five years' worth) dramatic breakthroughs are required. Gaining eight or ten months in measured reading skill in five months (good progress) is hardly good enough.

What is needed if breakthroughs are to occur, is a recognition that these *academic skills are intimately connected to the developmental or affective skills I've been describing.* Writing is not merely a mechanical manipulation of punctuation marks and parts of speech; feeling is very much a part of the process. With many freshmen, the inability to write effectively does not simply represent a lack of something to say or the technical skill to say it but also represents *a developmental need.* Students do have things to say, important things that they want to communicate to others, but fear intrudes. Fear may come from students' concern that their lack of grammatical proficiency will expose them to scorn or ridicule or it may come from the feeling that whatever they can express (even proficiently) will be so worthless that it, too, will invite criticism.[31] As the

Committee on the Student in Higher Education puts it, "Once the problem is recognized as . . . [developmental] and not lack of intelligence, and the teacher's attack moves from skill development to confidence development, these hurdles can fall and *skill can be demonstrated*."[32] I've added the italics because they underline an important concept: too much emphasis has traditionally been placed on the painful *acquisition* of skill and not enough on the display or demonstration of existing but suppressed skills.

Nearly every remedial skills program, at either two-year or four-year colleges, segregates remedial from "regular" students. True, there seem to be as many different kinds of remedial programs as there are colleges,[33] but one thing most have in common is that they create a dual-track skills system that sorts out the "dumb" students from the "smart." Even the remedial programs singled out for praise by B. Lamar Johnson in his book on innovative community colleges[34] or those cited as noteworthy by John Roueche and R. Wade Kirk[35] are all *remedial ghettos* in which students have to prove themselves before they're let out into the "real" college. And very few ever make it that far, even from the successful programs. Roueche and Kirk, for example, note that though a decent number do well in their "developmental" course, once they "transfer" (their word) into regular courses their grades fall dramatically, and only 35 percent of the remedial "graduates" complete even two years of study.[36]

A major reason for the failure of such programs *is the very fact that they exist*. Their existence itself contains an implicit message that almost guarantees failure. That message says to the remedial student: "You are inadequate. You must shape up. And to do that you need extra help only the instructors and this program can give you." Compensatory programs thus emphasize defects and deficiencies rather than strengths and competencies, ironically for those students who most need to develop positive feelings of self-worth.[37] Remedial students are often those with the least apparent motivation, coming from families with the greatest lack of educational tradition, and bringing with them the most intense antagonism toward school;[38] in other words, these students are least able to confront the latent messages emanating from the separate remedial programs in which they frequently find themselves. And it doesn't help to call these programs "developmental" or to identify these students as "provisional" or "high risk." (Incidentally, who's taking the risk? Presumably the college. But what does the school risk?[39]) It also doesn't help to rename the separate remedial counseling center "The Intensive Caring Center," as one two-year college proposed. The message is too blatant; the medical analogy too clear. The "dumb" kids know who they are in elementary school even when we disguise the slow class by calling it the "Sparrows." And the "dumb" kids in college know who they are as well. What we have to do is find out the ways in which they're "smart" and work from there.

Insight into means of helping students discover the ways in which they are "smart" may be found, among other places, in Carl Rogers's *Client-Centered Therapy*.[40] The basic therapeutic assumption, from which pedagogical analogies may be drawn, is that individuals have the capacity for self-initiated, constructive handling of their life situation. The approach itself involves the counselor or teacher focusing his/her whole attention and effort upon understanding and perceiving as the client (student) perceives and understands. This becomes, *in itself*, a striking demonstration of the worth and significance of the individual *and* also provides "operational evidence" that the counselor (teacher) has confidence in the client's potential for constructive change and development.[41] The more the counselor or teacher expects and relies upon the strength and potential of the client, the more he/she discovers that strength.

Traditional teaching assumes you can't trust the student. The teacher must supply motivation, information, organization for the materials, use examinations to measure progress and coerce students into the desired activities. Student-centered teaching assumes you can trust students to desire to learn in ways which will maintain or enhance self; you can trust them to use resources to serve these ends, to evaluate themselves in fundamental ways, to grow, *provided the atmosphere for growth is available.* That atmosphere depends largely upon the teacher's behavior. The classroom climate must in every way respect the integrity of the students— their aims, opinions, attitudes. This of course does not preclude an instructor's questioning, probing, challenging, disagreeing, etc. But it is important that teachers see themselves as members of the learning group rather than as the authorities for the group. They should rely on the capacity of students to sort out truth from untruth. They should recognize that the successful course is the beginning and not the end of learning. They should see that this kind of learning feeds the total self-development of students as well as improves their acquaintance with a given body of knowledge.[42]

There are a number of potential problems inherent in this approach. First there is the danger that classes will become group therapy. A therapeutic situation develops if tne teacher deals *only* with the emotionalized attitudes and feelings expressed in the classroom. However, if the instructor structures the initial sessions around the academic as well as the affective objectives and contents of the course, a nontherapeutic framework is established within which the group experiences will take place.[43] A minute amount of structuring goes a long way. The teacher, thus, remains quite powerful—and must be careful of that power. If, for example, instructors give "final" answers to questions directed to them or sum things up for the group at the end of the class, they are likely to find themselves again in the conventional role of expert and to discover that the group has regained its *de*pendence.

A colleague and I were coteaching a seminar a couple of years ago. We came out of one class feeling exhilarated—it was the finest thing we had ever seen happen in a classroom: the students had moved from insight to insight, getting into and beyond things in ways we had never experienced. We, too, had pushed to perceptions of group process and human understanding we had rarely encountered. We walked around and around the school's outdoor track after the class, retracing every marvelous moment. Ivan, though, was troubled by one doubt: something was wrong at the end. What was it? We finally came to see that when I had summed things up, I had taken for myself what had belonged to the group: by smoothing the jagged edges, by resolving the ambiguities in my summation, by reducing the tension that remained, I had taken responsibility for what had happened. I had deprived the students of *their* (our) accomplishment. I also had misperceived the value of *unresolved tension* at the end of an experience. I was so captured by the traditional tension-reduction model of motivation, which has so dominated American psychology,[44] that I couldn't see how true gratification often leads to heightened rather than reduced excitement. In Abraham Maslow's words, I had failed to understand that "the appetite for growth is whetted rather than allayed by gratification. Growth is, *in itself*, a rewarding and exciting process."[45]

Other problems involved in student-centered teaching include the danger of departmentalizing affective learning by the tendency to see cognitive, affective, aesthetic experiences existing in separate realms. It would be a mistake merely to add Affect 101 to English 101 in the curriculum with corresponding faculty specialists. There is just as much an affective challenge present, as we have seen, when students confront the blank page when trying to write as there are cognitive tasks present. And the seven-times table or differential equations for that matter have their affective and aesthetic as well as their cognitive components. What's needed, in effect, is that teachers—both those who emphasize the analysis of content and those who stress the feeling of experience—become more aware of the total way in which their students, as well as they themselves, deal with the complex reality of schooling.

Student-centered teaching has also at times neglected to emphasize the importance of students (and faculty) doing *more* than their-own-thing. A number of colleges, particularly during the tumultuous 1960s, adopted policies that encouraged their disaffected clientele to more or less do anything so long as it made them *feel* good. Thus the stories we all heard about students getting three credits or more for courses in sandal making or the *Kama Sutra*. Philip Werdell, for example, calls for the establishment of collegiate versions of sensitivity groups which would facilitate students learning what they want to know, and how to communicate with others.[46] But very little of this, *in itself*, is helpful for students who want to discover ways to *change* the conditions of their lives—especially in the absence of an understanding of what these students *need* to know in addition to what they *want* to know.

Finally, an overemphasis on affective learning is just as likely as traditional forms of learning to lead to the creation of various kinds of classroom expectations and rewards and punishments which may also interfere with academic motivation and attainment—the very opposite of what is presumably intended by the student-centered approach. If we assume that college students have been taught to compete with one another for the limited rewards dispensed by their earlier teachers, we can further assume that they will continue to do so in the newer kinds of classes I've been describing. If in fact their new teachers continue to bestow limited rewards for affective right answers, we should expect to find their students attempting to psych them out in old ways to find out what is going to be rewarded in new ways. I've seen too many students squirming in their seats, overeager to open their guts for teacher-facilitators seeking someone they can depend upon for emotional right answers when things start to drag a bit within the group. I've seen students condemn others for not being "open" or "honest" with the class—not so much because they feel openness or honesty may help their classmates "understand" or "grow" but rather to exhibit by comparison their own superior openness and honesty. This form of emotional tyranny then comes to replace more traditional forms of academic tyranny.

Just the other day I asked one of our students who had been in a class that emphasized affective learning why it "galled" him (his word) that a classmate had stopped coming halfway through the semester. "Because it would have done him good if he had come." Maybe he didn't feel it was doing him any good, I added. "Then he should have come to us to tell us why we weren't helping him. He at least *owed* us that much." Why, I asked, didn't you go to him to ask him privately why he wasn't coming or why he wasn't getting anything valuable from the class? As we talked further we began to think that maybe John himself wasn't getting as much from the class as he had thought. In the absence of required readings, term papers, and competitive grades the only thing that *seemed* to be required was attendance and participation. While scrambling for new kinds of rewards, one may look for the new "requirements" and resent others who reject both and accept guiltlessly a ripped-off, self-graded A.

Such problems notwithstanding, a student-centered approach emphasizing the integration of thinking and feeling offers the possibility that the old cooling-out may at last come to be replaced by a new heating-up. There is evidence that such an approach can work from some of the results of the programs I have been describing.

Among the important measures of how well students are doing are the rates at which they stay out of academic trouble (i.e. keep off probation) and the rates at which they complete their courses of study, transfer to four-year colleges, find jobs. The rate of probation is important because it usually foretells even worse trouble—academic disappearance or dismissal. It is variously estimated that up to 75 percent of students who get on probation never complete their educational objectives.

At Staten Island, approximately 50 percent of the students are placed on probation after their *first* semester. This figure drops a bit to between 40 and 45 percent by the end of the second term, but this drop is deceptive since a significant number of first-semester students are *gone* by the second semester and their disappearances ironically help cut the probation rate. In the programs I've been describing, only 7.2 percent are on probation after one term, with that figure more than halved at the end of the first year. This with a retention rate between these two semesters of nearly 90 percent.[47] Finally, an independent survey of the graduates of the past three years indicates that nearly 85 percent are either continuing their studies or are employed at work that they say is satisfying.[48] Not quite a mountain of evidence but perhaps enough to indicate the potential power of heating-up.

*People work in the places of learning, and people learn in the
places of working. Each experience is unique, but
scholarly preaching remote from practice tends to be as
sterile as practice becomes when it is detached from the
infusion of ideas. The best education is never purely
contemplative any more than the best job performance is
unadulterated action.*

—William Birenbaum
1969

EIGHT

CHOOSING A CAREER: EXPERIENCE IN THE REAL WORLD*

The choice of one's career is a *process* rather than an event, a process that begins in childhood. For the child the home in many ways is a workplace as well as a living-place, providing a variety of opportunities for very early career exploration: it is a hotel, a restaurant, a recreation center, a school, laundry, carpentry shop, etc. where parents, children, relatives, neighbors, assume many different work roles.[1]

The theory many have held until recently, that the process of choosing a career unfolds rather accidentally without the person having much control of the eventual choice, was founded upon statistical analyses of the career decisions of large numbers of individuals. Because significant numbers responded "It was an accident" to the question "How did you happen to become a

---

*This first appeared in a somewhat different form as "Experiential Education at a Community College" in *Implementing Field Experience Education.* (San Francisco: Jossey-Bass, 1974), pp. 1–12.

bookkeeper (or a lawyer, etc)?" a so-called accident
theory of decision making emerged and for a long time
dominated the thinking of social scientists. The other
major school of thought, the psychoanalytic theory,
holds that these choices occur primarily through uncon-
scious forces—a sadistically inclined person, for example, might become, via sublimation, a butcher or a
surgeon. Characteristic of both theories is the assumption that individuals are largely passive with respect to
the choice process, making choices either because they
are swept along by the overwhelming impact of a powerful outside stimulus or because they are propelled by the
strength of their basic impulses.[2]

A newer third theory, gathering both force and followers, sees occupational choice as a distinct part of the
natural pattern of growth and development of all individuals, occurring in stages throughout a substantial portion of adolescence and youth, with much of this process
quite responsive to the conscious desires and control of
individuals. If there are powerful constraints that tend to
limit freedom of choice or to render individuals passive,
it is more likely that choice will occur from forces that
are without than from those that emanate from within
the individual. Social constraints are seen to be at least
as powerful as those that are psychological—it is known,
for example, that young people from lower socioeconomic backgrounds have a narrower range of career
options than their more affluent counterparts; but then
again how many upper-class youths have chosen to be
carpenters in spite of the appearance of a so-called
counterculture?[3]

Eli Ginzberg and his colleagues at Columbia University have attempted to develop a general theory of what
might be called occupational development. They see

basically three distinct stages of growth: the fantasy period, the tentative choice period, and the realistic choice period. The first two span ages eleven through seventeen; the third occurs during the college years, or during the first few working years for those youths who do not enroll in college. During the later part of the period of tentative choice, as the result of having become more aware of their goals and values, older adolescents want to have the opportunity to test their choices in the world of experience; and thus, if they are headed that way, hope college will give them this opportunity. Most find, though, that because of their exclusive immersion in academic subjects, they gain little insight into the realities of the occupational world. If anything, college adds to their questions, presenting new ideas, new styles, and perhaps even new and additional confusion.[4]

Ginzberg seems to regret that this so often happens to college students; he would like to see them get on with the business of realistically narrowing their occupational choice making while in college by testing themselves through broader and deeper interactions with the real world. I, too, am critical of an education that consists of an exclusive immersion in academic subjects; but I have many more reservations about one that forces students, particularly community college students, to rush ahead into "realistic" choices. In fact, I feel that just the opposite has to occur—for our students the scope of tentative choices has to be broadened: their options have already been too narrowed for them by the social forces that affect their lives. The vocational education movement people, Ginzberg included, ignore the fact that the students they seek to enlist never had a wide range of fantasy or tentative choices to begin with and are usually locked into real choices prematurely. New students frequently have to buck their own personal stereotypes of various careers as well as confront their parents' expectations for them. They also have to deal with the prestige rankings of society and peers. All of this is enough for them to contend with without our encouraging an overhasty commitment to one occupation or another—particularly when those commitments do not reflect either their true aspirations or actual potential.[5]

College can have a constructive impact on career selection when students are introduced to the world of work and are helped to become aware of their true interests and to free themselves from the expectations others have for them.[6] An extensive program of internship or off-campus work/study options is just the sort of thing that can be most helpful. But before colleges proceed to set up such programs it is essential that they examine their assumptions both about the kinds of students to be served and about the hidden curricula functions of the kind of program to be established. This is important because there are choices to be made regarding the forms for these internship programs— choices from among those structures that encourage the confirmation of career choices already made or those that encourage continued self-definition and a broadening of occupational possibilities.

Recalling K. Patricia Cross's findings about the comparative aspirations of new and traditional students,[7] it would be a rather simple and clear-cut process to set up internships or off-campus study programs for these two types of students: For the traditional student, set up field study that is both humanistic and preprofessional. For the new student, set up off-campus work/study that is both specialized and prepractical. And in fact when two-year colleges go about setting up off-campus programs, up to 80 percent of them see the objective to be "career development," and plan accordingly. This means that the vast majority of *cooperative* education programs (as they're usually called at community colleges) follow the traditional high-school or engineering-school vocational education model.[8] According to this vocational education model, training is the objective. Students participate because they wish to acquire qualifications and skills for a predetermined area of employment.

Colleges serving traditional students also plan accordingly. Their *experiential* education programs (notice what a difference a name makes) tend to stress personal development. This model helps students explore occupational interests and skills as a means of exploring self, using the work experience as a means of supplementing classroom learning. And this means supplementing *all kinds* of classroom learning, general as well as specialized subjects and courses.[9]

But are these simple and clear-cut versions of field study the way to proceed? They are if we want to reinforce the current socioeconomic order while promulgating for new students an illusion of the rich possibilities for social mobility via universal higher education. However, if we want to help make the rhetoric that supports open access to higher education a functioning reality, we had better come up with learning structures, both on and off campus, that will enable new students to rise within the society in ways that reflect their true potential.

In field study the most overt message conveyed is that one learns by doing as well as by thinking and that the "outside" world is as valid a place in which to study as is the school. More covert and subversive messages include the demystification of the "teacher" as the only valid source of learning. This can be quite disruptive to the classroom routine. Leonard Plachta has written how traditional instructors may come to feel threatened by their students' exposure to learning through "non-teachers": the co-op student returning to campus after a sojurn in the "real world" is in a better position to question and argue with the professor, particularly with the professor who has been careless about keeping up with recent developments in his/her field.[10] Worse yet for school professionals is that off-campus study challenges the school's monopolistic claim that it is the best and only place to learn. No wonder then that so many academicians are reluctant to support awarding degree credit for off-campus work.

Additional hidden messages, and these are the ones that concern me here, are communicated by the placements themselves. Programs that place prelaw students in prestigious law firms or in public interest legal work are an extension of the way the sponsoring college regards itself and what it thinks are appropriate careers for its students. An off-campus program that places its students in health technology work or in computer maintenance programs delivers a different message. What is disturbing about this is that an Antioch, which primarily serves traditional students, is likely to offer experiential work of the former kind whereas a community college, which serves new students, is likely to offer the latter kind of internships. And since to a substantial degree the Antiochs and the community colleges are stratified according to the socioeconomic status of their students, the structures of their off-campus programs contribute to the maintenance of existing social and economic differences rather than to their reduction.

Most community college work/study programs are actually a part of the cooling-out function of their host institutions. In the only book-length study on the subject, Barry Heermann's *Cooperative Education in Community Colleges*, [11] this is rather clear in spite of the fact that he seems to favor the developmental over the vocational training model. Even in those programs he describes that are designed to help students define career objectives, there is no built-in awareness of how social forces affect aspiration and decision making.

When Heermann describes the benefits to the community of a comprehensive cooperative education program, virtually all of the benefits listed relate to *sustaining and preserving* the community as it is. And what this means for community college students and their families, as members of the community that Heermann wants to maintain, is that their rather low socioeconomic position is sustained and preserved as well. His objectives for the programs he suggests involve teaching students how to become "more readily adaptable to local [economic] needs" and making them "participants in the community's economic and social institutions" because then they will be "more sympathetic with and sensitive to its authority relationships and decision processes."[12] Not much heating-up can occur within co-op programs designed with such objectives in mind. It can occur, however, in a community college internship program that serves developmental needs of students both in career choice and in the larger process of maturation and self-definition.[13]

After students emerge from the Educational Development Seminar experiences I have described in the previous chapter, there is some real chance that they will begin to feel they have it within themselves to become whatever reflects their true abilities. As their basic skills improve, they become ready to work for academic credit at an internship. I do not see internships primarily as either job training or as exercises in how to be responsible on the job—although some of this is inevitably involved. Rather I see internships as part of more fundamental educational objectives: encouraging self-examination and self-definition. They are a means to help make real for community college students the possibility of becoming, say, a teacher by offering close contact with the school world. Perhaps a student will work at a teacher's side in a municipal high school where he/she can learn at close range that teachers are, alas, just people. Institutional structures are such that prior to this experience our student interns have virtually never known or spoken to teachers except as students. And social structures are such that few community college students have encountered teachers in noninstitutional settings. If via the coprofessional format of our internship program our students can come to demythologize teachers and begin to perceive them as people with both skills and limitations, then perhaps—if they choose—our students can become teachers themselves.[14]

As part of the larger process of self-definition we encourage students at Staten Island to sample a variety of different internships—sometimes as many as three or four during the course of a year. (Unfortunately nearly all other two-year colleges require students to keep the same placement throughout the entire term.[15]) We encourage switching internships because we have found that at first many students are reluctant to reveal their real dreams and aspirations. They have learned to live with drastically limited notions of success and with thwarted expectations. We have had many instances in which students began working as auto mechanic interns and then after a few weeks or months come in to tell us that they would really prefer to work with a high-school history teacher. And so at that point we immediately help them change internships rather than insisting that they wait until the beginning of a new semester. When these moments of redefinition come, we must be able to help students act as quickly as possible so as not to inhibit their search for appropriate careers.

I hasten to add that not all changes represent upward movement within the status hierarchy. And that is all to the good if these changes *also* represent choices arrived at as freely and with as little social pressure as possible. We had one student, for example, who initially expressed interest in working in a high-status position behind the scenes in the communications media—as a director or producer—but in the course of one year he dramatically "lowered" his aspirational level. He went from work in a film studio, to an off-campus job at a "radical" radio station (he became disillusioned when they treated him "like garbage" because of his lowly position—an apparent contradiction to their professed egalitarianism), to production work at the American Broadcasting Company's "College Scoreboard" program, and then finally to rather low-status work as a paramedic for the New York City Police Department. He loved the work and did brilliantly. His experience represents a real choice rather independent of social and parental pressures.

These kinds of changes are both facilitated and monitored within another Educational Development Seminar (the Internship Seminar) that runs concurrently with the off-campus work itself. (Incidentally, unlike many other two-year colleges, we set up internships on a one-work-day-per-week basis to fit realistically within the school, work, and commuting schedule of our students.[16]) In this Internship Seminar, again comprised of from fifteen to twenty interns and a faculty leader, students continue to shape or alter their plans in the light of what they learn from their work (and other academic) experiences. Without this seminar the desire to switch internships might reflect whimsy more than meaningful self-examination or thoughtful redefinition.

In addition, interesting work-related questions frequently arise. If, for example, interns in education perceive the frequent callousness with which schools treat their students, what can they do about it as mere community college students? Do they confront the administration of the schools where they are working, demanding that they act more humanely? Do they stifle their anger for the sake of keeping their jobs? Do they quit in frustration? These are real problems that have much to do with what it is to be a teacher.

One student was troubled by what she felt to be the inhuman way in which the teacher with whom she was working treated her third-grade class. This teacher felt her students were, in her words, "animals" (they were the lowest track third-grade class); and according to our student, Cathy, the class's undisciplined behavior was beginning to convince her that the teacher was right. But she was troubled because as part of our seminar she had read *Summerhill* and Herbert Kohl and John Holt, etc.; and their analyses of the disruptive behavior of children in schools tended to indict the institution rather than the children. But still Cathy's experience was creating the kind of frustration and bitterness that was turning her against the children. She felt she was beginning to resemble an all too familiar frustrated New

York City schoolteacher after only a month on the job. She was miserable. To try to test who was right—the third-grade teacher or John Holt—we had Cathy role play first the teacher she was working with and then a John Holt–style teacher. The rest of us played the students. In addition to enabling us to reconnect with our own third-grade experiences, valuable in itself, the exercise helped Cathy see how different classroom structures and different teacher expectations dramatically affect the classroom environment. Obviously not all the problems evaporated; but she did see that when she allowed a certain structured disorder, the children (the rest of us) began to become responsive to classroom learning. Cathy continued to work at the school and got the teacher to agree to allow her to work privately with the five most "hopeless" cases. The assistant principal found Cathy a private place (a used-book storage closet), and she began to try to apply some of *her own* methods. It wasn't easy and by no means did she achieve miracles. But her students' reading scores showed a measurable improvement and they stopped behaving like "animals"—at least with Cathy.

Also in these Internship Seminars we examine the concept of work itself. Many students today are rejecting or at least questioning the Protestant Ethic which teaches one to seek life-affirming satisfaction through work. One part of the so-called youth culture would like work to be neither essential nor inevitable; life-affirming satisfactions should be sought in various ways. But they learn, partly through their internships, that the world of work is still basically structured according to the older ethic; and so for these students, particularly, unless bridges can be built between the old ethic and the new, schooling remains irrelevant. One way of at least locating the foundations for these bridges is to help students discover specific kinds of work that reflect the new ethic. Community college students, who come primarily from working-class and lower-middle-class backgrounds, have a rather circumscribed view of the world of work. They often perceive work to be an unrelentingly dreary struggle for inadequate wages. They are generally unaware of some of the newer, more exotic, perhaps more satisfying work situations. One student, committed to the new work ethic, was about to drop out of school because everything Staten Island had to offer seemed inevitably to lead to a "straight," nine-to-five, jacket-and-tie kind of job. But as a result of a series of internships that began in a photography studio and ended with him working at the Sierra Club, he discovered that one might both make a living and find satisfaction doing conservation work. He did so well at the Sierra Club, provoking them to get interested in fighting to preserve a wilderness area in eastern Canada, that they encouraged him to apply to Syracuse University's School of Forestry. Their letters of recommendation helped him gain admission with a large financial aid package.

Once again, while attempting not to be overcritical of other community colleges struggling, as we are, with their internship programs or too pompous or self-serving about Staten Island's, I should mention what Heermann calls the "career practicums" of other colleges. There are a few that stress, as we do, the sharing of work-related problems to help students find that the problems they are encountering are often not unique. But again it seems that the old vocational education model is frequently the one emulated. For example, the kinds of topics suggested for examination in the practicums focus, among other things, on "today's secretary," "retailing: a new look," "banking: an innovative service," along with more promising topics such as "the psychology of work" and "the social role of business."[17]

In addition to structuring an off-campus work/study program flexible enough so that as students go through the process of self-definition they can serve a variety of internships, we have found it valuable *not* to offer up a menu of work/study opportunities as is common at many colleges. As much as possible, what we do instead is individualize our placements: When a student tells us that he/she wants to work in a psychiatric setting we spend a considerable amount of time in first helping the student define just what kind of work he is seeking. We of course often present various options drawn from past experience, but the focus is always on helping students define and refine their preferences. A preselected list of internships limits choice. Our individualized approach, we feel, is limited only by the students' growing strength and imagination.

To help this process, obviously, one also needs an internship director of equal strength and imagination. Our director of internships, Carl Takakjian, is sensitive to the idea that his role is to facilitate choosing rather than directing or controlling it. In addition to the lengthy talks he has with students as they go about trying to define their futures, he often gets them involved in seeking out and setting up the internships themselves. This takes more time. Sometimes it also means that we lose potential internship sites because students aren't as effective in setting them up as is our director. It would obviously be easier for him to pick up the telephone and set something up in the anthropology department of New York's Museum of Natural History, but if students can make this contact themselves it helps reduce our director's all-powerful image and reinforces the students' sense of their own growing confidence and strength. So we try to get them involved in the entire process and gladly risk whatever confusion or untidiness may result from their participation.

Something else is important that should be apparent from the examples of specific internships I have cited: ABC Sports, Sierra Club, the Museum of Natural History. These are all "quality" internships, the best possible placements. All too often community college interns complain that the work they are given to do is both repetitive and menial. Indeed various studies have confirmed this.[18] Thus the quality of the placement is critical. We have our own hidden message here—though we try to make it explicit: nothing but the best for our students. People accustomed to second best begin to think of themselves as second best. This is the usual experience for most of our students. We would as much as possible like to reverse this—not to turn the tables in the society but rather to help our people develop a positive sense of self-worth. And helping them find quality internships facilitates this.

After watching the Olympics on television Danny told us that, *although it was impossible,* he would like to work with the Wide World of Sports people. It was the "although it was impossible" that we were concerned about—not that we couldn't set it up but that Danny believed it was impossible *for him.* After all, he was just a community college student with a 2.6 grade point average. And although Danny, as indicated earlier, only remained at ABC for a short time, moving on to paramedical work, the process of helping him understand why he felt it was impossible as well as his helping in significant ways to set up the placement taught him a great deal about his power and worth that should be valuable to him in whatever he does in the future.

There is another by-product of "quality" placements. When we first contacted ABC (and many other places) they, too, thought it was impossible to work with community college students. If they had allowed student interns to work with them, it had always been, for example, Bennington or Antioch students. Their notion, initially, was that the proper kinds of internships for community college students might be to help maintain and repair ABC's computers or air conditioners. So in addition to working with Danny's image of himself we also had to work with ABC's image of Danny. If left unexamined and unchallenged, they both together could have contributed to defeating him.

How the type and quality of an internship communicates via hidden messages can be seen dramatically in another example from a couple of years ago. One incident had a great deal to do with shaping the development of our internship program at Staten Island. It happened during the first year of open admissions in the City University of New York (1970–71) when I was the director of our Preparatory Skills program. Toward the end of that year I was talking with Brian, one of our brightest students, about his plans for the summer. He told me how difficult it was to find jobs but that he had solid leads at a supermarket and at a gas station. I knew he was interested in college teaching or administration and asked how these summer jobs related to that aspiration. Obviously, he told me, only in that they would bring in some money. While talking with him I remembered a job from the summer before that a Yale sophomore, Mike, had secured for himself. Mike was also interested in college teaching and administration, and when he went to the Yale Placement Office to look for help, they set him up for the summer working as an intern in the office of the president of Staten Island Community College, William Birenbaum! Not only did he get paid rather handsomely but he was also able to earn academic credit. And when I thought about the difference in the way Brian would spend his summer it made me furious. We discussed all of this at great length and we decided that it would be a good idea for Brian to see our placement counselor to find out what kinds of things she had to offer. He also decided that when she asked him what he wanted to do for the summer he would tell her that he wanted to work for Kingman Brewster, president of Yale. (The fact that when Brian came up with this idea we both laughed about it also taught us something about the differences between Yale and S.I.C.C. and how those differences have affected all of us.) He did go to our placement counselor and the few openings she had were for stock-clerk jobs at Sears and the like. When he told her about wanting to work for Kingman Brewster she looked at him as if he were literally crazy. Well, Brian did get "crazy" about this. He learned via these covert messages just what S.I.C.C. was expecting of him and became determined to do something about it. He didn't go to Yale for the summer but did get to go there to take some courses the following spring semester. He finished his baccalaureate in three years—just about unheard of for open-admissions students[19]—and is now enrolled in Columbia University's Ph.D. program in anthropology with a sizable fellowship.

Obviously a few examples are not infinitely generalizable, but through the years we have had more than just a few Cathys, Dannys, and Brians. It is becoming clear that by putting the hidden curriculum to work for students in egalitarian ways, by building an experiential education program to release rather than to contain potential, schooling—even at the college level—can serve notions of personal development and equality.

Our problem is this: the present structure of relationships between senior and junior colleges suggests that we take our innovating, our experimenting, out of the hides of our students, who then pay a price later on when they try to transfer to a senior institution.

—Seymour Eskow
1969

NINE
THE TRANSFER TRAUMA

We began to rethink our whole approach to transfer as a result of a series of experiences that culminated one day in my colleague Joe Harris's office. A former Staten Island Community College student who had transferred to Middlebury College stopped by one hot June day to tell us about his junior-year experiences in Vermont. It was tough but he was doing very well, getting all A's and B's, and seemed headed toward law school. While José was telling us about one of his political science courses, the school's transfer counselor stuck his head in about another matter. He recognized José—not that he had helped him transfer to Middlebury, Joe Harris had done that; it was just that after José was accepted there was a good deal of publicity about it (not too many Puerto Rican community college students ever get into places such as Middlebury) and our transfer counselor got in on some of the reflected glory. When he heard how well José was doing and that he was a prelaw student, our counselor told José that if he kept it up he would help him get into Brooklyn Law School. This offer was made in all generosity and its significance passed right over Joe and me and José that day. But later that week we realized that the cooling-out functions of community colleges—for José at least—were reaching out beyond the two years allotted to community colleges. Our transfer counselor had tried to convince José to transfer to Brooklyn College in the first place—and had lost him; now a year later he was getting set to cool him out to Brooklyn *after* José got his B.A.

Now what's wrong with all of this? Aren't Brooklyn College and Brooklyn Law School good places? Yes, they're good places all right. What's wrong is the *automatic* way in which we were trying to send José to them. José is a really first-rate student and should have a wide range of realistic options from which to choose. When I applied to college and graduate school, I too was a first-rate student. As an upwardly mobile middle-class person the only thing automatic about my applications to college and graduate school was that I was automatically going. Unlike José, for me the process was full of choices: Brooklyn College—or its equivalent—was my "safe school." And the difference was not just that my family could more or less afford to send me to M.I.T. or Princeton or Columbia—my choices. Nowadays, with colleges looking to widen and deepen the "pool" from which they select students there are scholarships for José, as well as work/study monies, Economic Opportunity Grants, National Defense Loans, etc. No, the problem for José involves how community colleges function to limit rather than expand choosing, the way they help the Josés select schools to which to apply for transfer, and thus reinforce the limited academic aspirations that are a part of working-class culture.

When all this became clear to us, we looked into the operations of our transfer office. We were dismayed by what we found. When you enter the office, you're faced by a bookcase full of college catalogs. An impressive sight that upon closer examination reveals its limitations. Virtually all of the catalogs are from colleges that are a part of the city and state systems of which Staten Island Community College is a member. These are the schools to which transfer is easiest and in many instances automatic. For students thinking or dreaming about other more exotic places, the bookcase offers very little. Then when they get to see the transfer counselor himself, pretty much all he does is give them the application forms for what he deems to be the appropriate city or state colleges. If they raise questions of other possibilities, he often raises a skeptical eyebrow which is sometimes enough to discourage further inquiry. If they persist, he has no concrete information available. And as the school's only transfer counselor, he's in a hurry. He has to meet the transfer needs of hundreds of students. In June 1973, for example, Staten Island awarded more than a thousand associate's degrees. About half of our graduates were going on to other colleges. In addition, hundreds more transferred without receiving their degrees. Numbers of this size encourage handing everyone seeking transfer counseling an application for Brooklyn College.

But in addition to those students who find their way to the counselor's office, there are many others who might transfer but have no idea whatsoever how they should proceed. Most students never see a counselor. The only relationship they have with their advisers is to get biannual perfunctory signatures on their registration forms. Most advice concerning transfer comes from fellow students. And many students don't get even this frequently inaccurate kind of information. So it isn't surprising that come each May and June dozens of students who are about to graduate or who have run out of credits they are allowed to take at S.I.C.C. (sixty-eight or so) come wandering to various offices looking for transfer help. Many others just drift away. But even for those who find someone to talk to, most deadlines for application have passed and the choices they have are virtually nil. Occasionally we can help hustle a student or two into some place that hasn't yet filled its quota of transfer students. But this is an inadequate process for an institution that has historically defined a substantial part of its uniqueness to be close, effective counseling.

A recent conference of transfer personnel from the city and state Universities revealed that S.I.C.C.'s process is the rule rather than the exception. Uppermost in the minds of the conferees was not the facilitation of the transfer process, the dissemination of information to eligible students, or the opening of more transfer options. Rather, it was the old "articulation" problem of how to assure that the credits students earn at community colleges are accepted at the four-year colleges to which they transfer.[2]

How has this situation come about? One has to look again at the history of how community colleges developed and at their social and hidden functions. The most important thing to recall is that public community colleges *began exclusively* as transfer institutions and only much later began to expand their offerings to include vocational courses. It is only since the 1940s that community college legislation, reflecting what are seen as the new social functions of two-year colleges, has emphasized vocational and technical programs. Many writers since that time cite the obvious need for more highly trained workers as the result of technological expansion; this is the need that the community college is now supposed to be uniquely suited to meet.[3]

In addition, we have seen, there is a more covert but at least as powerful social need served by the junior college: the need to absorb and sort out the hordes of new students who have started to demand their piece of the higher education action. This trend began at the end of World War II when hundreds of thousands of veterans sought admission to college under the G.I. Bill. In the 1960s at places such as C.C.N.Y., protesting students, occupying the City College campus, pressured the City University to accelerate its open-admissions program— CUNY opened its doors to all high-school graduates in September 1970, five years ahead of schedule. And where did most of these new students go? To community colleges—whether or not they wanted to become technicians. Community college enrollments have tripled and quadrupled since 1950 while the growth in four-year-college enrollments has "merely" doubled. Four-year colleges and universities not only feared being inundated by numbers, they also feared inundation by illiteracy. The four-year colleges and universities in effect said: Let the community colleges handle both the "salvaging" of "late-bloomers" through their noted remedial programs and also let them handle the cooling-out of "latent terminal" students, sending on to us as transfer students only a relatively small number of the literate.

The tip-off to how this unspoken covenant between two- and four-year colleges works is revealed by examining the parallel history of the formal and informal "articulation" arrangements that have developed between two- and four-year institutions with regard to the transfer of students and their credits. In the early days of community colleges there was relatively little social pressure to expand higher educational opportunities more-or-less equally to all socioeconomic groups. As a result there was relatively little pressure on four-year colleges to be particularly generous in accepting transfer students or their credits—even though junior colleges were originally set up at the behest of four-year colleges specifically as college-parallel institutions. As late as 1965 it was not uncommon for up to 50 percent of community college students to lose some credit when transferring[4] or for senior colleges to arbitrarily reduce all community college grades to senior-college C's or even to obliterate all grades earned at a community college and to have transfer students in a sense begin all over again with a zero grade point average.[5]

But slowly things began to change. Various minority groups began to perceive the real economic functions of higher education and how this is linked to the tracking and cooling-out functions of community colleges. They began to demand more than equal access to higher education; they began to demand equal *results*. Equal results meant more B.A.'s, and thus the pressure was on four-year colleges to become more flexible in their admission of transfer students and the transfer of their credits.[6] By 1955 the principle of strict course parallelism had given way in most parts of the country to "equivalency" as the basis for course acceptability.[7] This concept of equivalency meant that although four-year college X required its "native" students to take English Composition 101, it no longer denied its transfer students credit for their junior-college Introduction to Composition 100 course if it were considered to be generally equivalent to Composition 101. The next step, the emerging current situation, was for four-year colleges to accept an entire package of community college credits—if students have earned an associate's degree. In effect the university now says: "We will accept as transferable what you say is transferable." The "ultimate," according to Frederick Kintzer, is for "full in-faith acceptance of the associate degree, including technical-vocational credits and without regard for the high-school records."[8] But there are problems with both the current and ultimate position: First, many (and in some schools most) students transfer *prior* to earning an associate's degree; they, therefore, still face significant loss of credit when transferring. Second, if recent faculty feeling in the City University of New York is a straw-in-the-wind regarding the transfer of technical-vocational credits, the ultimate position is a long way off. The executive committee of the University Faculty Senate stated that:

> Articulation policies should be based on academically sound principles and not simply on the mistaken, short-term expedient of attempting to satisfy a universal demand for the baccalaureate degree. Whatever value a liberal arts baccalaureate degree has will quickly disappear [if technical credits become transferable] at least so far as CUNY is concerned, if the degree becomes simply a statement of the fact that the student has earned 128 credits in a program characterized by neither rational form or content.[9]

Although some view this to be a reactionary position, it indicates that the CUNY faculty at least perceived some of the real social forces impelling CUNY and other systems to reexamine their transfer procedures. Kintzer chalks up the new flexibility to a growing enlightenment on the part of university officials; the CUNY faculty more accurately sees the impetus behind a more open system emanating from new and powerful social and political forces that want to equalize the results of as well as access to higher education.

But even if we were to achieve Kintzer's "ultimate position," would the results of higher education really be equal for the working-class and lower-middle-class students who typically enter college via community colleges? Many would respond affirmatively. Dorothy Knoell and Leland Medsker, for example, in their often cited study, *From Junior to Senior College*, found that: (1) Demographically, community college students who transfer are quite like "native" students who begin at four-year colleges (except that the community college students come from somewhat poorer and less well educated families); (2) At least 75 percent of transferred students go on to get their B.A.'s; (3) Although transferred students' grades declined less than one-half point during their first semester at their new college (−0.3 points), this was virtually overcome by the time they graduated.[10]

All of this sounds good until examined closely; but let me take these findings point by point:

(1) Yes, students who transfer are demographically similar to native students. But up to 75 percent of first-semester community college students declare themselves to be transfer students, and of these only about one-third ever go on to other colleges. An enormous number drop out, get cooled-out, pushed out, disappear, etc. Demographically, these dropouts tend to come disproportionately from among racial and economic minority groups, from the least well educated families, and from the lowest achievers in high school. No wonder, then, that those who get through the communi-

ty college filter and go on to a four-year college are similar to the students who began there. This is not dealt with at all by Knoell and Medsker nor is it commented on by others who do cite their findings to demonstrate the effectiveness of community college transfer programs. Indeed, they are all rather casual about this high nontransfer rate of community college B.A.-aspirants. Perhaps the calm of Knoell and Medsker and their followers results from their feeling that substantial numbers of community college B.A.-aspirants seem doomed to failure: "It is very possible that, if [the] one third to one half of the present enrollment in transfer courses *destined to fail* or to become discouraged and quit had been required to start college experience in an appropriate program, society might have many more technicians than is currently the case" (my italics).[11]

(2) Knoell and Medsker claim that at least 75 percent of transferred students earn baccalaureates. *But* that is only three-quarters of the 25–30 percent of community college students who actually go on to transfer. This means, by their calculations, that only 14–17 percent of the original community college B.A.-aspirants ever get their degrees. Compare this to the approximately 50 percent graduation rate of B.A.-aspirants who enter college via four-year colleges. Again, none of this is examined by the major writers. Nor is there any comment about another remarkable and related finding reported by Knoell and Medsker: that there is some evidence that although California has one of the nation's highest percentages of high-school graduates attending college, at the same time its percentage of baccalaureate recipients in the college-age group is below the national average. They speculate that the large proportion of lower-division students enrolled in junior college may be

a factor in this seeming discrepancy.[12] I know of no more significant evidence to support my assertion that one of the community college's most significant social functions is to *limit* rather than to increase the number of students who go on to receive the baccalaureate and thus help to maintain the value of the B.A. in the face of minority-group and lower-class social pressure.

(3) Finally, a word must be said about the decline in transferred students' grades during their first semester at four-year colleges. Although the Knoell-Medsker study indicates that this decline is more or less made up in subsequent semesters, there are significant but infrequently perceived consequences that result from this decline.[13] First, a −0.3 decline in grade point average frequently tips transferred students' averages under the probationary limits of their new colleges. Although being on probation does not inexorably lead to dismissal, it frequently does. More important, being placed on probation has a demoralizing effect on students—particularly transferred students who come to four-year colleges somewhat uncertain of themselves and of their ability to succeed.

Even more significant is the fact that declining grades negatively affect a transferred student's ability to secure financial aid.[14] Elite private colleges have usually been open about the relationship between academic performance and the amount of financial aid a student receives. For example, the director of financial aid at Mount Holyoke writes, "Since, among applicants with need, academic excellence is the key to being offered assistance, the . . . applicants selected for scholarship help are of extraordinary ability."[15] Less selective four-year colleges have less openly tended to follow the example of their elite brother and sister institutions; they too have generally allocated their limited financial aid funds for transferred students according to academic achievement in addition to demonstrated economic need. So a −0.3 decline in G.P.A. coupled with inadequate financial aid resources causes many transferred students to withdraw; Knoell and Medsker state that after transfer, financial problems ranked first among the various causes associated with students withdrawing from college. They also say that since it costs significantly more to attend a four-year college, transfer students may develop unrealizable collegiate aspirations at the less expensive community colleges since during that time their financial situation will not have improved enough to make attending a four-year college realistic.[16] What they advocate in the name of more realism is, in effect, more cooling-out: the problem would be no problem if more transfer students would switch into two-year terminal or career programs. A more constructive realism would involve not being so casual about the −0.3 G.P.A. decline and doing something about the regressive financial aid policies that apply particularly and specifically to transferred students.

If as I've claimed transfer programs have not succeeded (with obvious and significant exceptions for many individual students who began at community colleges and went on to become successful teachers, engineers, businessmen, etc.), what would constitute a successful program? First, it is obvious that the kind of transfer office and transfer counseling described at the beginning of this chapter would have to go—not just the bookcase full of obsolete catalogs and limited choices but the service concept they represent. Community colleges can't just open an office and wait for the "clients" to appear at the right time (before transfer application deadlines), asking the right questions ("What kind of New York State Scholar Incentive grant can I expect if I transfer to a unit of the State University rather than to a unit of the City University?"). Community college students from working-class homes are less knowledgeable than middle-class students about application deadlines and procedures, scholarships, the differences between large and small colleges, residential college life versus commuter life, private versus public colleges, etc. Nevertheless, the current transfer-counseling model makes the middle-class assumption that community college students know all of this and all the transfer counselor has to do is supply the appropriate answers to the right questions. What is needed is an aggressive concept that sees itself as part of the *teaching* process. This process must reflect an awareness of the regressive, unacknowledged social and political functions of community colleges and must attempt to thwart them and replace them with more egalitarian methods. Beginning in the first semester rather than the last, there must be a systematic plan to teach students about the details and possibilities of various transfer options.

An effective transfer procedure should be linked with the kind of counseling we have tried to build into our Educational Development and Internship Seminars at Staten Island. Part of the function of these seminars is to help students begin to make long-range plans for themselves that include transfer. They also, hopefully, lead students to finding teacher-counselors to whom they can come for transfer information during their sophomore year. This eliminates the impersonal service-center approach of the usual community college transfer office.

To strengthen our approach to facilitating transfer we have been experimenting with a special program for second-year students. It emerged a couple of years ago from our realization that barriers to successful transfer involve a good deal more than just lack of information.

We had been working with a small group of students to help prepare them for possible transfer admission to Yale. Our work began with us passing along some basic information about Yale to a few students who expressed interest in eventually going on to law or medical school. We felt that if they were to be admitted and graduate they would have a very good chance of realizing their aspirations. We had some contacts at Yale and started talking about the possibilities. Basic information was obviously needed: One student had never heard of Yale—she thought Yale was a company that manufactured locks. Another student with nearly a straight A average who had become interested in Yale one day decided not to apply because the scholarships that were available to her, she told us, were inadequate. When we wondered why she felt this way since we knew Yale to be one of the wealthiest universities, she showed us the token scholarships *listed in the Staten Island Community College catalog*: twenty-five dollars from the American Legion, fifty dollars from the Italian Club of Staten Island, etc. She didn't know that if she were admitted to Yale, *Yale* not S.I.C.C. would provide the money.

As part of the Yale-transfer program we arranged for these students to take courses at Yale's Center for the Study of the City during the spring semester at no cost to either S.I.C.C. or the students. The people at Yale were most generous. We all went up there one day just before the semester was to begin to make the final arrangements, meet the professors, get the reading lists. Everything went very well. But in the car on the way home a colleague and I began to pick up some very negative vibrations from the students in the back seat. We asked what was the matter. Incredibly, they told us they were depressed because *it hadn't worked out*, that we hadn't "scored." They were literally sitting there with the reading lists in their hands while at the same time telling us that Yale had reneged on its promise to allow them to take courses! They claimed the professors we met had been hostile, and in spite of what they had promised would not let them actually take the classes. We obviously discussed this at great length both then and later. We all came to feel that their past conditioning to expect and accept failure had caused them to transform a successful experience into a more familiar and easier to accept failure situation.[17]

We attempted to structure our transfer program to struggle with this kind of problem. The program continues and extends the EDS concept into the sophomore year, helping students reformulate and monitor their earlier plans. But its specific objectives involve helping students select, apply to, and be accepted by a four-year college (with adequate financial aid), and develop whatever skills they will need to be successful there. Part of what we do is informational; but for the most part we are concerned with helping students deal with transfer trauma. It might very well be that the decline in grade point average that transferred students experience is more the result of the social and cultural shock they encounter when moving from a familiar setting to a new college than any lack of basic academic skills. It typically takes students at least one semester to begin to feel at home at a new college, to begin to understand how it works, to learn who has the power to get things done, how to cut through red tape, how to get to know the social leaders, etc.* At most community colleges a great deal of atten-

---

*Since community college students are the only college students who must transfer if they seek a B.A., they are forced, in a sense, to go through the adjustment and resulting lower grades of two first semesters. This puts community college students at a further disadvantage to students who enter college at four-year institutions. Just one more example of how community colleges are structured for failure.

tion is focused on how to prepare students in the academic or "hard"-skills area but very little is paid to teaching the personal or "soft" skills that are at least as important. The transfer program attempts to work in both areas.

With regard to "soft" skills, we continue the work begun in our EDS's, with students exploring their educational biographies so as to make their schooling coherent to them. Affective learning continues to be stressed. For example, we have developed a series of exercises and experiences designed to help students build or strengthen the skills they will need to confront the difficulties of going on to a new and in some cases dramatically different social and cultural scene. If students are planning to transfer to a residential college, this may very well be the first time they have been away from home. If they are planning to transfer to a private or elite state college or university, this may be the first time they have ever been out of a working-class or ghetto culture. If students are planning to transfer to a college with stiff academic expectations, this may be the first time they have been taken seriously as students—and this presents unique problems: an environment that expects and *rewards* only success may be a difficult one for them to survive in. But adaptive and survival skills *are learnable*.

We have developed some survival or initiative experiences (we call them that) which we ask our transfer students to undergo. One exercise involved our asking the students to locate two faculty members between 12 noon and 2 P.M. one Saturday afternoon. We told them that we would be together some place within the five boroughs of New York City. That was it. We gave them no additional clues. The exercise was not just to see if they could find us (they did—within an hour and a half) but also it was designed to help them understand how they go about confronting difficult problems. We did this by having them reconstruct the steps they went through in locating us. Why hadn't they "staked out" our houses in an attempt to follow us? Why had some worked as a group, dividing up the assignments, whereas some had worked on their own? Why had they depended so much on the telephone? Why had some given up without trying? Why when they had successfully located us did they feel let down? When we first posed the problem, they had said it was impossible; so after finding us why did they belittle their achievement by calling it "too easy"? After a series of such exercises students got to be quite good at solving "impossible" problems. More important, they began to expect success and to enjoy it.

To help students deal with the shock of transferring from a community college with its decidedly working-class student body and culture to a four-year college with its very different milieu, we set up other experiences for the transfer group. For example, we arranged for interested students to spend a week living with "alternative" families. We chose the families so they would be similar to those that send their children to the kinds of colleges to which our students would be transferring. We were concerned that our students might feel diminished in these kinds of homes, that they would think their alternative parents to be better people than their own parents because they were more affluent. When we discussed these feelings openly, we found that this did not happen. In fact, we had a couple of experiences in which some of our students had to deal with opposite feelings. One student, for example, said that when he arrived at the only moderately posh Central Park West apartment of his family-for-the-week, he immediately felt they could not be good people because of their bourgeois lifestyle. But during the course of the week he came to learn they were just people—not "rich people": When they woke up in the morning they were just as grouchy as his people. He also discovered that they were unhappy about some of the things their children were doing just as his parents were unhappy with some of his behavior. He came to see as well that racial and class oppression are not just applied from those above onto those below and that his initial hostility was in part an expression of his own doubts about himself and his discomfort at being in an unfamiliar environment.

In addition to visiting families, we have our transfer students visit colleges—for a day if they are in the area to two or three days if they are farther away. The first-hand information they gather is obviously valuable—it brings a college catalog to life and sometimes reveals the deceptions of public relations people. More valuable is the experience of taking initial steps to survive at a different college, to sample dormitory life for the first time, to sit in on classes, to try to relate to a new group of students. Following these brief campus visits, which usually occur during the fall semester, we encourage students, if possible, to spend the month of January taking courses while in residence at four-year colleges that conduct discrete mini-semesters at that time. This gives many of our students their first real taste of living away from home for a sustained period of time. It also gives them the chance to try out their developing academic skills in a new setting. And finally, if students are thinking of applying to the school they're attending, it gives the student and the college an opportunity to check each other out. Our students generally have found that they can do the work, and this helps reaffirm their growing sense that they can be academically successful. Perhaps some of these experiences will reduce transfer trauma and the usual decline in G.P.A. that results from it.

In the nonacademic or soft-skill areas other things happen during January that are just as important but more difficult to define or measure. Debbie had never spent *one* day or one night away from home prior to joining a Transfer Seminar group. When her group planned to go away together for a weekend of work and fun—with faculty members—she had a great deal of difficulty telling her parents that she wanted to participate, much less getting their approval. Therefore, when on her own she decided to fly out to the University of Redlands in California to participate in their January semester, we were shocked and a little nervous that her parents would blame us for putting such an idea in her head. But she confronted them and won their permission to go. Although faculty members received a few late-night telephone calls from her parents while Debbie was away and apparently not calling them as much as they would have liked, both the faculty and the parents survived. Debbie more than survived; she thrived in California in the confidence that she at least knew that she could make independent choices and make them work. She is currently doing very well living and studying in England as a Friends World College student. In a strict sense we didn't "teach" any of this to Debbie. We did, however, structure our Transfer Seminar environment so that she could acquire these valuable soft skills.

A few words about hard skills. I've already written about how work on basic skills is an important part of a successful first-year program (see chapter 7). But the work must continue and can be integrated in interesting and effective ways into a second-year transfer program.

We attempt to help students practice the specific kinds of skills that will be required at the kinds of schools to which they are applying. If, for example, we have a student who is serious about transferring to an experimental college that emphasizes independent studies and learning via educational contracts, we attempt to *simulate* that experience for that student at our school. If, on the other hand, we have students who are interested in transferring to so-called traditional colleges that emphasize highly structured, scholastically demanding work, we attempt to simulate these kinds of educational experiences for those students, including the same kinds of objectives and standards, as well as grading policies, that their new colleges will apply. This too, we hope, contributes to reducing the trauma of transferring and the decline in G.P.A.'s transferred students experience.

I've mentioned that a successful transfer program also must be able to deal with the barriers that separate two- from four-year colleges. While our students are attending various colleges during the January semester, we take the opportunity to work in our own way on the institutional barriers that separate two- and four-year colleges. As indicated earlier these barriers still exist and must be assaulted if community colleges are to develop successful transfer programs. The articulation between colleges within the same state or municipal system has been improving in recent years, and although much still needs to be accomplished, especially with regard to the transfer of certain community college credits, we have decided to put most of our energies to work trying to establish liaisons with four-year colleges outside our systems. In general we are well received. Many fine four-year colleges are excited about the possibility of widening their pool of applicants by working with our transfer program.

They have been willing to take the "risk" of accepting some of our students, particularly because they feel the students' experiences with us are of the sort that prepare the students to have a good chance of being successful. As a result of our program, the performance of students during January semesters, and the accumulating evidence of success of those who have transferred and thrived at Amherst and Smith and Berkeley, many colleges that rarely if ever admitted community college transfer students have begun to do so—with adequate financial aid.[18]

Often we have had to encourage colleges to reexamine and modify long-standing policies regarding community college applicants, for fewer than one institution in five has any aid set aside for transfer students.[19] I recently visited with the director of admissions and financial aid at a fine northeastern private college. He was intrigued by the idea of establishing a relationship with us. But when it came time to discuss financial aid for potential applicants, he said, "God, our school has a policy— rather arbitrary I admit but a policy nonetheless—not to give any aid whatsoever to first-semester transfer students. They have to show us they can do well before we'll give them any money." Since in the past they had only accepted transfer students from other private four-year colleges (students who could afford the tuition and room-and-board costs) it wasn't necessary for them to have a financial aid program for transfer students. When I pointed out that this policy would automatically exclude nearly all of our students, the director told me that they had never before realized this. Since that conversation, the college has in fact begun to accept some of our applicants, for the first time with scholarships and other forms of financial aid.

This year one of our students applied to Sarah Lawrence. Part of the application form asked for a detailed family history, not just the names, ages, and educational backgrounds of the applicant's father and mother, but similar information about paternal and maternal grandparents. In addition, the application required details about the entire family's occupations, including names of firms, titles, etc. The only thing missing was a request for everyone's income. Both the student and her counselor, Elinor Azenberg, were quite upset that this kind of information might affect admission to Sarah Lawrence, particularly since this information might hurt community college students' chances since their parents and grandparents couldn't be expected to contribute very much money to the college.

Ellie wrote to the dean of the college, asking "What is the purpose of this form? . . . Our inference was that admission decisions were influenced at Sarah Lawrence either by social or educational background or by the family's ability to support the college's endowments. In either case, admission wasn't to be based solely on the student and his or her personal ability but upon externals beyond their control." It is nice to be able to report that in part because of this letter Sarah Lawrence plans to eliminate these kinds of questions from their application.

Often, however, there are disappointments. Brown University, for example, rejected one of our best and most interesting students with the advice to him that "community college students should aspire to lesser colleges." Bill had a 3.7+ average at S.I.C.C. During his last semester there he took twenty-two credits and received A's in all seven courses. He is a master tool and die maker, having spent eight years between high school and college learning and working in the trade. He came to S.I.C.C. with the desire to become a labor lawyer. He dreams about getting labor and small manufacturers together to assure the survival of the quality work that only these kinds of small shops can do. While at S.I.C.C., he designed and built on his own an enormous radio telescope and won a Ford Foundation Upper Division Scholarship that pays up to 50 percent of all his college expenses as a transferred student. If Brown feels that Bill should aspire to lesser places, which community college student can aspire to places such as Brown?

When another student applied to Barnard College, also with a nearly perfect average, also somewhat older than the usual college sophomore, and also offering an extremely rich, "nontraditional" series of life experiences, she got the same kind of reception—though not nearly so blatant. Juanita Bodden had written to Barnard requesting an application fee waiver. She did mention that she had been nominated for a Ford Foundation scholarship and included the application itself which contained an extensive autobiographical statement. The associate director of admissions' letter to her was curt and to the point: We might waive the fee if you can get a "statement of extreme need" from your adviser, financial aid is seldom available for transfers, your foreign-language proficiency is questionable, in the meantime why not apply to the adult School of General Studies (their "night school") since most of Barnard's students are between sixteen and twenty-one.

Juanita was furious and fired a letter back to the associate director. She told her that she had been accepted by Princeton and had received financial aid to supplement the Ford scholarship. At Princeton, too, the majority of students are between sixteen and twenty-one; but unlike Barnard, Princeton took her extra years to be an asset. And although Princeton, too, has a language requirement, they were making arrangements for her to take a language, whereas Barnard seemed to be holding it against her. She deeply resented Barnard's attempt to cool her into the decidedly inferior but just as costly School of General Studies. She concluded: "Not only do we deserve you, but you also deserve us. . . . Princeton, Amherst, and Smith recognized our ability and have accepted us. Both the colleges and the students have benefited from the experience. But as long as places like Barnard continue to maintain their present policy on community college transfers, then the educational system in this country is still in grave trouble."

Experiences such as these indicate a structured commitment to immobility built right into our public and private system of higher education. In Michigan, for example, *by law* community colleges are not allowed to publish private colleges' degree requirements in their catalogs.[20] This is obviously an outrageous example of a state-mandated mechanism for maintaining social stratification. Very rarely are the mechanisms that open—but overt or covert, they are there nonetheless.

*Within ten years I want to place all my students in
    top bureaucratic positions of H.E.W. and change that
    whole goddamn place! So that it begins to serve human
    beings and not the bureaucrats who serve them. This
    means the students have to be prepared to talk the
    Man's language, for one thing. I can go into a meeting
    of bureaucrats and start talking street talk and get
    nothing; and I can go and start talking about optimum
    feasibility and bullshit like that and they'll listen.*

—Walter Tubbs, Jr.

1972

TEN

LESS HIERARCHICAL INSTITUTIONS

Institutions are communications media, and if in part the medium is the message, the messages most institutions in our society communicate concern how to exist within hierarchical relationships: how to behave when you have power, how to try to get it, how to act when you are powerless. It is obvious that if we want a different, less hierarchical society, we need to begin to restructure our institutions so that they will deliver more egalitarian messages.

In the realm of higher education this would not only require changing the way in which schools are governed by redistributing power among all members of the school community, but restructuring our various collegiate systems themselves. At the very least this would mean *the elimination* of junior or community colleges since they are the most class-serving of educational institutions. The elimination of these institutions would of course not spell the end of higher educational opportunities for students from low socioeconomic backgrounds; they, along with everyone else would be able to enter directly into B.A.-granting schools. This would alter the decidedly second-class status attached to community colleges and their students and also end the academic and social trauma experienced by junior-college students when they are forced to transfer to senior colleges if they seek B.A.'s—as most of them do. Coupled with this "de-hierarching," public systems of higher education should consider awarding a single university-wide B.A., or graduate degree rather than having individual units within a system award their own degrees of widely different prestige. In California, for example, this would mean that graduates would receive a University of California degree rather than a separate degree from Berkeley, U.C.L.A., or Santa Cruz. Thus competence—the ability to do the work, perform the job— would become the determining factor for graduate school admissions, employment, etc.[1]

But, the cry is frequently raised, aren't we already "producing" too many B.A.'s? What about all those people with baccalaureates who can't find jobs and are forced to drive taxi cabs? It is claimed that there is a limit, even in affluent, advanced nations such as ours, to the number of people who can be employed in professional, managerial, or even semiprofessional fields. Occupational education advocates such as Norman Harris variously estimate that by 1980 perhaps only 25 percent of the labor force will be required for such "people-oriented" work for which a B.A. seems appropriate. Thus if we plan our colleges and the degrees they offer, our recruitment, admissions, counseling, and retention policies to produce more than this 25 percent, we shall be preparing, in his words, "a blueprint for disaster."

With incredible arrogance he concludes, "To put it bluntly, we already have an oversupply of philosopher-kings. The era of the educated unemployed is not just around the corner—it is here!"[2]

Harris and those of his persuasion totally misunderstand the reality behind their claim that there is something inevitable about that 25 percent figure. They also fail to see the intrinsic rewards of a liberal education—even for a cab driver. In my earlier chapter, The Hidden Functions of Schooling, I attempted to show how future manpower-needs projections and the corresponding distribution of students within the different strata of the higher educational systems are manipulated to fulfill preconceived notions of appropriate work hierarchies and to preserve the mythological idea that the top, by its nature, has only so much room for talented people. If we can manage to control and manipulate markets and employment opportunities (so that for example about 20 percent of *all* workers' jobs are related to automobiles), why not a similar manipulation in favor of "people-oriented" work?[3]

I'm both concerned and suspicious about current efforts to put limits on such educational opportunities as new students are for the first time entering colleges and universities in significant numbers. It seems more than coincidental that, in spite of cutbacks in some educational expenditures, just when collegiate opportunities are expanding to include students who have hitherto been excluded we get proposals to establish B.A. quotas or even to deschool. Such proposals can only lead to a further hardening of the social status quo. Right now these proposals are particularly troublesome, since depressions and recessions are particularly good times to advance such regressive ideas. Though many see a leveling off or decline in college enrollments during these times, the fact is that enrollments are actually continuing to increase—as was the case during the Great Depression. Young people frequently choose to study their way through economic downturns. And the current recession is no exception. The director of admissions at Colorado State University put it this way: "Young people continue with school because they figure they'll take their chances of studying for four years and then be able to get a . . . job when they've graduated." He noted that at his school, applications for admission for 1975–76 were about 40 percent higher than during the previous year.[4]

But at a time when jobs for people with B.A.'s, or all jobs for that matter, are scarce (*The New York Times* noted that job opportunities for 1975 college graduates as compared with 1974, were down by 18 percent[5]), shouldn't young people be encouraged to take a realistic, hard look at the value of a college education; at the very least shouldn't they get themselves into some sort of postsecondary, career-oriented education? Isn't there a real danger that we are generating, in James O'Toole's words, a "reserve army of the *under*employed"?[6] For example, when in the spring of 1975 Bronx Community College advertised fifty government subsidized, rather low-level tutoring jobs for unemployed college graduates at $7,800 per year, more than a thousand applied. Of these thousand, over half had graduate degrees from Columbia, Berkeley, and the like.[7]

My response to O'Toole would be that since virtually all graduate students at Columbia and Berkeley still come from backgrounds of relative social and economic privilege, times of hardship are more than ever *not* the times to close the doors of higher education in the faces of the less privileged. Doing so would obviously tend to solidify inequalities.

We already have a sign of this tendency in the fact that the proportion of blacks enrolling in college is declining after years of increase. In 1972, 8.7 percent of freshmen were black; by 1974 the percentage had fallen to 7.4.[8] If colleges are no longer recruiting black students with the same vigor they showed in the late 1960s and early 1970s, isn't it clear that we can anticipate lower-class white ethnic students will receive the same treatment in the near future? Their short day in the academic sun also appears about to end.

Frank Newman, president of the University of Rhode Island, feels that if there has to be a competition among young people, he would rather have them compete for jobs than compete to get into college.[9] With affirmative-action programs and the like, this would mean that women and blacks and the children of the working class would at least have a chance to get good jobs and assert more power within the society.

Perhaps the idea embodied in the epigraph of this chapter provides the guidance we need to change things in fundamental but careful ways: people first have to learn "the Man's language" without succumbing to the Man's ways. The best kind of liberal education can teach that; it can also prepare new students to do more than stammer or look at their feet when they come to sit in society's paneled boardrooms. Many a "community leader" has been ineffective when sitting in the conference room of the Ford Foundation, many a union leader has settled for less than was necessary because he or she has not been able to match either confidence or verbal skills with management negotiators.

Critically important, though, to sitting in the room

with one's values intact is the understanding that having a B.A. or advanced degree doesn't make you a better person. And this requires that we all begin to see hierarchical relationships for what they are: historical rather than natural constructs that serve either political or economic forces. One analysis has it that hierarchical arrangements are needed only during times of scarcity in order to regulate the production and distribution of limited goods and services. In a postscarcity society such as ours, supported by a technology that has both the potential to produce a surfeit of goods and to liberate us from onerous toil, a more egalitarian, less hierarchical structure is possible.[10]

But schools continue to function around the assumption that hierarchy is both natural and inevitable, and continue to prepare students for predestined unequal experiences. The classroom presents all too many opportunities to learn one's place. With the expansion of bureaucracy in the schools paralleling the deepening bureaucracy of the rest of society, a third party in addition to the teacher and student has more and more entered the educational picture—the administrator. The lessons one needs to learn in order to function in this new tripartite structure have become an important socialization function for the modern school—students are being prepared to operate within complex and ultimately alienating adult work structures.[11]

So far attempts at far-reaching school reform have usually failed. Liberal solutions as well as conservative proposals all miss the structural basis of inequality. Liberal environmentalists who blame inequalities on unequal opportunity as well as conservative Jensenites who claim a genetic basis for social differences both believe that in our meritocracy people rise or fall according to their ability. If a bright, capable, poor black person fails to do well, liberals argue, it may be because of limited opportunities; conservatives feel genetic deficiencies may be the problem. Neither group admits that in a society like ours there is limited room at the top, and that no matter how schools try to increase reading scores or open their doors, all the best efforts are doomed to fail unless the structure of opportunity is changed. [12]

We have learned to adjust all too well to the idea of social scarcity, of just so much room at the top. Our strivings usually assume a hierarchy of positions and accept a relativity of success which demands, among other things, that our happiness depends upon someone else's disappointment.

Even those people who find themselves in quite subordinate positions function in nonconspiratorial ways to help sustain their own and others' dominance *and* subordination. I once had the unpleasant experience of trying to convince a group of high-school guidance counselors to encourage bright black and Puerto Rican students to apply to a number of good four-year colleges that had put aside a decent amount of scholarship money for them. They still insisted, however, on sending these students to two-year colleges. Their attitude, blatantly, was that if when *they* went to school they had to strive to make it through four-year colleges, these obviously inferior kids should be forced to struggle through two-year colleges. Clearly racism was involved in their feelings, but their resistance to my proposal had at least as much to do with how it offended *their well-developed sense of place—their own and their students'.* Ivan Illich gives an insight as to how people, with the school's assistance, learn to put themselves and others into appropriate places by coming to believe that the world is a place in which everything can be measured and vertically arranged:

> People who submit to the standard of others for the measure of their own personal growth [which in fact is *not* measurable] soon apply the same ruler to themselves. They no longer have to be put in their place, but put themselves into their assigned slots, squeeze themselves into the niche which they have been taught to seek, and, in the very process, put their fellows into their places, too, until everybody and everything fits.[13]

Sociologists Seymour Lipset and Reinhard Bendix add that the potential for social change is defused in America because of what they call our "ideological egalitarianism." We remain optimistic about the fairness of the way power and status are distributed. We act as if social and economic differences, though significant, are both accidental and temporary since we all have essentially equal chances to achieve unequal statuses. The emphasis on equality and opportunity in American ideology, they claim, makes class and status differences less important than in other societies. Ironically, therefore, though social distinctions are greater in America than in many places in which Horatio Alger is not part of the national mythology, things are less likely to change here in fundamental ways than in places where the ideology is less egalitarian.[14]

Peter Blau and Otis Duncan claim that the lack of clamor for basic change results from the fact that though chances are quite limited for social mobility there is considerably more opportunity in America for people from the lower strata to move into elite strata than in other societies. This movement, limited though it may be, sustains an ideology of mobility which both recognizes *and significantly exaggerates* the potential for such upward movement.[15] Also, this relatively high rate of social mobility ironically helps preserve social inequality—the appearance of fairness reconciles people to whatever places (high or low) *they achieve.* As Blau and Duncan put it: " . . . chances of mobility make men less dissatisfied with the system of social differentiation in their society and less inclined to organize in opposition to it."[16]

The schools' role in this is to *ritualize* the ideology of the society, particularly the unrealizable aspects of that ideology: true equality of opportunity, real freedom, progress, efficiency, etc. Rituals are the connection between ideology and practice. When the practice falls short of the ideal, the ritual preserves at least the illusion of the possibility of the ideal by pretending that it still exists. Schools connect our "ideological egalitarianism" to the practice of unequal and unfair rewards by preserving the illusion that only brains and dedication are required for success and that we live in a democratic meritocracy. The reality is that as things now stand, schools, jobs, class structures are all hierarchically ordered. Thus opportunities for mobility are structurally limited to begin with. The inequalities that affect the future begin at birth. The ritual of school helps us pretend these differences are not important and that what happens to us is objective, fair, and ultimately all our own doing.[17]

There have been many attempts to reform institutions of higher education; rarely, though, have these attempts been applied to state-wide systems or networks of institutions. Even less often have the reformers attempted to challenge the critically important hierarchical structures of these institutions. And nearly never have there been innovations at two-year colleges amounting to anything beyond more of the same in new guises. It is ironic to note that most experiments or new programs in higher educational alternatives are almost always exclusively available to fill the needs of discontented *traditional* students and not at all to fill the needs of so-called new students. These students have to endure a nearly universal diet of traditional studies within traditionally structured institutions. Independent study, affective learning, educational contracts, residential living-learning communities—the now almost traditional panoply of experimental education—are available in scores of elite colleges which rarely recruit or admit lower-class students.[18]

Even at that, there has been some harsh criticism of late of some of these attempts at innovation. Paul Dressel feels that much of what passes for experimentation at colleges and universities is actually only "faddism and tinkering." Changes in grading practices, alterations in the calendar, freshmen seminars are often just grafted onto existing programs without much rethinking of the totality of the education experience or without attempting to modify the views or practices of the faculty.[19] "Freedom" of this variety frequently means doing your own thing, however meaningless, and "participatory governance" without significant changes in the structures of power too often results in endless discussions. Innovators at times naïvely seem to assume that society will stand transformed when confronted by their revolutionary love.[20] If presented with the opportunity to enter these new collegiate structures, new students usually react with skepticism. Many times they seem to feel that they do not want to continue to be experimented upon (they often have been the unwitting victims of "special" or "compensatory" programs in the lower schools that promised a great deal and delivered very little). By avoiding such innovations, nontraditional students seem to be saying: They may be excellent models for personal growth, but will they enable us to get jobs?[21]

Offering alternative courses cannot do much more than quiet discontent unless the structures within which they are set are also altered. No matter how enticingly relevant the courses, no matter how charismatic or interactive the teachers, the environment itself remains the most powerful teacher and continues to deliver latent messages that contradict what appears to be going on in the new courses. In a·competitive, hierarchical setting the most sought after teacher-facilitators are often still at best merely charismatic entertainers no more effective than the skillful lecturers to whom they are supposed to provide an alternative: they still retain nearly total control of the learning situation and tend to monopolize both insight and luminosity. An environment that promotes cooperation and multiple options, that actively helps students assert control of their academic lives, rejects the notion of the teacher-star. No one person can become so visibly important. Whatever competition there is is generated within oneself, and a powerful teacher-star may actually interfere with this process. In the best new programs, teacher-stars have dimmed as students develop insight and become luminous.

Real change rarely happens, usually only the trappings of it are present. Perhaps this is why so many colleges, after tinkering with the fad of experimentation, turn back to more orderly ways—convinced of the validity of the tried-and-true. In 1969, for example, Brown University revamped its curriculum, made grades optional, dropped nearly all course requirements—a dramatic series of steps for an Ivy League college. But now, it seems, most Brown students prefer to get grades and pursue traditional programs of study. In the words of *The New York Times*, "professors teach largely the kinds of courses they did before, and many of the innovations are shriveling up." This is taken as a national trend— college students, we are told, are jettisoning idealistic talk about self-discovery in favor of grade-grubbing to get into law or medical school.[22]

As with so much else, when innovation comes to two-year colleges it too is second best. A recent inventory of innovative college-level programs prepared for the Carnegie Commission on Higher Education presents an interesting comparison between the different kinds of experimental programs one finds at junior and senior colleges.[23] As we've already seen, at most four-year colleges each student negotiates an individual "contract" with the college and in doing so agrees to complete certain seminars, field work, and independent study over a four-year period. The school agrees to facilitate the student's "intellectual and affective growth and independence."[24] At innovative two-year colleges, according to the Carnegie inventory, one encounters computer-assisted teaching, autotutorial capacities, TV instructional methodologies, and the like. Delta College in Michigan is singled out as one of the nation's fifteen most innovative community colleges "because of its success in promoting instructional innovation in its programs in autotutorial nursing, team-teaching geography, intensified learning, open-circuit TV instruction," etc.[25] The hidden curricula messages, however, at places like Delta, reinforce or are identical to the latent messages of their traditional brother and sister colleges: At experimental two-year colleges one learns via machines because one is being prepared to work with machines; at innovative four-year colleges one learns independently because one is being prepared to live and work that way.[26]

Other ideas for new structures for new students are more subtle but equally regressive. One of my favorites comes again from the Carnegie Commission, which proposes having more and more nontraditional students go into *noncollegiate* postsecondary experiences: skills training, part-time studies, national service, proprietary schools, open universities, "learning pavilions," the armed forces, etc., in the name of "alternative channels to life, work, and service."[27] So a few years after their first report on two-year colleges advocated that just about everyone should enroll in a community college, the commission now seems to turn from that idea toward this new one. One can't help but suspect that this suggestion for semi-deschooling has as much to do with controlling the "production" of B.A.'s as the earlier proposal—and is just as regressive. The Carnegie Commission, it would appear, remains mired in hierarchical thinking.

There is nothing inevitable (nor has there ever been) about our dual structure of separate two- and four-year colleges. The two-year model is hardly the only way to satisfy the demand to "democratize" higher education. Even Leland Medsker, one of the leading spokesmen for junior colleges, saw back in 1960 that there were a number of options from which choices could be made: "As each state faces the unprecedented task of providing opportunities for a college population predicted to double in the next ten years, it must decide whether to expand the capacities of four-year colleges or to decentralize higher education by two-year colleges, or both."[28]

The City University of New York faced that decision only a few years ago when they instituted their nationally-scrutinized open-admissions program. They could have chosen to democratize their system by opening the doors to their four-year colleges rather than dumping most low-achieving students into the community colleges. They had had four or five years of solid experience prior to the first year of open admissions with a special program (SEEK) that admitted students with the poorest possible academic backgrounds directly into the most elite senior schools such as City, Brooklyn, Queens, and Hunter Colleges. SEEK provided extensive counseling services, effective developmental courses, an initial no-failure learning environment, free textbooks and supplies, and a weekly stipend for each student ranging up to fifty dollars per week depending on financial need so students could more or less be freed from the need to work to support themselves or their families. The program had a remarkable success—at CUNY's most elite City College, as the plans for open admissions were being drawn, it was known that *84 percent* of SEEK students returned for at least a third semester.[29] Nonetheless, this success did not appear to influence the course of open admissions. The planners chose instead to embrace a concept of separate-but-equal rather than follow the SEEK precedent.[30]

Shortly after the turn of this century another idea was around that if adopted would have significantly altered our educational hierarchy. It was known in shorthand form as the "6-4-4" plan. It called for six years of elementary education followed by four more in another institution which would include the equivalent of the last two elementary and the first two high-school years, culminating with four more in a third institution to include the last two years of high-school studies and the traditional freshman and sophomore years of college. It was even suggested at the time that this four-year junior college would offer a full baccalaureate degree to its graduates. College presidents such as Harper of Chicago, Butler of Columbia, Eliot of Harvard, etc. were favorably disposed to shortening the B.A. in this manner. A key element in this plan was that the 6-4-4 pattern was to be for *all* students, not just for the low-achieving new students traditionally shunted to the two-year junior college. In the early days of the American Association of Junior Colleges, the idea was debated and most of the leaders supported it on the grounds that it made psychological and developmental sense: The proposed divisions between the three new schools corresponded better to what were known to be the stages of adolescent intellectual and personal development than the current educational structure. A number of four-year junior colleges were established, but by 1955 all were out of existence.[31] What happened to such a seemingly good idea?

As William Crosby Eells pointed out back then, the four-year junior college had the problem of having to live in the world of reality, not theory.[32] For one thing, there was the imperative of intercollegiate athletic competition: the four-year junior college did not readily fit into existing patterns of organized and highly profitable play. Still another reality was the vested interests of school administrators: a school system organized on the 6-4-4 plan required a smaller total administrative staff than one set up on the 6-3-3-2 plan. In California, however, at one time there were up to seven four-year junior colleges. Now there are none though it is generally acknowledged that not one of them closed for purely educational reasons.[33] Today, the AAJC does not even discuss the four-year format for community colleges; they have never been known to get involved in losing battles. Too bad, for the 6-4-4 plan culminating in a B.A. would have gone a long way toward eliminating many of the *structural* second-best features of the current system.

Of course there have also been many attempts through the years to convert existing two-year colleges into four-year institutions. Rarely, though, have these been conscious attempts to reduce the way in which institutional stratification contributes to the support of social differences among people. Of the eighty-nine two-year colleges that became four-year colleges between 1948 and 1968, most did so because there were no senior colleges close enough to home for their transfer students to attend.[34] Often, incredibly, for reasons difficult to decipher, this conversion enabled the new four-year college to act *more* like a two-year college than before the transition. In a Carnegie Commission study of colleges in transition the one case study of such a change is of Pueblo Junior College's metamorphosis into Southern Colorado State College. The author is happy to point out that since 1965, along with a steady rise in the number of B.A.'s and B.S.'s awarded, there has been a dramatic *three-fold increase* in *technical* two-year degrees.[35] It may be that because the new four-year college feels more secure with its wider diversity of options, efforts can be redoubled with equanimity to cool as many students as possible into terminal programs. Programmatic comprehensiveness, without the complementary impulse to activate students' full potential, may wind up merely providing an array of options for students to fall back upon as they come to "discover" the limits of their ability.

It is not enough to build new structures; what goes on within them must also be new, as well as what goes on within the people attempting to participate in these new possibilities. To discover models for such change it's best to look outside of educational institutions to the world of work. For it is there that some of the most important methods for reducing hierarchical relationships are to be found, and it is there that we can discover profound lessons for our schools.

The traditional work situation is as hierarchically structured as anything in our society. In grossest terms there is the boss at the top and the workers arranged in various strata below. The "boss" may include top company executives, boards of directors, powerful stockholders, or school principals; the "workers" may include just plain workers as well as people with supervisory responsibility—foremen, office managers, deans, etc. But whatever the arrangement, whatever the blending of roles and responsibilities, the closer one approaches those with the decision-making power on the organizational chart, the fewer the people one encounters. In fact most such charts are classic expressions of the pyramidal arrangements that are so pervasive in our various institutions.

This traditionally structured work situation is not of divine origin; it is based upon assumptions about human nature and human potential that are open to serious challenge. These assumptions include the view that workers are incapable of formulating decisions on their own, that they are only able to follow instructions and at that only under the threat of punishment. This body of beliefs was best articulated and promoted at the turn of the century by Frederick W. Taylor; in fact his influential ideas for industrial efficiency became known as Taylorism.[36] It is somewhat difficult, to say the least, to reconcile this view of human potential to larger democratic theories for our society: if you can't trust workers to make decisions concerning their working arrangements, how can you trust them to participate in the governmental processes of the nation? Well it seems you can't, according to powerful contemporary democratic theory. Joseph Schumpeter, among others, in his extraordinarily influential book *Capitalism, Socialism and Democracy*[37] has criticized the arguments in favor of increasing people's participation in the governance of their own lives on the evidence that the widespread apathy and disinterest of ordinary citizens could threaten the stability of the Western democracies. He claims these societies owe their stability not to direct, continuous citizen participation but to the development of a leadership cadre more or less responsible to the people via frequent elections.

All of this industrial and social theorizing assumes that ordinary people to a large degree are afflicted by their so-called authoritarian personalities and as a result if left to their own devices might upset the stability of the system—they might even embrace a totalitarian society. (We've encountered this concept before when attempting to describe how community college students, similarly affected, are allegedly unable to learn much more than secretarial or auto repair skills.[38]) But there is much empirical evidence, and it is growing, that participation in the workplace and in the other institutions of society is vitally important in a modern theory of democracy and that such participation conforms to a more satisfactory *and accurate* view of human nature than that propounded by Taylor, Schumpeter, and other Social Darwinists. The more libertarian view of human nature sees people as endowed with thinking and creative powers that *need* to be fulfilled. It is best defined by what psychologist Abraham Maslow calls the "hierarchy of needs"—that human beings are constantly working toward fulfillment: "Apparently we function best when we are striving for something that we lack, when we wish for something that we do not have."[39] It is the object of that striving that varies hierarchically according to circumstances. The lowest needs are physiological and it is difficult to feel other, higher needs until these have been satisfied: "For our chronically and extremely hungry man, Utopia can be defined as a place where there is plenty of food."[40] Other needs in ascending order are the need for safety, the need for belongingness and love, the need for esteem, and finally the need for "self-actualization"—for self-expression, creativity, meeting challenges. The need for self-actualization for certain individuals can be as powerful as hunger for others still at the lowest level of need. For people with this need only less hierarchical institutions and relationships which permit more participation provide the possibilities for fulfillment. In more advanced technological societies, where lower-level needs are fulfillable, the higher needs are more present and thus we have, for example, the blue- and white-collar blues and even revolts among workers.[41] If we assume that all humans have the potential and need for self-actualization, then hierarchical institutions by their nature must be frustrating to the majority.

There is also evidence that participation in and of itself has other positive psychological consequences; it might, in Carole Pateman's words, "also be effective in diminishing tendencies toward non-democratic attitudes in the individual."[42] Participation in the workplace, for example, helps people develop the personal confidence necessary to the development of the "democratic character," the antithesis of the authoritarian personality democracy must allegedly be protected against. But this dialectic between opposite psychological and social types presents something of a double bind, particularly for those low-socioeconomic-status people supposedly afflicted with authoritarian personalities. Because of their social situation, they frequently find themselves in the lowest-level jobs which provide little or no opportunity to develop the personal skills necessary to participate in any direct way in the governance of their own lives—in fact, many claim that society must be protected from their participation. Additionally, we set up various service institutions for them and their children based upon the assumption that their authoritarian characteristics are unchangeable, though the rhetoric of these institutions pretends otherwise—their schools for example are usually the most oligarchical and authoritarian in structure. These institutions, then, prepare them for or reconcile them to the dull, repetitive, uncreative work that is their "inevitable" lot in life. A vicious, double-bound cycle of interlinked self-fulfilling prophecies in which it appears that society is doing everything it can to objectively and fairly meet their needs.

But as I've indicated, there is increasing evidence of the ability of these low-level or "afflicted" workers to participate in and even take control of their own work lives. Donald Jenkins has written a book to demonstrate that not only is this now a world-wide phenomenon but it is also a more efficient, *more profitable* means of doing business. Participatory management which involves workers having a *real* say in the way in which goods are produced, the office or factory is organized, the profits are distributed, etc., exists within many U.S. major corporations: Texas Instruments, Corning Glass, Monsanto, Syntex, Procter & Gamble, etc.[43] It would be naïve to assume that corporate giants such as these allow a measure of worker democracy primarily because such involvement reduces their employees' sense of alienation and boredom: obviously, if it weren't profitable, they wouldn't allow it.

There's a lesson here as well for those of us interested in the reform of schools: Unless we can convince the educational powers-that-be that it's in their best interest and in the nation's best interest to allow the schools to change, to become—among other things—less hierarchical, the schools simply won't change. Is such a thing likely or even possible? Perhaps. Let me try one scenario. *New structures for the schools may be possible if policy makers come to see new structures for the society to be inevitable.* According to this argument, the forms of schooling would have to be changed to serve new social needs. One compelling view of inevitable new structures for society which would require new forms for schools is contained in a recent article by Emile Benoit. He forecasts the emergence of a powerful "world social movement for human survival" which may become "the major social movement for the remainder of this century." He cites pollution, food shortages, and shortages of raw materials as the principal threats to the survival of the world's growing population and thus supports a policy of "selective growth." This policy would encompass "a shift from goods production to services and leisure; from status-displaying goods to goods yielding mainly intrinsic satisfaction; from resource-depleting and polluting goods to resource-conserving and pollution-combating goods"; etc.[44]

In such a society, current educational practices would quickly become obsolete (just as when we moved from

an agricultural to an industrial society the then traditional practices became obsolete and had to be and were
fundamentally altered). And though there are many
signs that we are well on our way toward the service
society Benoit projects, our schools are still organized in
such ways to produce graduates for a goods-producing,
industrialized society, a society we're coming less and
less to resemble: Perhaps much of our students' discontent with schooling is the product of their sense of this
contradiction. School is frequently irrelevant to them,
they tell us, because it doesn't relate to the real world out
there. It may then be in the best interest of the schools to
seek restructuring along more cooperative and less competitive lines,[45] stressing a people orientation rather than
a thing orientation—all of this according to a newly
defined, less hierarchical *self-interest*. Schools in this
way would *continue* to serve the dominant interests of
the society; it's just that society would see its best
interests in very different ways.[46]

A less apocalyptic view of social change would see
such things as the benefits derived from worker democracy or from successful experiments in broad-based
forms of participatory school governance as not in
themselves leading to a new and better society but rather
as institutional models pointing toward preferable future
social arrangements. Such school and work situations
are, in this view, places to practice new forms of interaction to liberate *part* of one's spirit, teaching one less
hierarchical values and modes of behavior—perhaps as
part of the preparation necessary for more fundamental
societal changes. This might be considered to be a
homeostatic view of institutional or social change. Homeostasis is the principal which states that systems tend
to seek equilibrium; if a stable system is disrupted, for

example, it attempts to establish a new stasis. Innovative programs within schools, or experimental schools within larger systems, if they are both effective and sustain themselves long enough, may force their host institutions or systems to seek a new equilibrium that seriously deals with their presence. Sometimes when host institutions or systems turn to deal with innovations in their midst, they deal with their challenging presence by ruthlessly killing them off. However, institutions frequently enough bend in the direction of their experimental programs to justify this technique for educational reform.[47]

I trust that I am not being overly optimistic, particularly at this time, in my belief in these possibilities for institutional reform. I know that in the current economic climate, there are overwhelming pressures for regressive change in the name of austerity. I've seen one proposal, for example, by the head of a major system of two- and four-year colleges to flush students out of school even faster than in the past. He advocates removing the matriculation of students who do not complete at least nine credits in a semester. In this way the colleges would save both financial aid monies and tuition subsidies as these now non-matriculated students would have to pay much higher tuition bills. I've also seen a recent proposal by the president of a senior college, pressed to save money, that calls for the conversion of a neighboring comprehensive junior college into a technological training center. This in spite of the fact that the two-year college in question has the highest percentage of its graduates going on to receive B.A.'s of any community college in the state. It should be obvious that I oppose what they and others are advocating. Though the recession may conveniently provide the camouflage to con-

ceal such reactionary social purposes, hard times must
not be allowed to cause the principal sufferers to become
the only permanent victims.

Finally, for the kind of school reform I am suggesting,
it is essential that those of us seeking change examine
our own relationship to hierarchical structures *and* the
extent of our own stake in preserving them. Because as I
have come to learn, change in the world outside depends
upon personal change within individuals.

I can now, in conclusion, only speak of my own
experience. To begin with, I know that as a nontenured
faculty member inevitably seeking tenure and promotion
in the City University *the very act of writing this book for
me is partly an act that both acknowledges and accepts
the university hierarchy*: my work world at a time of
budget cuts and faculty "retrenchment," is now more
than ever governed by publish-or-perish, up-or-out imperatives. But as someone working to reduce the irra-
tional power that accrues by itself to role differences,
how do I reconcile my own needs to take on an even
more powerful title and role? Just as I try to help students
stuck in the same hierarchies that enfold me to understand how these various forms of stratification have
shaped their lives, *with their help* I, too, try to understand my needs to be defined, to define myself by my
place within "the system." I can't "teach" them any of
these things unless I am going through the same process
myself; I can't teach very much more than I know. Much
more has to be discovered, and these discoveries must be
mutual. We are inexorably connected, the students and
I; and therefore must work things out that way.

As the teacher I used to be nervous about what I knew.
I felt it gave me too much power among my students.
Even after I realized the problem of teaching for right

answers (though I was quite good at it), my knowledge still seemed to give me more power and authority in the classroom than I felt I either deserved or wanted. I was correct about the "deserved" but misperceived the "wanted" because I did in fact want to control the flow of things in the room—if not the "answers."

I learned to deal with my hierarchical needs by acknowledging them to the students as much as possible and together making them (*and* the students' needs to be subordinate) a part of the discussion of every class in which any of us sensed it to be a problem. It became important then to stop for a few moments a discussion of *Portrait of the Artist as a Young Man* if Debbie was seen to be talking to Neil through me. If someone noticed me sitting at the "head" of the circle, he or she might interrupt a class on the Protestant Ethic to check out what I was doing. Through this process my nervousness about my own knowledge diminished, as did *theirs.* I began to see my knowledge, my experience as part of my contribution to our mutual communication. I began to stop using it as a tool for the expression of my need for power over their minds. Classes I couldn't manipulate or control no longer were such a threat to me as I began to discover the truth in the old pedagogical cliché that an effective teacher learns as much as he or she teaches.

I've even found that existing within less hierarchical structures has helped me to endure. Among other things, it has helped me escape some of what I used to call "my responsibilities." In traditional bureaucratic situations, at the very least, you would know where the buck stopped. Within newer forms of doing business, it sometimes appears that it never stops; but many of the same problems arise anyway and there's no one around to blame, or challenge for redress.

But the struggle to define myself less hierarchically is far from over—and is not without its ironies. Recently something happened to me in my role as "director of an experimental program" which taught me that through the years—even when working toward more equal relationships—perhaps what I was really doing was learning how to survive.

A number of penetratingly bright students came by to talk about an instructor who they claimed was having a negative effect on them—in his own way, he was telling them how dumb and powerless they were, and this was upsetting them terribly. As director they wanted me to do something about it. I had similar feelings about this instructor and told them so. I also told them about our participatory procedures: how on our Personnel Committee (which deals with such problems) I had only one vote out of eight, how students have half the total number of votes, etc. But they still wanted *me* to do something to right a clear injustice. Well, we talked about how bad it would be for me to have the arbitrary power to fire him (my talking with him, my officially observing his negative effects on students and writing memos to the file about it, none of that had any effect on ameliorating the situation). I asked the students if they would like it if I had that power and decided to let someone go because I disagreed with his or her teaching style. "But," they persisted, "you stand for an educational philosophy opposite to the one he represents." I pressed them to tell me what they would do if they were in my place. "We don't know," they shot back, "but *you* should know what to do."

I gave them a by-now-familiar lecture on how it was ironic that the most powerless people in this situation— the instructor's students—actually had the most power to deal with the problem, that even if only four or five of them were willing to confront the risk of losing credits they could take control of the class, turn it around, get it back to the subject, stop his abusing students, etc. That's the nonhierarchical message: an analysis of where the power traditionally lies and how to organize to balance it. But between us, there's no question in my mind that the instructor will still get tenure.

A BRIEF CRITICAL BIBLIOGRAPHY

There have always been critics of the community college. Before even a dozen junior colleges existed, Alexis Lange, for one, was complaining that they were wrong to offer only college-parallel transfer courses, that junior colleges should focus as well on the practical arts.[1] This early criticism set the direction for most of what followed and in fact is the pattern of thinking for the majority of today's most influential critics: Nothing is fundamentally wrong with two-year colleges; Yes, the teaching and counseling is not all it claims to be, but the basic objectives and functions are commendable; If anything is wrong, it's that community colleges are not doing enough of what they're doing; Something for everybody, more of the same.

True, there have been and are a few voices that challenge the assumptions of this collective vision, but they have largely been ignored or discounted. Charles Monroe has even found labels for them: "the left-wing critics—college students, liberal professional educators, militant writers, and Marxists."[2]

With only slight oversimplification, the major critics of two-year colleges of the past ten or fifteen years may be grouped in three or four clusters. The first group consists of those I propose to call the official critics. They are usually found to be affiliated with the American Association of Junior Colleges, the Carnegie Commission on Higher Education, the Center for Research and Development in Higher Education at the University of California in Berkeley, and peripherally with the Educational Testing Service and the College Entrance Examination Board—a powerful conglomeration of corporate higher educational management. The official criticism calls for the development and expansion of the community college movement essentially along its currently charted course. Community colleges should continue to free themselves from structural subservience to four-year colleges and universities. They should develop their own unique "identity," which usually means they should expand their technical and vocational programs. They should become more "comprehensive," offering something for everybody: transfer courses, terminal programs, adult education opportunities, golden-age programs, paraprofessional institutes, etc.

The next major category of critics expresses what I will call the left-official view. These critics are official in that they often share some of the same sponsorship as the official critics: the Berkeley Center; the Department of Health, Education, and Welfare; etc. But, more important, they are official in that the conclusions they reach, the recommendations they propose also advance things-as-they-are: community colleges should continue to expand—pretty much in their present form—to absorb the increasing number of nontraditional students seeking a college education. But these critics are *left-official* in that they pay at least lip-service to some of the more radical criticisms of schools: they agree that there is a hidden curriculum in schools, including two-year colleges, that is as powerful as the more familiar reading-'riting-'rithmetic that comprises the overt curriculum; schools, including community colleges, serve custodial functions, screen, sort, and channel students; etc. But as I've indicated, what they wind up proposing conforms to the official position.

An interesting subgroup of the left-official camp might be called the antiuniversity group. Along with Christopher Jencks and David Riesman they see community colleges (at least potentially) standing as antiuniversity forces against the nation-wide university movement that has all but transformed American higher education into a machine for producing scholars for the research establishment. Graduates from the dozen or so most powerful universities have propagated this vision of higher education as the primary function of colleges and universities. It is only some of the more influential experimental colleges *and* the community colleges that have resisted. To the antiuniversity critics, community colleges have at times provided innovative alternatives to the university model in that they are student oriented rather than subject-matter oriented, practical rather than theoretical, open-doored rather than elitist. Ironically, although their critique of educational systems is egalitarian, the implications of what they propose (the expansion of antiuniversity community-colleges-as-they-are) would help sustain rather than reduce the current antiegalitarian systems.

The final group consists of the radical critics. What

significantly distinguishes them from all other critics is
their assertion that in spite of their democratic and
egalitarian rhetoric, two-year colleges at their very essence support and help sustain the current social status
quo. Through cooling-out and other regressive devices,
they help protect the social advantages that accrue to the
affluent students who attend prestigious four-year colleges and universities. My problem at times, with the
radical critics is not with their analyses of higher educational systems but rather with their proposals. They, too,
often seem to accept the inevitability of what exists, and
call only for a few reforms that would make things more
humane for the students. Some radical critics even wind
up advocating more of the same and thus may, in a
sense, share more in common with the official or left-
official critics than they might like to admit.

Major official critics include Leland Medsker. His *The
Junior College: Progress and Prospect*—sponsored by the
Carnegie Corporation, carried out at the Berkeley Center for the Study of Higher Education—is a classic
statement advocating comprehensiveness for the junior
college. For Medsker, the need for comprehensiveness
(something for everybody) emerges from the obvious
diversity of the community college's student body: This
diversity imposes on the two-year college the responsibility of providing an equally varied educational program.[4]
But as we have seen, community college students tend to
cluster in the transfer programs and aggressively avoid the
career curricula. And so to implement a diverse educational program, Medsker calls for social engineering: a
"task to be performed . . . is that of convincing promising high school graduates that it may be wise for them to
prepare as technicians."[5] So linked to the concept of
comprehensiveness is the rather unpleasant fact that to

achieve it, it is necessary to convince students to pursue studies they don't want.

Other official community college voices belong to the leaders of the American Association of Junior Colleges. Two recent studies are David Bushnell's *Organizing for Change: New Priorities for Community Colleges*[6] and the president's view, Edmund Gleazer, Jr.'s *Project Focus: A Forecast Study of Community Colleges.*[7] Both draw on data from a nation-wide survey of two-year colleges (956 of them) in which students, faculty, and administrators were interviewed or given questionnaires, among other things to determine their views on the long-range goals of community colleges and to discern discrepancies between the desired goals and the present situation.

Bushnell sees a consensus among students, faculty, and administrators for increased comprehensiveness as the long-range goal of community colleges—with a particular emphasis on the growing viability of terminal programs. Thus, what he comes to advocate for the modern two-year college is just such an expanded comprehensiveness with counselors playing the key role of convincing students that there are many well-paying and socially useful occupations that require less than a baccalaureate degree.[8]

Gleazer's new book, *Project Focus*, at first appears to be a long way from the punishing tone of his first book, *This Is the Community College*. The new work is full of rather contemporary school criticism that almost justifies placing it in the left-official critics' category. Some of this criticism, for instance, "The mission I am proposing here assumes no rigid patterns and schedules to satisfy either the 'custodial' or 'rite of passage' function,"[9] results in some interesting if limited suggestions.

Gleazer, for example, wants to avoid the questionable dichotomies commonly used to classify courses and programs: it is wrong, he feels, to separate academic from vocational, college from noncollege. But as in his earlier book, he is still bedeviled by the two-thirds who not only will not transfer but who continue to avoid the many excellent vocational programs available to them. He knows these programs are considered to be of low status, that they have traditionally been used as a dumping ground for "dumb" (his word) and disruptive students.[10] But in spite of such criticism he still accepts as inevitable that two-thirds *will not* transfer.

The second group of critics, the left-official critics, also eventually come down to offering change-without-reform.[11] Representative of this school of criticism is William Moore, Jr. in his highly acclaimed *Against the Odds: The High Risk Student in the Community College.*[12] Although his overall view of community colleges in my judgment is accurate, he misperceives *the causes* for these failures and thus the programs he recommends will do little to alleviate the problems he sees so clearly. According to Moore, the causes of the community colleges' troubles are timid administrators, ill-prepared teachers, mediocre counselors, tradition-bound curricula, etc. What's missing is that *Against the Odds* almost totally fails to place two-year colleges in their actual social or political setting and thus winds up contributing to the very problems it describes.

How his failure to perceive the real causes for academic pathology destroys the possibility for meaningful reform can be seen in the limitations of the general curriculum that Moore proposes as an antidote to the deficiencies of other remedial programs. It is a separate and unequal program for low-achieving students who are placed in it, segregated from "high-ability" students, as the result of low test scores and poor high-school averages. The general curriculum essentially consists of a basic-skills program bolstered by a watered-down liberal arts program—euphemistically referred to as General Education. Moore calls it the "Three-R's-Plus Curriculum"—an apt enough description.[13] But he fails to see how in the past these kinds of compensatory programs have themselves contributed to sustaining the limited success and massive failure of students.

In chapter 3 I discussed one aspect of the thoughts of the most prominent left-official critic, Arthur M. Cohen—director of the E.R.I.C. Clearinghouse for Junior Colleges and contributing editor (for community colleges) of *Change* magzine. I attempted to show how Cohen comes to design a two-year college *totally* committed to cooling-out *while at the same time* detailing the regressive social functions of cooling-out. He sees many of the social causes of the community college's failures, but he misses some of the most crucial. There is, for example, virtually nothing in *A Constant Variable: New Perspectives on the Community College*[14] or in his other writing that relates students' socioeconomic backgrounds to their academic achievement. Cohen fails to see that students in the various tiers of the higher educational system are not randomly distributed nor are they merely sorted out as the result of differing cognitive capacities. Schools indeed teach inequality, as he perceives, but *not* on the basis that some children are smart and others aren't or that some are schooled and others aren't.

The findings of the influential Newman Commission also belong in the left-official category. Although the bulk of their *Report on Higher Education*[15] is devoted to the problems facing four-year colleges and universities, there is enough specifically about community colleges to get a clear perspective on their thinking concerning them. Essentially what they point out are disturbing trends in our senior higher educational institutions toward uniformity, growing bureaucracy, overemphasis on academic credentials, isolation of students and faculty from the world—in other words, "a growing rigidity and uniformity of structure that makes higher education reflect less and less the interests of society."[16] They go on to say that although the student population seeking higher education is becoming ever more diverse—in class and social background, age, academic experience, and ability—colleges and universities have come more and more to assume that there is only one mode of teaching and learning—the academic mode.[17]

As a result, they are attracted to the community college movement. What they see there is precisely the kind of diversity they believe is needed to revitalize higher education. They thus feel a need to save community colleges from certain destruction as they move toward duplicating the university model—"The two-year institutions are not yet set in concrete, but the molds are being formed."[18] The point they miss, as they longingly look to the community college to rescue the soul of higher education, is that although it is true that for the two-year college the cement of traditional academic forms has not set, community colleges have long since been set in a concrete mold of their own: the concept of comprehensiveness and the various versions of cooling-out that make it work. In fact, the very mold the Newman Commission itself proposes for two-year colleges.

In many ways the Newman Commission belongs with

the antiuniversity critics since their analysis of the problems in higher education parallels Jencks's and Riesman's. In their book *The Academic Revolution*,[19] Jencks and Riesman do not draw out the plan for a revolution in higher education but rather describe one that has already occurred. This revolution was the triumph of professional scholars in the struggle for domination of the nation's colleges and universities. The victorious model, with its advocacy of an intellectual meritocracy, has brought with it the pervasive arrogance and elitism that has done very little to increase social mobility or reduce inequality in America—in spite of praising the opportunities for these inherent in the concept of mass higher education.

Is there any relief from the academic onslaught? For Jencks and Riesman there are a few glimmers of hope— among the few antiuniversity institutions they describe there is the flickering light of the community colleges. Although they are quite aware of many of their limitations (they sort, screen, cool-out, provide a safety valve for four-year schools, and in the end cost as much or more *per graduate* as traditional colleges), they at least provide some resistance to the academic revolution. Community colleges, they claim, show comparatively little regard to professional academic opinion about how an institution of higher learning should be run and consequently teach both subjects and students whom most scholars regard as worthless. Ironically, for this reason, two-year colleges might thus provide a real alternative to the dominant academic structure of the American university.

But Jencks and Riesman totally misperceive the actual socioeconomic character of the students who attend two-year colleges, they misread the data, and thus wind up asserting that community college students, on the average, *are more affluent than four-year college students*.[20] And since they miss this crucial point, their desire to see community colleges offer an antiuniversity diversity of learning opportunities (i.e., vocational programs) means that what they come down to recommending is socially regressive.

Another antiuniversity critic, who doesn't even see the problems Jencks and Riesman see, is Judson Jerome. The section of *Culture Out of Anarchy* devoted to community colleges borders on romantic fantasy. He is so entranced by the antiuniversity possibilities of two-year colleges that he sees them *now* in his image of the college of the future. Notice how his envisioned college of the future is very much like what comprehensive community colleges are reputed to be: "Our present schools and colleges will, I believe, wither away and be replaced by a much more comprehensive set of institutions serving the whole population: all ages, all classes, continually, on a basis of essentially free access."[21]

The last and numerically smallest group of critics are the radicals. Perhaps the first of these is William Birenbaum. On the relationship of two-year colleges to the status quo, Birenbaum has written: "Far from upsetting the status quo of American higher education, the junior colleges shore it up. Far from contributing something new in substance, the two-year colleges strengthen the status quo in a higher educational system desperately in need of reform."[22]

Broadening this analysis beyond the higher educational realm, Birenbaum established the foundation for the radical criticism in 1969 in *Overlive: Power, Poverty, and the University*:

The stratifications of American society are honored in the stratifications of the unfolding new educational plans [for higher education]. This is a politically pragmatic response to the challenge. It accepts the shortcomings of the lower systems and perpetuates them, projects them into the future lives of the people who have been damaged. It permits the higher educational system to do something at a time when the people will not allow it to do nothing. . . . It results in the enlargement of the power of the university without disturbing its ancient prejudices. . . . Something for everybody is not enough, especially if the "something" is the further institutionalization of what is not working well.[23]

It might be said that the radical criticism of community colleges is an explication of this text.

Birenbaum asserts that if education is to have a chance to make a difference it will be necessary to consider why various programmatic attempts to alleviate inequality have failed. They have failed because they rarely have been addressed to the powerlessness of the people and their communities. In his words, most poverty programs and university uplift projects have naïvely viewed power "merely as a quantity rather than as a process." They assume that increasing the amount of food, housing, educational facilities will in itself fundamentally alter the patterns of exploitation. This traditional approach fails because it does not even begin to balance the power between the deprived and the powerful.[24]

Thomas Corcoran is another radical critic. But with regard to progressive recommendations, there is much to be desired in his "Community Colleges: The Coming Slums of Higher Education."[25] In fact, he might almost be considered to belong to a critical category of his own—that of the "cooled-out critic." He articulates and accepts the radical critique of community colleges. But he feels that the current structures will continue—it is naïve to believe in the possibility of fundamental change. And so one has to offer *realistic* suggestions. The problem with Corcoran is not that he chooses to be realistic but *how* he chooses to be realistic. What he offers in the name of realism—more vocational education—ironically would only support and further solidify the very conditions that he attacks. He is then a radical critic cooled-out to accept the reality and inevitability of second best, just as community college students are cooled-out to accept the inevitability of second best terminal programs.

Finally, Jerome Karabel is a radical critic who is particularly good at demonstrating how the expansion of vocational programs *in itself* has enabled community colleges to play their regressive social role. His article "Community Colleges and Social Stratification,"[26] is a rich mine of radical criticism. Unlike Corcoran, Karabel recognizes that access to higher education is not the critical question; what is critical rather is what happens to people once they get there. And what happens once students get to two-year colleges is less than felicitous. Among other things, recent data indicates a pronounced class bias in the composition of students enrolled in vocational and career programs: they are lower in every measure of socioeconomic status than transfer students.[27] It would appear that the tracking system that sets two-year colleges at the base of the higher educational pyramid is considerably subtler with socioeconomic and racial tracking also taking place *within* community colleges.

NOTES

NOTES TO THE INTRODUCTION

1. For another account of the effects of tracking on an individual student see Thomas Cottle, "What Tracking Did to Ollie Taylor," *Social Policy*, July/August 1974, pp. 21–24.

2. Tracking, however, in new forms remains very much a part of a New York City high-school education. Schools now offer "special interest electives" to selected students and award "Regents" and "non-Regents" diplomas to graduates who prepare for and successfully take state-wide Regents examinations: Iver Peterson, "Schools Use New Ways to 'Track' Students," *New York Times*, July 2, 1975, p. 38.

3. *Beyond the Open Door* (San Francisco: Jossey-Bass, 1971), p. 92.

4. "The 'Cooling-Out' Function in Higher Education," *American Journal of Sociology* 65 (1960): 569–76.

NOTES TO CHAPTER 1

1. Gene Maeroff, "Colleges Face Year of Economic Worry," *New York Times*, September 7, 1974, pp. 1, 30.

2. Educational anthropologists such as Jules Henry and George Spindler, among others, have made an immense contribution to understanding the frequent contradictions between schools' stated and unstated functions. Useful compilations of such writing include *Education and Culture: Anthropological Approaches,* George Spindler, ed. (New York: Holt, Rinehart and Winston, 1963); *Anthropological Perspectives on Education,* M. L. Wax, S. Diamond, and F. O. Gearing, eds. (New York: Basic Books, 1972). See also Richard Schmuck and Patricia Schmuck, *Group Processes in the Classroom* (Dubuque, Iowa: William C. Brown Co., 1971).

3. *Life in Classrooms* (New York: Holt, Rinehart and Winston, 1968), p. 31.

4. For an interesting discussion of this see Robert Dreeben, "The Contribution of Schooling to the Learning of Norms," *Harvard Educational Review* 37 (Spring 1967): 211–37; idem, *On What Is Learned in School* (Reading, Mass.: Addison-Wesley Publishing Co., 1968).

5. Dreeben, "The Contribution of Schooling," p. 229.

6. See, for example, Benjamin Bloom, Allison Davis, Robert Hess, *Compensatory Education for Cultural Deprivation* (New York: Holt, Rinehart and Winston, 1965).

7. *Culture Against Man* (New York: Vintage Books, 1965).

8. *Deschooling Society* (New York: Harper & Row, 1970–71), p. 1.

9. Ibid., p. 39.

10. This even extends to the way, for example, children have fun. In our schooled (and of course media-oriented) society, we've come to professionally organize our street games into baseball Little Leagues and "Midget Football Associations." Here, too, there is a pronounced detachment of feeling from action.

11. Michael Katz, *The Irony of Early School Reform: Educational Innovation in Mid-Nineteenth Century Massachusetts* (Boston: Beacon Press, 1968), p. 43.

12. *Twenty-First Annual Report of the Massachusetts Board of Education Together with the Twenty-First Annual Report of the Secretary of the Board,* 1859, p. 66.

13. Ibid., p. 117.

14. *Education and the Rise of the Corporate State* (Boston: Beacon Press, 1972), p. 76. David Cohen and Marvin Lazerson reach similar conclusions in "Education and the Corporate Order," *Socialist Revolution* 23, May/June 1971, pp. 14–46.

15. Michael Katz, *Class, Bureaucracy, and Schools: The Illusion of Educational Change in America* (New York: Praeger Publishers, 1971), pp. 31–32, 33.

16. Katz, *The Irony of Early. School Reform,* pp. 49, 92. These ideas, incidentally, are still very much alive. Diane Ravitch in a recent article, "Moral Education and the Schools," also sees schools emphasizing appropriate modes of belief and behavior: *Commentary,* September, 1973. Spiro Agnew, until recently a rather good litmus paper of popular thinking, still sees education as the cure for urban crime and vice: "We know that juvenile delinquency and adult crime, drug abuse and the general feeling of alienation and drift among our young people have deep-rooted causes that begin early in life. Every human being needs a sense of purpose, a goal to strive toward, and the pleasure of accomplishment when that goal is reached. It is a need that is built into the human soul and psyche. Career Education offers hope that every American will have the chance to fulfill this need before disenchantment and despair give rise to serious defections from society": Address to the Convention of the American Association of School Administrators, Washington, D.C., February 16, 1972.

17. Katz, *Class, Bureaucracy, and Schools,* p. 33.

18. "Recruiters Snap Up Job-Trained 'Grads' of Two-Year Colleges," June 10, 1965.

19. As Frank Jennings has noted, "the junior college would provide the kind of education and training that would convert

students into tax-paying and responsible citizens. The junior college would take the older adolescent off the streets . . . and prepare him for the job market": "The Two-Year Stretch: Junior Colleges in America," *Change,* March/April 1970, p. 19.

20. "Junior College Department of Civic Education," *School and Society* 2 (1915): 442–48.

21. New York: Holt, Rinehart and Winston, 1940, pp. 23–24.

22. Robert Sproul, *Before and After the Junior College* (Los Angeles: The College Press, 1938), p. 19.

23. *The Community College* (New York: McGraw-Hill Book Co., 1950), p. 60. The conservative ideology that underlies the writings of the junior colleges' founding fathers is most completely revealed in Gregory Goodwin's unpublished doctoral dissertation, "A Social Panacea: A History of the Community–Junior College Ideology" (E.R.I.C. ED no. 093 427).

24. *Why Junior College Terminal Education?* Terminal Education Monograph no. 3 (Washington, D.C.: American Association of Junior Colleges, 1941), pp. 31–33.

25. "Major Issues in Junior College Technical Education," *The Educational Record* 45 (Spring 1964): 128–38.

26. A satirical look at the meritocratic society of the year 2034 may be found in Michael Young, *The Rise of the Meritocracy* (Harmondsworth, England: Penguin Books, 1958).

27. *The Conspiracy of the Young* (New York: Meridian Books, 1971), p. 210. A concise statement of this position can also be found in Martin Carnoy's introduction to *Schooling in a Corporate Society: The Political Economy of Education in America* (New York: David McKay Co., 1972), and in Marvin Lazerson, "Revisionism and American Educational History," *Harvard Educational Review* 43 (May 1973): 269–83. Also, an interesting third-stream position has emerged as the revisionists have pursued their analyses of the real functions of schooling. They insist, in a sense, that it doesn't matter who's correct (those who claim that schools are for the development of all or those who argue that schools serve inequality and the

status quo) *because schools can't make a difference anyway—even if they tried.* Either genes or environment or race or socioeconomic status or parents' educational attainment or luck are more powerful factors in influencing one's future than anything schools can do to reduce or sustain inequality. For examples of this third-stream genre see Coleman et al., *Equality of Educational Opportunity* (Washington, D.C.: U.S. Government Printing Office, 1966); Jencks et al., *Inequality: A Reassessment of the Effect of Family and Schooling in America* (New York: Basic Books, 1972); and the Rand Corporation Study for the President's Commission on School Finance, *How Effective is Schooling? A Critical Review and Synthesis of Research Findings* (Santa Monica, 1972).

28. *The Great School Legend: A Revisionist Interpretation of American Public Education* (New York: Basic Books, 1972), pp. 3 ff.

29. Ibid., p. 4.

30. For contemporary alternative views that acknowledge similar data but which conclude that the schools were more concerned with instructing the young in how to cultivate the political virtues needed to run a democratic society than with generating social mobility, see R. Freeman Butts, *The Education of the West: A Formative Chapter in the History of Civilization* (New York: McGraw-Hill Book Co., 1973); Carl F. Kaestle, *The Evolution of an Urban School System: New York City, 1750–1850* (Cambridge, Mass.: Harvard University Press, 1973); and Stanley K. Schultz, *The Culture Factory: Boston Public Schools, 1789–1860* (New York: Oxford University Press, 1973).

31. "The Modern School in Retrospect," in *The Modern School of Stelton* (Stelton, N.J.; privately printed, 1925), pp. 115–19.

32. Katz, *The Irony of Early School Reform*, pp. 45 ff.

33. *Twenty-Eighth Annual Report of the Massachusetts Board of Education,* 1866, pp. 83–84.

34. Katz, *The Irony of Early School Reform*, p. 84.

35. Ibid., p. 53.

36. Ibid., p. 91.

37. Ibid., pp. 84 ff.

38. "The Integration of Higher Education Into the Wage System," mimeographed (Cambridge, Mass., 1972), pp. 30–31. See also his "Schooling and Inequality from Generation to Generation," in T.W. Schultz, ed., *Investment in Education: The Equity-Efficiency Quandary* (Chicago: University of Chicago Press, 1972), pp. 219–51.

39. Ivar Berg's *Education and Jobs: The Great Training Robbery* (New York: Praeger Publishers, 1970) is the best-known work on educational inflation: the title tends to say it all. R. Collins also finds schooling to be ineffective at teaching job-related skills below the level of such professions as law, medicine, etc. If anything, schools help reproduce status differences by emphasizing and rewarding high-status modes of behavior. He writes: "In this light, any failure of schools to impart technical knowledge . . . is not important; schools primarily teach vocabulary and inflection, styles of dress, aesthetic tastes, values and manners"—all of which are more important for success than educational or technical requirements: "Functional and Conflict Theories of Educational Stratification," in B. R. Cousin, ed., *Education: Structure and Society* (Harmondsworth, England: Penguin Books, 1972), p. 187. See also Lester Thurow, "Education and Economic Equality," *The Public Interest* 28 (Summer 1972): 66–81; and Gerald Somers, *The Effectiveness of Vocational and Technical Programs* (Madison, Wisc.: Center for Studies in Vocational and Technical Education, 1971), which concludes that "many students, at all school levels, were able to enjoy higher wages *by moving out of their field of training* when they entered the labor market" (my italics), (p. 206).

A 1974 study of the effectiveness of community college vocational programs revealed that only 16 percent of the graduates got jobs for which they were trained and eight out of ten who did were only earning the minimum wage: Wellford Wilms, *Public and Proprietary Vocational Training: A Study of Effectiveness* (Berkeley: University of California Center for Research and Development in Higher Education, 1974).

40. A classic statement of this position may be found in Clark Kerr et al., *Industrialism and Industrial Man* (Cambridge, Mass.: Harvard University Press, 1960).

41. Murray Milner, *The Illusion of Equality* (San Francisco: Jossey-Bass, 1972), pp. 36 ff.

42. Ibid., p. 69.

43. New York: Praeger Publishers, 1962.

44. Ibid., p. 3.

45. Ibid., p. 14.

46. *The American Occupational Structure* (New York: John Wiley & Sons, 1967), p. 70.

47. Ibid., p. 424.

48. *The Academic Revolution* (New York: Doubleday & Co., 1968), pp. 72–73.

49. C. Wright Mills in *White Collar: The American Middle Classes* (New York: Oxford University Press, 1951) and Herman Miller in *Rich Man, Poor Man* (New York: Thomas Y. Crowell Co., 1964) also see little reduction in inequality despite increasing overall prosperity. For Mills, this is primarily the result of the marked increase in the number of menial white-collar occupations which give the illusion if not the reality of upward mobility. For more evidence of how two-year colleges protect low-achieving middle-class students from excessive downward mobility see J. M. Katz, "The Educational Shibboleth: Equality of Opportunity in a Democratic Institution, The Public Junior College" (Ph.D. diss., U.C.L.A., 1967). A couple of dissenting views might be noted. Stephen Thernstrom sees upward mobility and reduced inequality to be difficult but a historical reality in his *Poverty and Progress: Social Mobility in a Nineteenth Century City* (Cambridge, Mass.: Harvard University Press, 1964). H. Schelsky sees schools, particularly higher education, playing a significant role in reducing inequality: "Family and School in Modern Society," in A. H. Halsey, J. Floud, and C. A. Anderson, eds., *Education, Economy, and Society* (New York: Free Press, 1965), pp. 414–20.

50.   Christopher Jencks, "Social Stratification and Higher Education," *Harvard Educational Review* 38 (Spring 1968): 306–7.

51.   New York: McGraw-Hill Book Co., 1970, p. 5. Frederick Kintzer's even more recent analysis indicates how two-year colleges protect middle-class students from downward mobility—at public expense: "The Community College Transfer Student," in Dorothy Knoell, ed., *Understanding Diverse Students, New Direction for Community Colleges* (San Francisco: Jossey-Bass, 1973), pp. 1–14.

52.   And as one might expect, black youths also aren't being served very well by two-year colleges. Allen Ballard, in *The Education of Black Folk: The Afro-American Struggle for Knowledge in White America* (New York: Harper & Row, 1973), writes: "Black children are being directed into two-year colleges precisely at that time when B.A.'s and M.A.'s are becoming the keys to an adequate livelihood in this society" (p. 95). Anthony Monahan arrives at similar conclusions in "Making It at the Inner City's Proving Grounds," *Chicago Tribune Magazine*, April 16, 1968, pp. 22–23, 38–44.

53.   On this very point see John Felty, *A Feasibility and Planning Study for an Experimental, Two-Year College for Rural and Urban Youth* (Washington, D.C.: Office of Education, 1969).

54.   *Profile of the Community College* (San Francisco: Jossey-Bass, 1972), p. 208.

55.   Joe Rempson, "Minority Access to Higher Education in New York City," *The City Almanac* no. 7, August 1972. David Lavin is more optimistic. See his CUNY-sponsored study, "Student Retention and Graduation at the City University of New York: September 1970 Enrollees Through Seven Semesters" (New York: City University of New York, 1974). See also Gene Maeroff, "City U. Open Admissions Held a Success," *New York Times*, March 17, 1974, pp. 1, 52; and Barry Kaufman and R. Botwinck, "Student Retention and Graduation at the City University of New York: Fall 1970 to Spring 1974" (New York: City University of New York, June 1975).

56.   Ellen Trimberger presents data to show the differential dropout rates among the various classes of students in the City University: the poorest drop out at a 39 percent rate during their first year in a CUNY community college (and at a 30 percent rate at senior colleges); the middle group drops out at a 20 percent rate during their first year at either a two- or four-year college; while the richest and most able group drops out at only a 10 percent rate: "Open Admissions: A New Form of Tracking?" *The Insurgent Sociologist* 4, 1 (Fall 1973): 39. Again, for a more optimistic view see Elaine El-Khawas and Ann Bisconti, *Five and Ten Years After College Entry: 1971 Followup of 1961 and 1966 College Freshmen*, Research Report, vol. 9, no. 1 (Washington D.C.: American Council on Education, 1974).

57.   "The Community College," in W. K. Ogilvie and M. R. Raines, eds., *Perspectives on the Community-Junior College* (New York: Appleton-Century-Crofts, 1971), pp. 38–40.

58.   Spiro Agnew, "Toward a 'Middle Way' in College Admissions," *Educational Record*, Spring 1970, p. 111.

59.   Alexander Astin, *Predicting Academic Performance in College* (New York: Free Press, 1971); idem, *College Dropouts: A National Profile* (Washington D.C.: American Council on Education, 1972); idem, *Preventing Students from Dropping Out* (San Francisco: Jossey-Bass, 1975).

60.   Astin, *Predicting Academic Performance*, p. 29.

61.   Ibid., p. 29.

62.   Even good friends of community colleges such as Arthur M. Cohen and Florence Brawer concede this is one of their functions: ". . . public community colleges do the preliminary sorting and screening of the students, allowing all young people . . . to enroll but passing on to the university at the junior year only those who have demonstrated competence in college-level studies. Often spelled out in . . . [state master plans] is the expectation that many . . . will be shunted into terminal basic studies or occupational curricula": "The Community College in Search of Identity," *Change*, Winter 1971, p. 56. The Folger Commission provides additional evidence of

how well two-year colleges do at controlling the flow of students through higher educational systems: John Folger, Helen Astin, A. Bayer, *Human Resources and Higher Education* (New York: Russell Sage Foundation, 1970), pp. 175 ff.

63. Blau and Duncan, *The American Occupational Structure*, p. 157. Specifically, Figure 4.5 (p. 157) for exact percentages. I should add here their qualification to this radical finding: they see much of this downward mobility to be the result of the social consequences of high-status students dropping out of senior colleges, thus completing less than four years of college (p. 160). I'm certain this makes it difficult to derive a distinctive picture of the results of a community college education, but it does not alter the fundamental outline of my argument.

64. "Quality in Higher Education," *Current Issues in Higher Education—1958* (Washington, D.C.: Association for Higher Education, September 1958), pp. 8–13.

NOTES TO CHAPTER 2

1. Edmund Gleazer, Jr., "Analysis of Junior College Growth," *Junior College Directory* (Washington, D.C.: American Association of Junior Colleges, 1961), tables 6 and 7, pp. 41–42.

2. Carnegie Commission on Higher Education, *The Open-Door Colleges: Policies for Community Colleges* (New York: McGraw-Hill Book Co., 1970), pp. 33 ff. It is difficult at this time to see the future of college enrollments clearly. As Selden Meneffee points out, the bloom is off the boom as the result of the ending of the draft and lowered birth rates: "Finding New Directions," *Change*, Summer 1974, pp. 54–55, 63. There is now an emerging body of two-year college literature on how to keep the bloom in the boom by reaching out still further to new clients—women, veterans, the handicapped, older adults. If one projects enrollment figures from the 1963–73 decade through to 1985, the community college percentage of the college market can be expected to increase from 23 to 41 percent. However, if one extends the figures from the shorter

period, 1968 to 1973, the projection sees liberal arts colleges and universities increasing their share of the market at the expense of the two-year institutions. In sum, things are difficult to predict. See Edward Fiske, "Education Uncertainty," *New York Times,* April 18, 1975, p. 36; and the Carnegie Foundation for the Advancement of Teaching study, *More Than Survival: Prospects for Higher Education in a Period of Uncertainty* (San Francisco: Jossey-Bass, 1975).

3. Between 1870 and 1900, for example, the total population doubled whereas enrollments in higher education increased four and a half times: Ralph Fields, *The Community College Movement* (New York: McGraw-Hill Book Co., 1962), p. 17. See also John Brubacher and Willis Rudy, *Higher Education in Transition: A History of American Colleges and Universities, 1636–1968* (New York: Harper & Row, 1968), p. 262.

4. Carnegie Commission, *The Open-Door Colleges,* p. 34.

5. "The Progress of Educational Development" (Discourse delivered before the Literary Societies of the University of Michigan, Ann Arbor, 1855), p. 32.

6. Alexis Lange, "The Junior College, With Special Reference to California," *Proceedings of the National Education Association* (Washington, D.C., 1915), pp. 119–24. See also W. R. Harper, "The High School of the Future," *The School Review* XI (1903): pp. 1–3. For an extensive account of Lange's contribution to the junior-college movement see Jesse Bogue, *The Community College* (New York: McGraw-Hill Book Co., 1950), pp. 331–37. Also, for a discussion of the four methods of establishing junior colleges—"amputation," "stretching," "decapitation," and "independent creation"—see Lloyd Dell Reed, *Jesse Parker Bogue: Missionary for the Two-Year College* (New York: Carlton Press, 1971), pp. 44 ff.

7. For a fuller discussion of the reasons for the failure to Germanize the structure of American education see Clyde Blocker, Robert Plummer, and Richard Richardson, *The Two-Year College: A Social Synthesis* (Englewood Cliffs, N.J.: Prentice-Hall, 1965), p. 26. See also Michael Brick, *Forum and Focus for the Junior College Movement: The American Associ-*

ation of Junior Colleges (New York: Teachers College Press, 1963), p. 86.

8. William Crosby Eells, *The Junior College* (Boston: Houghton Mifflin Co., 1931), p. 47.

9. William Rainey Harper, *The Trend in Higher Education* (Chicago: University of Chicago Press, 1905). p. 378.

10. William Rainey Harper, "The Small College: Its Prospects," *Journal of Proceedings and Addresses*, National Education Association, 39th Annual Meeting, July 7–13, 1900, pp. 74–80. Ken August Brunner feels, in fact, that at that time Harper was more concerned with the fate of these weak four-year colleges than with the establishment of junior colleges for their own sake: "Historical Development of the Junior College Philosophy," *Junior College Journal* 40 (April 1970): 30–34.

11. "President's Annual Report, University of Chicago, July, 1902," in *Decennial Publications of the University of Chicago*, vol. I (Chicago, 1902), p. xcvi.

12. "Ancient History," *Junior College Journal* 1 (May 1931): 503–4.

13. See Elbert Fretwell, Jr., *Founding Public Junior Colleges: Local Initiative in Six Communities* (New York: Teachers College Press, 1954).

14. Eells, *The Junior College*, pp. 54–55. In what follows, I am indebted to Eells's still excellent version of the historical development in California. See especially his chapter on the subject in *The Junior College*, pp. 88 ff.

15. *California Statutes*, 1907, Chapter 69, p. 88.

16. It has been pointed out that in addition to the "pure university" ideology, Lange and Jordan also embraced the popular racist eugenics of their times. For them, the junior college would also protect the university from genetically inferior southern and eastern European types: Gregory Goodwin, "A Social Panacea" (Ph.D. diss., E.R.I.C., no. ED 093 427), pp. 33 ff.

17. Lange, "The Junior College, With Special Reference to California," pp. 119–24.

18. Ibid., p. 124.

19. A. A. Gray, as early as 1915 in an article in *The School Review*, noticed and applauded Fresno's initiative. He welcomed their attempt to begin to reorganize higher education "on a more vocational basis": "The Junior College in California," *The School Review* 23 (1915): 468.

20. Quoted in Eells, *The Junior College*, p. 93.

21. Quoted in C. L. McLane, "The Junior College, or Upward Extension of the High School," *The School Review* 21 (1913): 166–67.

22. Ibid., p. 167.

23. C. L. McLane, "The Fresno Junior College," *California Weekly*, July 15, 1910, p. 539.

24. McLane, "The Junior College," p. 166.

25. Alexis Lange, "The Junior College—What Manner of Child Shall This Be?" *School and Society* 7 (1918): 211–18; idem, "The Junior College as Integral Part of the Public School System," *The School Review* 25 (1917): 465–79. Lange traveled up and down the length of California admonishing junior-college administrators to prevent the wrong students from attempting to prepare for transfer to the elite universities where such training would be harmful to them—considering their intellectual limitations. Instead, he encouraged them to direct their students toward vocational subjects: Brick, *Forum and Focus*, p. 22.

26. For a thorough comparison of the California junior-college laws through 1929 see table 9 in Eells, *The Junior College*, pp. 118–19.

27. The first period, which I've already described, extending from 1850 to 1920, encompasses the development of the junior-college idea and its implementation, albeit limited, in separate institutions offering the first two years of the bacca-

laureate curriculum: James Thornton, *The Community Junior College*, 3rd ed., (New York: John Wiley & Sons), p. 71.

28. Brick, *Forum and Focus*, p. 71.

29. It is interesting to note in this regard that in 1926, when the University of Minnesota offered Leonard Koos the opportunity to become the first professor of higher education in the nation, he declined because of his conviction that the junior-college movement, with which he was becoming increasingly identified, was part of secondary and not higher education: Goodwin, *A Social Panacea*, p. 102.

30. Quoted in Brick, *Forum and Focus*, pp. 119–20.

31. See Doak Campbell, "Effects of the Depression," *Junior College Journal* 3 (April 1933): 381–82. Generously funded New Deal programs such as the Civilian Conservation Corps and the National Youth Administration motivated many in the AAJC to admonish themselves for missing out on the opportunity to mount similar vocationally oriented programs. C. C. Colvert, an AAJC president in the early 1940s, chastised the membership in his presidential address in 1941:

> Had not we of the junior colleges been so busy trying to offer courses which would get our graduates into the senior colleges instead of . . . offering appropriate and practical courses—terminal courses—for the vast majority of the junior college students, we might have thought to ask for, and as a result of having asked, received the privilege of training these young people.

"Terminal Education and the National Defense," *Junior College Journal* 11 (May 1941): 496.

32. Walter Eells, "Executive Secretary's Report," *Junior College Journal* 11 (May 1941): 503.

33. Brick, *Forum and Focus*, p. 126.

34. Ibid., pp. 94 ff.

35. Eells, *The Junior College*, p. 289.

36. The earliest statement I've found of the university's concern about being overwhelmed by great numbers of students is from Edmund Jones's 1905 inaugural address as president of the University of Illinois. Rather than being drowned by the ten thousand students whom he sees wanting "the kind of work offered in the freshman and sophomore years of the University," he would prefer to see these students "scattered over the state at fifty other institutions"—junior colleges: "Ancient History," *Junior College Journal* 5 (December 1935): 143. Ten years later, James Angell found that those universities most eager to accept transfer students from newly formed junior colleges were those "where . . . the press of undergraduate students is so great as seriously to embarrass the facilities of the institution." Those universities, however, struggling to attract as many students as possible, continued to prefer to admit their own freshmen than to accept transfers: "The Junior College Movement in High Schools," *The School Review* 23 (1915): 292. In 1920, Alexis Lange claimed that "the junior colleges will tend to prevent annual cloudbursts of freshmen and sophomores from drowning the university proper": "The Junior College," *Sierra Educational News* 16 (October 1920): 483. More recently, James Bryant Conant also advocated shunting as many students as possible into two-year colleges so that universities can become "first-rate scholarly institutions." Otherwise the press of new students will cause a deterioration in the quality of the faculty and "more than one promising center of research and professional education will become a training institution: *The Citadel of Learning* (New Haven: Yale University Press, 1956), p. 71.

37. Earle Ross, *Democracy's College: The Land-Grant Movement in the Formative State* (New York: Arno Press and *The New York Times*, 1969), pp. 153, 181.

38. Edward Danforth Eddy, Jr., *Colleges for Our Land and Time: The Land-Grant Idea in American Education* (New York: Harper & Bros., 1957), p. x.

39. Grant Venn, *Man, Education and Work: Postsecondary*

Vocational and Technical Education (Washington, D.C.: American Council on Education, 1964), p. 46.

40. Ibid., p. 56.

41. On this see the so-called Douglas Commission Report, formally *The Report of the Commission on Industrial and Technical Education*, Boston: Commonwealth of Massachusetts, 1906.

42. Venn, *Man, Education and Work*, p. 65.

43. For more on this see chapter 5 herein, especially those sections that deal with testing.

44. "The Second Transformation of American Secondary Education," in Reinhard Bendix and Seymour Lipset, eds., *Class, Status, and Power: Social Stratification in Comparative Perspective*, 2d ed. (New York: Free Press, 1966), p. 441.

45. "I.Q. in the U.S. Class Structure," *Social Policy*, November/December 1972—January/February 1973, p. 80. See also Timothy Healy, "The Case for Open Admissions: New Problems—New Hopes," *Change*, Summer 1973, pp. 24–29.

46. Ken Brunner, "The Training of Subprofessional Personnel in the U.S.," mimeographed (Paper prepared for the International Conference on Middle Level Manpower, San Juan, Puerto Rico, October 10–12, 1962), pp. 12 ff.

47. *Higher Education Act of 1972*, p. 87.

48. Between 1950 and 1970 the proportion of middle-level technical workers increased from 7.1 percent to 14.5 percent of the work force: Bureau of the Census, *The American Almanac* (New York: Grosset & Dunlap, 1971), p. 2250.

49. On this see Eli Ginzberg, "Education and National Efficiency in the U.S.A.," in A. H. Halsey, J. Floud, and C. A. Anderson, eds., *Education, Economy, and Society* (New York: Free Press, 1965), pp. 68–79. Additional signs of the vocationalization of graduate education may include the fact that an increasing number of school systems are requiring their elementary and high-school teachers to have master's degrees. Also, various cities have similar requirements for their social

workers. All of this, in addition, may signal a downward shift in the status of teachers, social workers, etc.

50. Phebe Ward, *Terminal Education in the Junior College* (New York: Harper & Bros., 1947), pp. 6–7.

51. Ibid., p. 7.

52. *Higher Education for American Democracy*, 6 vols. (New York: Harper & Bros., 1947–48).

53. Ibid., I:41.

54. On the controversy, see Gail Kennedy, ed., *Education for Democracy: The Debate Over the Report of the President's Commission on Higher Education* (Lexington, Mass.: D. C. Heath & Co., 1952).

55. It also appears that Zwerling's law has been operative in other industrialized societies. A. H. Halsey, for example, has shown how it has worked in Britain and Russia. Britain is moving rapidly toward a three-tiered higher educational system that parallels ours: Oxford and Cambridge are the elite national universities that enroll mainly children from the upper classes and prepare them for positions of influence and leadership. The local universities (Sussex, London, York, etc.) enroll upper-middle-class people and prepare them for upper-middle-level work. A newer third tier of schools composed of Colleges of Advanced Technology and Teacher Training Colleges, corresponding roughly to our community colleges, offer courses of three years' duration and prepare middle- and lower-middle-class people for decidedly middle-level jobs: "The Changing Functions of Universities in Advanced Societies," *Harvard Educational Review* 30 (Spring 1960): 119–27. See also A. H. Halsey, "British Universities and Intellectual Life," in Halsey, Floud, and Anderson, eds., *Education, Economy, and Society*, pp. 502–12; and Eric Ashby, *Technology and the Academics* (particularly chapter 3) (New York: Macmillan Co., 1958).

56. Quoted in Kennedy, ed., *Education for Democracy*, p. 32.

57. F. M. McDowell, *The Junior College*, Bureau of Educa-

tion Bulletin 32 (Washington, D.C.: U.S. Government Printing Office, 1919); Leonard Koos, *The Junior College Movement* (Boston: Ginn and Co., 1925); W. C. Eells, *The Junior College.*

58.   John Gardner, "National Goals in Education," in *Goals for Americans: The Report of the President's Commission on National Goals and Chapters Submitted for the Consideration of the Commission* (New York: Spectrum Books, 1960), p. 81.

59.   New York: Harper & Row, 1961.

60.   Gardner, "National Goals in Education," p. 85.

61.   Ibid., pp. 90–91.

62.   A. Wolfe, "Reform Without Reform: The Carnegie Commission on Higher Education," *Social Policy*, May/June 1971, p. 20.

63.   Carnegie Commission on Higher Education, *The Open-Door Colleges*, p. 15. Jerome Karabel, in "Perspectives on Open Admissions," talks about the real issue of open admissions at the City University—the future distribution of privilege—issues carefully avoided but between the lines of the Carnegie Commission report: in Logan Wilson, ed., *Universal Higher Education: Costs, Benefits, Options* (Washington D.C.: American Council on Education, 1972), p. 265–86.

64.   *The Open-Door Colleges*, pp. 4–5.

65.   Ibid., pp. 15–16.

66.   Ibid., p. 52.

67.   *The Carnegie Commission on Higher Education* (San Francisco: Jossey-Bass, 1973), p. 71. Additional criticism may be found in Norman Birnbaum, "The Politics of the Future" and W. Roy Niblett, "The Commission's Work: A View From Abroad," both in *Change*, November 1973, pp. 29–37, 38–44. See also, Donald McDonald, "A Six Million Dollar Misunderstanding," *The Center Magazine* 6 (September/October 1973): 32–50. But by far the best is Alan Wolfe's "Reform Without Reform," (op. cit.): it is the only one that exposes the socially regressive aspects of the commission's work.

68. Mayhew, *The Carnegie Commission*, pp. 5–6.

69. "The Community College in Search of Identity," *Change*, Winter 1971–72, pp. 55–56.

70. *A Master Plan for Higher Education in California, 1960–1975* (Sacramento: California State Department of Education, 1960), p. 58. A. J. Jaffe's and W. Adams's "Two Models of Open Enrollment" is rather good on how this master plan is fundamentally a ratification of the higher educational status quo: in Wilson, ed., *Universal Higher Education*, pp. 223–51.

71. M. Deutsch, A. Douglass, and G. Strayer, *A Report of the Survey of the Needs of California in Higher Education* (Berkeley: University of California Press, 1948), p. 26.

72. The suggested proper ratio in another such document— *Five Years of Progress: Florida's Community Junior Colleges* (Tallahassee: State Department of Education, 1963), p. 10.

73. *A Master Plan for Higher Education*, pp. 72 ff.

74. Jerome Karabel's "Protecting the Portals: Class and the Community College" contains some good material on how community colleges now use the mass media to sell their vocational education programs: *Social Policy*, May/June 1974, pp. 12–18.

75. *A Master Plan for Higher Education*, pp. 79–81.

76. Ibid., p. 65. A more appreciative view of the California plan—and others—may be found in Roger Yarrington, ed., *Junior Colleges: 50 States/50 Years* (Washington, D.C.: American Association of Junior Colleges, 1969).

77. *Report of the Joint Committee on the Master Plan for Higher Education*, draft (Sacramento: California State Legislature, February 1973), p. 59.

78. Ibid., p. 60.

79. The idea of the pure university is alive and well in the eyes of futurologists such as Alvin Eurich. By the twenty-first century he sees strong liberal arts colleges and universities at last cut loose from the first two years of higher education

"since these now come almost wholly within the province of the junior colleges": "Higher Education in the Twenty-First Century," in John Margolis, ed., *The Campus in the Modern World* (New York: Macmillan Co., 1969), pp. 101–12.

80. Legislative Document no. 30, Albany, N.Y., 1948, p. 28.

81. Ibid., p. 28. See also *Matching Needs and Facilities in Higher Education*, Legislative Document no. 31, Albany, N.Y., 1948.

82. *Education Beyond High School: The Regents Plan for the Development of Post Secondary Education* (Albany: New York State Department of Education, 1972), pp. 251–52.

83. Ibid., p. 101.

84. Ibid., p. 258.

85. Ibid., p. 255. And these nightmare institutions may actually be coming into existence. Richard Rinehart claims that more than half the colleges and universities in America are considering the institution of such programs: "Articulating Career Education at Associate-Degree and Baccalaureate-Degree Levels," in Norman Harris, ed., *Updating Occupational Education* (San Francisco: Jossey-Bass, 1974), pp. 93–103. Alan Gross even has a name for these four-year, two-year colleges: "communiversity": "Communiveristy—A New Approach" (E.R.I.C. no. ED 100 471, 1974).

86. *1968 Master Plan of the Board of Higher Education for the City University of New York*, draft (New York: The City University of New York, 1968), chapter 1, pp. 3–4.

87. Ibid., chapter 2, p. 4.

88. Ibid., chapter 2, pp. 2–3. A *New York Times* editorial of September 12, 1974 decrying a $9.5 million cutback in state funding for the City University sees these cuts channeling more students into transfer programs rather than into more appropriate (but more costly) vocational programs.

89. *1968 Master Plan*, chapter 3, p. 7. For more on how tracking works *within* two-year colleges, see Fred Pincus, "Tracking in the Community Colleges," Research Group One

Report no. 18 (Baltimore, 1974); and E. J. Brue, H. B. Enger, and E. J. Maxey, "How Do Community College Transfer and Occupational Students Differ?" American College Testing Program Report no. 41 (Iowa City, 1971).

90. *1968 Master Plan*, chapter 1, p. 16. For more on this see D. Rosen, S. Brunner, and S. Fowler, *Open Admissions: The Promise and the Lie of Open Access to American Higher Education* (Lincoln: University of Nebraska, 1973). It is particularly good on how the 1968 master plan was scrapped and replaced by one that moved open admissions up from 1975 to 1970, and also on how the channeling features of the original plan were carefully preserved. The pros and cons of CUNY's plan are effectively aired in *Open Admissions: The Pros and Cons* (Washington, D.C.: Council for Basic Education, 1972). Ellen Trimberger's "Open Admissions: A New Form of Tracking?" *The Insurgent Sociologist* 4 (Fall 1973): 29–43, is a careful presentation of how New York City's seemingly more egalitarian system is just as socially stratified as California's clearly segmented system. And finally, Allen Ballard's *The Education of Black Folk* (New York: Harper & Row, 1973) details how linking level of college admissions to high-school average or rank in graduating class (CUNY's policy) helps preserve a racially segregated society (p. 128).

91. Friedrich Schonemann, "A German Looks at American Higher Education," in Paul Schilpp, ed., *Higher Education Faces the Future* (New York: Liveright, 1930), p. 120.

NOTES TO CHAPTER 3

1. The enormous power of counselors in directing students' educational and career choices is well documented in Aaron Cicourel and John Kitsuse, *The Educational Decision-Makers* (Boston: Bobbs-Merrill Co., 1963).

2. "I.Q. and the U.S. Class Structure," *Social Policy*, November/December 1972–January/February 1973, pp. 65–69.

3. "The 'Cooling-Out' Function of Higher Education," *American Journal of Sociology* 65 (1960): 569–76.

4. Burton Clark, *The Open Door College* (New York: McGraw-Hill Book Co., 1960), p. 68.

5. Ibid., p. 69.

6. Ibid., pp. 71-75.

7. Charles Monroe in *Profile of the Community College* (San Francisco: Jossey-Bass, 1972) says a community college is doing very well if half its students return for a second year (p. 208).

8. Clark, *The Open Door College*, p. 165.

9. Clark, "The 'Cooling-Out' Function," p. 573.

10. Joseph Katz, Marvin Hoss, and Robert Vargas, *The Search for Independence* (Belmont, Cal.: Brooks/Cole Publishing Co., 1968), p. 82.

11. "On Cooling the Mark Out: Some Aspects of Adaption to Failure," *Psychiatry* 15 (1952): 451-63.

12. Ibid., p. 457.

13. "The Junior College, With Special Reference to California," *Proceedings of the National Education Association*, Washington, D.C., 1915, p. 21.

14. Ibid., p. 22.

15. New York: Holt, Rinehart and Winston, 1940, pp. 4, 30, 113, 137-38.

16. New York: Houghton Mifflin Co., 1968, pp. vi, 52, 66.

17. Ibid., p. 67.

18. For more evidence of subtle versions of cooling-out see James Thornton, *The Community College* (New York: John Wiley & Sons, 1960). It has gone through three important editions; in publishers' terms it has had a high rate of "adoption" for graduate school courses in higher education and thus has had a significant impact on current teaching and counseling practices at two-year colleges. (See especially pp. 73-74, 267 ff.) B. Lamar Johnson, *Islands of Innovation Expanding: Changes in the Community College* (Beverly

Hills, Cal.: Glencoe Press, 1969), pp. 41 ff.; and Monroe, *Profile of the Community College*, pp. 39 ff., contain other examples. For a detailed explication of how counseling and cooling-out is particularly effective when students are from different ethnic, racial, and socioeconomic status than their counselors (the usual situation), see Frederick Erickson, "Gatekeeping and the Melting Pot: Interaction in Counseling Encounters," *Harvard Educational Review* 45 (February 1975): 44–70.

19. See for example, Leland Medsker, *The Junior College: Progress and Prospect* (New York: McGraw-Hill Book Co., 1960), pp. 186–87; and Monroe, *Profile of the Community College*, pp. 145–47.

20. Public Law 85–864 passed by Congress in 1958 provides for federal support for college-level counseling.

21. Quoted in "The Illinois Public Junior College: A Program Review," (Springfield, Illinois: Illinois Economic and Fiscal Commission, January 1973), p. S-1.

22. Ibid., p. 7.

23. *Personnel and Guidance Journal*, June 1967, p. 976.

24. Ibid., p. 975.

25. Ibid., pp. 974–75.

26. *Junior College Student Personnel Programs: Appraisal and Development* (Washington, D.C.: American Association of Junior Colleges, 1965).

27. *Junior College Personnel Programs: What They Are and What They Should Be* (Washington, D.C.: American Association of Junior Colleges, 1967). Also widely distributed (seventy-five thousand copies in print) and also formulating methods for cooling-out is Gilbert Wrenn, *The Counselor in a Changing World* (Washington, D.C.: American Personnel and Guidance Association, 1962).

28. *Junior College Student Personnel Programs*, p. 7.

29. Ibid., p. 7.

30. Ibid., p. 8.

31. On this see Alexander Astin, *Predicting Academic Performance in College* (New York: Free Press, 1971), pp. 29–31; and Bruce Eckland, "Social Class and College Graduation," *American Journal of Sociology* 70 (July 1964): 36–50.

32. *Junior College Student Personnel Programs*, pp. 41–42.

33. Ibid., p. 42.

34. *Dateline '79: Heretical Concepts for the Community College* (Beverly Hills, Cal.: Glencoe Press, 1969), p. 156.

35. *A Constant Variable* (San Francisco: Jossey-Bass, 1971), pp. 181–82.

36. Ibid., p. 98.

37. Ibid., p. 136.

38. The future second-best community college will be well stocked with textbooks now rolling off the presses with what publishers call "adjusted texts" written in simpler language, using fewer abstractions but more repetition of the concepts. These new texts will help assure that even those kinds of students who in the past have come alive and been "salvaged" by their community college experience will have an even more difficult time in the future encountering real college-level material: Iver Peterson, "College Textbooks Being Simplified to Meet the Needs of the Poor Reader," *New York Times*, November 7, 1974, p. 47.

39. *Measurement and Evaluation in Guidance* 4 (October 1971): 163.

40. Ibid., p. 170.

41. "An Investigation of the 'Cooling-Out' Process in the Junior College as Indicated by Changes of Major," (E.R.I.C. no. Ed 039 868, 1969), p. 29.

42. Ibid., p. 30; Leonard Baird, "Patterns of Educational Aspirations," *American College Testing Research Report*, no. 32, December 1969, pp. 55–73. There are some, of course, who refuse to accept the thought that community colleges

practice cooling-out. David Bushnell and Mary Kievit, for example, not only perish the thought but also claim that students like what happens to them at two-year colleges: they see them as providing opportunities for increased earning power and higher social status; "Community Colleges: What Is Our Job?" *Change*, April 1974, pp. 52–53.

43. Students, for example, seem to have been able to entirely avoid Bronx Community College's seven-year-old Division of Plastics Technology. Though it has a building of its own, spent hundreds of thousands of dollars on modern equipment and promotional brochures, only twenty-six students have ever completed the two-year course of study and at present *not one student* is enrolled: Michael Kaufman, "City U Division of Plastics Lacks Nothing but Students," *New York Times*, May 2, 1974, p. 49.

NOTES TO CHAPTER 4

1. In this discussion I am indebted to Mark Blaug's *An Introduction to the Economics of Education* (Harmondsworth, England: Penguin Books, 1970).

2. Quoted in Blaug, ibid., p. 2.

3. Mimeographed, Lancaster, England: University of Lancaster, September 1972.

4. *Who Benefits from Higher Education and Who Should Pay?* (Washington, D.C.: American Association for Higher Education, 1972), p. 26.

5. Blaug, *Introduction to the Economics of Education*, p. 23.

6. Carnegie Commission on Higher Education, *Higher Education: Who Pays? Who Benefits? Who Should Pay?* (New York: McGraw-Hill Book Co., 1973), p. 17.

7. Ibid., p. 16; and see Leland Medsker and Dale Tillery, *Breaking the Access Barriers: A Profile of Two Year Colleges* (New York: McGraw-Hill Book Co., 1971), p. 115.

8. Carnegie Commission, *Higher Education: Who Pays?*,

p. 46. A 1967 census study indicates the differential in median earnings for graduates of colleges of different qualities: with a B.A. from a low-ranked institution median income was $7,881; the figures were $9,752 and $11,678 for medium- and high-ranked institutions: U.S. Bureau of the Census, "Men With College Degrees: March 1967," *Current Population Reports*, p. 20 (180).

9. New York: Basic Books, 1972, pp. 27, 223. The Carnegie Commission also attempted to estimate the advantage of attending a private college rather than a public college. They conclude that ". . . the representative student who attends a tax-supported public institution will receive an income 15% higher than the average male at age 50. . . . The private college alumnus is anticipated to have an income 27% above the nonattender. . . ": *Higher Education: Who Pays?*, p. 84.

10. "If a student gives up or delays taking an income-producing job to go on or return to college, he or she obviously has an additional cost of attending college over and above actual expense outlays. For some students (or potential students) this is a major factor in determining attendance, and it should be considered a cost of attending college": *Higher Education: Who Pays?*, p. 49.

11. Lexington, Mass.: D. C. Heath & Co., 1970, p. xiii.

12. Ibid, pp. xiii–xiv.

13. Ibid., pp. 2–3.

14. Ibid., p. 15. Alan Wolfe, however, contends that federal taxes are also regressively collected and that without fundamental tax reform all parts of the higher educational system will continue to redistribute money unequally: "Carnegie Again," *Social Policy*, November/December 1974, pp. 60–63.

15. Chicago: Markham Publishing Co., 1969, p. 69.

16. Ibid., p. 67.

17. Ibid., p. 73.

18. Ibid., pp. 42–44.

19. Ibid., p. 76.

20. Ibid., p. 71.

21. Ibid., p. 65.

22. Ibid., p. 22.

23. "Community Colleges and Social Stratification," *Harvard Educational Review* 42 (November 1972): 342.

24. Though Louis Hausman estimates that "the figure of $200,000 is widely accepted as the average net incremental lifetime value of a college degree": "Pressures, Benefits, and Options" in Logan Wilson, ed., *Universal Higher Education* (Washington, D.C.: American Council on Education, 1972), p. 9; the familiar $200,000 amount has been revised downward so that now $20,000 to, say, $50,000 is the more generally agreed upon figure. See Richard Eckaus, *Estimating the Returns to Education* (Berkeley: Carnegie Commission on Higher Education, 1973); Walter Adams and A. J. Jaffe, "Economic Returns to the College Investment," *Change*, November 1971, pp. 8–9, 60; and Theodore Schultz, "Optimal Investment in College Instruction: Equity and Efficiency," in T. Schultz, ed., *Investment in Education* (Chicago: University of Chicago Press, 1972), pp. 2–30.

25. Hansen and Weisbrod, *Benefits, Costs, and Finance*, pp. 77–78.

26. Ibid., p. 72.

27. Ibid., p. 78.

28. W. Lee Hansen and Burton Weisbrod, "The Distribution of Costs and Direct Benefits of Public Higher Education," *Journal of Human Resources*, Fall 1967, pp. 16–38.

29. "The Distributional Effects of Public Higher Education in California," *Journal of Human Resources*, Summer 1970, p. 361.

30. Ibid., p. 364. Robert Hartman contends both Hansen and Weisbrod *and* Pechman are correct: the system is remarkably both progressive and regressive! It all depends upon how

you compile your data: "(1) Poor people pay taxes and very few of them use public higher education. Those who do, gain thereby; those who don't don't. [And though he doesn't mention it, they help subsidize more affluent students.] (2) Middle income people are heavy users of the system. Their taxes don't cover the costs. (3) A few rich people use the system and gain handsomely thereby. The rest of the rich pay substantial taxes and get no direct return": "A Comment on the Pechman-Hansen-Weisbrod Controversy," *Journal of Human Resources*, Fall 1970, p. 521.

31. Pechman, "The Distributional Effects of Higher Education," pp. 19–20, 26.

32. Ibid., p. 222.

33. Hansen and Witmer make precisely this same point in "Economic Benefits of Universal Higher Education": ". . . individual rates of return have held roughly constant [since at least 1939] in the face of the universalization of secondary education and the growing participation in higher education. . . . The individual's rate of return for the completion of two years of college, however, has more often than not been less than 10 percent; hence, it compares less favorably with the return that can be earned in other investments. In short, the magnitudes of rates of return confirm that the completion of high school represents a wise economic decision and that a four-year college education pays off. But the efficiency of two-year college programs is less clear-cut": in Wilson, ed., *Universal Higher Education*, p. 28.

34. Christopher Jencks et al., *Inequality: A Reassessment of the Effect of Family and Schooling in America* (New York: Basic Books, 1972), p. 222.

35. Carnegie Commission, *Higher Education: Who Pays?*, p. 44.

36. *California Student Resources Survey, 1972* (Sacramento: The California State Scholarship and Loan Commission, 1972), p. 193.

37. Carnegie Commission, *Higher Education: Who Pays?*, p. 46.

38. Ibid., pp. 11, 91.

39. Partly in response to some of these inconsistencies, the Carnegie Commission published *Tuition* (New York: McGraw-Hill Book Co., 1974). They argue here that they were neither trying to benefit private at the expense of public colleges nor were their proposals regressive. They in fact want to make things more equal by increasing direct grants to low-income students. But even such increases have not stemmed the decline, since 1972, in enrollments of blacks in the nation's colleges: for example, from 8.7 percent of all freshmen in 1972 to 7.8 percent in 1973: "Minorities Drop in U.S. Colleges: First Slash Since Mid-60's Is Linked to Economics," *New York Times*, February 3, 1974, p. 43.

Incidentally, Marilyn Gittell in a recent essay challenges the new conventional wisdom emerging from Coleman, Jensen, Jencks, etc., that additional funding for schools, compensatory education programs, etc., are inevitably doomed to fail: "Coleman's report written in 1966, did not take into account major federal funding which had just begun to be filtered to local districts, yet Coleman data has been continually referred to as proving that compensatory education is a failure": "Education and Equality: Social Darwinism Revisited," in Alan Gartner, C. Greer, and F. Reissman, eds., *What Nixon is Doing to Us* (New York: Harrow Books, 1973).

40. Carnegie Commission, *Higher Education: Who Pays?*, p. 108. There have recently been powerful counterproposals to increase the tuition in public colleges so that middle-income families (usually defined as those earning $15,000 or more a year) can take on more of the burden of college costs. See, for example, *The Management and Financing of Colleges* (New York: Committee for Economic Development, 1973) which recommends raising tuition up to 50 percent of institutional costs. Some have pointed out the regressive nature of such proposals. First of all, only 20 percent of the students in college come from families earning $15,000 or more; and even assuming they could pay the increased tuition, such proposals if implemented would drive poorer people away from the colleges they are just now beginning to enter: see Fred Hechinger, "Class War Over Tuition," *New York Times*,

February 5, 1974. There is also evidence that if tuition were raised as proposed, factors other than cost would inhibit low-socioeconomic-status students from attending college—it seems that well-educated parents with low incomes are more likely to contribute to college costs than poorly educated parents with high incomes: see John Lansing, Thomas Lorimer, Chikashi Moriguchi, *How People Pay for College* (Ann Arbor, Michigan: Study Research Center, 1960).

NOTES TO CHAPTER 5

1. *The Junior College Movement* (New York: Holt, Rinehart, and Winston, 1940), p. 2.

2. *Secondary Education in California—A Preliminary Survey* (Sacramento: California State Department of Education, 1929), p. 71.

3. Tyrus Hillway uses 1943 data gleaned from the American Council on Education's Psychological Examination to make much the same point: the scholastic aptitude of the average junior-college freshman is lower "than it is for freshmen in standard four-year colleges and universities," but there is still considerable overlap: *The American Two-Year College* (New York: Harper & Bros., 1958), p. 86.

More than a decade later, Harold Seashore examines data from twenty-four thousand junior-college freshmen who took the College Qualifications Test in 1957. He, too, cites the overlap but also indicates that the proportion of high-ability students in two-year colleges is smaller than in four-year colleges and the percentage of low-ability students is higher: "Academic Abilities of Junior College Students," *Junior College Journal* 29 (October 1958): 74–80.

4. *A Study of the Academic Ability and Performance of Junior College Students* (Princeton, N.J.: Educational Testing Service, 1965).

5. William Cooley and Susan Becker analysed Project TALENT data which consisted of 1960 test results from 440,000 high-school seniors. It gave them the opportunity to compare the ability levels of students who went to junior col-

leges, four-year colleges, and of young people who did not go on to college at all—the first large-scale opportunity to make this kind of survey. They found that in verbal, mathematical, and other measures of cognitive ability there is a slightly greater tendency for the junior-college students to be more like the noncollege students than the four-year-college students. However, this study, too, mentions the overlap in that a third of the two-year students scored higher than the mean scores of the four-year-college students: "The Junior College Student," *Personnel and Guidance Journal* 44 (January 1966): 465.

6. "Academic Description and Prediction in Junior Colleges," in *The Two-Year College and Its Students: An Empirical Report* (Iowa City: American College Testing Program, 1969), pp. 108–20.

7. Ibid., p. 117.

8. *Social Policy*, November/December 1972—January/ February 1973, pp. 65–96.

9. Socioeconomic status is a complex variable to attempt to measure, but nearly everyone agrees that it includes at least the student's family income (often estimated on the basis of the father's occupation since children rarely have an accurate sense of how much their parents earn), the level of the father's educational attainment (grade-school education only, high-school graduate, some college, a B.A., etc.); the number of books in the home; whether or not the student has a room, desk, typewriter, etc. Something else that nearly everyone also agrees about is that on all of these measures of S.E.S., two-year students fall significantly below the S.E.S. level of four-year-college students. K. Patricia Cross, for example, finds that junior-college students fall between the noncollege and four-year group on every index of socioeconomic status: "Higher Education's Newest Student," in Terry O'Banion and Alice Thurston, eds., *Student Development Programs in the Community Junior College* (Englewood Cliffs, N.J.: Prentice-Hall, 1972), p. 28. In addition, Max Raines cites American Council on Education data to show the median family income for incoming junior-college students to be between $8,000 and $9,000 per year whereas it's $12,000–$13,000 per year for

incoming four-year students: "Characteristics of Junior College Students," in W. K. Ogilvie and M. R. Raines, eds., *Perspectives on the Community Junior College* (New York: Appleton-Century-Crofts, 1971), p. 178. Leland Medsker and Dale Tillery concur: *Breaking the Access Barriers* (New York: McGraw-Hill Book Co., 1971), pp. 40 ff., as does David Bushnell, citing the most recent data available as of this writing: *Organizing for Change* (New York: McGraw-Hill Book Co., 1973), pp. 24 ff. Bruce Eckland adds an interesting and disturbing wrinkle to this. Past research had indicated that though social class is related to who goes to college, class is *not* related to who graduates. His study, however, suggests that class and college graduation *are* significantly related, particularly among "average" students—the kind who enter community colleges: "Social Class and College Graduation," *American Journal of Sociology* 70 (July 1964): 36–50.

10.   For more on the relationship between "success" in life and the number of years one remains in school, see chapter 4 herein.

11.   See Chapter 1 herein for a fuller discussion of this.

12.   Motivation, for example, a key to success, has been seen to be class-related. Bernard Rosen has written about what he calls "the achievement syndrome" in which class-transmitted personality characteristics such as one's motivation and value-orientation influence a student's capacity to take advantage of his/her intelligence and opportunities ("breaks") or to compensate for the lack of them: "The Achievement Syndrome: A Psychocultural Dimension of Social Stratification," *American Sociological Review* 21 (April 1956): 203–11. See also Joseph Kahl, "'Common Man' Boys," an interesting study of the personal characteristics of working-class and lower-middle-class boys who went on to make it at elite schools: in A. H. Halsey, J. Floud, and C. A. Anderson, eds., *Education, Economy, and Society* (New York: Free Press, 1965), pp. 348–66. Herbert Hyman's "The Value Systems of Different Classes" describes how some of the hidden injuries of class affect one's life chances: in Rinehard Bendix and Seymour Lipset, eds., *Class, Status, and Power* (New York: Free Press,

1966), pp. 488–99. And see Natalie Rogoff, "Local Social Structure and Educational Selection," which points out how even the characteristic values of the local community affect one's educational progress and opportunities for future success: in Halsey, Floud, and Anderson, eds., *Education, Economy, and Society*, pp. 241–51.

13. Thomas O'Connell, president of Berkshire Community College, expresses repugnance at his students' speech patterns: varying degrees of nonstandard English, double negatives, pronoun and verb errors, and lots of localisms. In his words, language "untouched by previous school experience": *Community Colleges: A President's View* (Urbana: University of Illinois Press, 1968), p. 65.

14. Though Daniel Yankelovich cites recent evidence that "youth culture" values have powerfully influenced blue-collar youths since the late 1960s: *The New Morality: A Profile of American Youth in the 70's* (New York: McGraw-Hill Book Co., 1974).

15. "Differential Characteristics of Entering Freshmen at the University of California and their Peers at California Junior Colleges," (Ph.D. diss. University of California, Berkeley, 1964).

16. H. Dale Tillery, "Report to the Conference for Chief Personnel Administrators on Implementing the Open Door," Pacific Grove, California, January 10, 1964.

17. J. R. Warren, for example, compared junior- and senior-college students and found that the four-year students were adventuresome, impulsive, and involved, while the two-year students were cautious, prudent, and controlled; they were also the most apprehensive and rigid, least autonomous, most authoritarian, and least flexible in their thinking: *Patterns of College Experience,* U.S. Office of Education Cooperative Research Project S-327, (Claremont, Cal.: College Student Personnel Institute and Claremont Graduate School and University Center, October 1966).

J. M. Richards and L. A. Braskamp echo these findings and also suggest social and educational policies that they claim relate to these social-scientific realities, policies for example which lead to curricula tracking and its social consequences. Junior-college students, they say, are less concerned with personal and intellectual development. In general, these students can be described as pragmatic individuals who seek vocational training (this in spite of the fact that they most frequently avoid career programs) whereas four-year colleges attract more talented students "who are intellectually oriented, who plan a degree in one of the traditional subject areas, and who expect to take part in a wide variety of activities in college": "Who Goes Where to Junior College?" in *The Two-Year College and its Students*, p. 80.

Others reaching identical conclusions include Charles Collins in a monograph widely distributed by the AAJC—*Junior College Student Personnel Programs: What They Are and What They Should Be* (Washington, D.C.: American Association of Junior Colleges, 1967); and L. Goldberg and J. T. Dailey in their unpublished manuscript, "Research on Academic Degree Projections: The Identification and Development of Talents of 1960 High School Graduates," (Project TALENT, Palo Alto, Cal., 1963).

18. *Student Characteristics: Personality and Dropout Propensity* (Washington, D.C.: American Association of Junior Colleges, 1970), p. 49.

19. Ibid., p. 50.

20. "Toward an Empirical Typology of Junior College Subcultures," (E.R.I.C. no. ED 013 076, 1967).

21. "Goodbye, Pygmalion," *Change*, March 1975, pp. 52–53.

22. Recently, however, there has been some criticism of the data on the authoritarian personalities of working-class people. It has been pointed out that much of this data derives from elusive material that reveals as much about the attitudes of the writers as their subjects. See for example Louis Lipsitz, "Working Class Authoritarianism: A Reevaluation," *American Sociological Review*, February 1965, pp. 27–43; Richard Hamilton, *Class and Politics in the United States* (New York: John Wiley & Sons, 1972); and Andrew Levison, *The Working-Class Majority* (New York: Coward, McCann & Geoghegan, 1974).

23. Paul Heist and George Young, *Omnibus Personality Inventory: Manual* (New York: The Psychological Corporation, 1968), pp. 10–12.

24. Ibid., p. 2.

25. Herbert Gans's *Urban Villagers* (New York: Free Press, 1962), among other things, is one of the best studies of working-class values and family life available and might profitably be read in the context of an analysis of the value distortions present in such instruments as the O.P.I., where many of the laudable qualities he sees to be part of working-class culture are denigrated. See pp. 27 ff. for example.

26. K. Patricia Cross, *The Junior College Student: A Research Description* (Princeton: Educational Testing Service, 1968); *Beyond the Open Door: New Students to Higher Education* (San Francisco: Jossey-Bass, 1971).

27. There is some thought that it is difficult if not impossible to accurately characterize in sweeping terms large groups of students on the basis of the kind of data Cross derives from student questionnaires. See as an example Alexander Astin et al., *The American Freshmen: National Norms for Fall 1973* (Los Angeles: American Council on Education and the University of California, n.d.).

28. Cross, *Beyond the Open Door*, see particularly chapter 4 therein, "Interests of New Students," pp. 56 ff.

29. Ibid., pp. 92 ff.

30. Ibid., p. 157.

31. Ibid., p. 166.

32. Ibid., p. 145.

33. San Francisco: Jossey-Bass, 1972, p. 196.

34. Ibid., p. 196.

35. Ibid., p. 190.

36. Ibid., p. 200.

NOTES TO CHAPTER 6

1. *The Irony of Early School Reform* (Boston: Beacon Press, 1968), pp. 211, 214–15.

2. *Young Man Luther* (New York: W. W. Norton & Co., 1958), pp. 34–35.

3. *The Great School Legend* (New York: Basic Books, 1972), pp. 154–55.

4. For more on the mechanisms of "conscientization" see Peter Berger, Brigitte Berger, and Hansfried Kellner, *The Homeless Mind: Modernization and Consciousness* (New York: Random House, 1973), pp. 175 ff.

5. "Politics of the Classroom," *Social Policy*, July/August 1973, p. 67.

6. Ibid., p. 67.

7. Ibid., pp. 68, 79, 80.

8. New York: Center for Social Research, The Graduate School and University Center, City University of New York, 1972.

9. For more on how sitting in a circle by itself changes nothing unless you also deal with the teacher's need to control and the class's complicity, see Michael Rossman, *On Learning and Social Change: Transcending the Totalitarian Classroom* (New York: Vintage Books, 1972), pp. 15–18.

10. See for example Victoria Steinitz, Prudence King, and Ellen Shapiro, "Ideological Development in Working-Class Youth," *Harvard Educational Review* 43 (August 1973): 333–61.

11. "Campus Missionaries: The Laying On of Culture," *The Nation*, March 10, 1969, p. 297.

12. Ibid., p. 300. Alan Wolfe covers similar ground in "Working with the Working Class," *Change*, February 1972, pp. 24–29.

13. For more on this see Samuel Bowles, "Cuban Education and the Revolutionary Ideology," in Martin Carnoy, ed., *Schooling in a Corporate Society: The Political Economy of Education in America* (New York: David McKay Co., 1972), pp. 272–303.

NOTES TO CHAPTER 7

1. New York: Harper & Row, 1957.

2. See for example A. W. Chickering, *Education and Identity* (San Francisco: Jossey-Bass, 1969); Nevitt Sanford, "Higher Education as a Social Problem," in N. Sanford, ed., *The American College* (New York: John Wiley & Sons, 1962), pp. 10–73; Mervin Freedman, *Impact of College*, (Washington, D.C.: U.S. Government Printing Office, 1960).

3. Kenneth Feldman and Theodore Newcomb, *The Impact of College on Students* (San Francisco: Jossey-Bass, 1973), pp. 29 ff.

4. Ibid., p. 112. For more on this see J. C. Stanley, "A Design for Comparing the Impact of Different Colleges," *American Educational Research Journal* 4 (1967): 217–28.

5. Feldman and Newcomb, *The Impact of College on Students*, p. 145.

6. A good example of this is T. M. Newcomb's study of the radical changes that occurred among students from upper-middle-class conservative families during their stay at liberal Bennington College: *Personality and Social Change: Attitude Formation in a Student Community* (New York: Dryden Press, 1943).

7. The best review of this sticky methodological problem may be found in Stephen Withey et al., eds., *A Degree and What Else? A Review of the Correlates and Consequences of a College Education* (New York: McGraw-Hill Book Co., 1971).

8. *Beyond High School: A Psychosociological Study of 10,000 High School Graduates* (San Francisco: Jossey-Bass,

1968). A recent Daniel Yankelovich survey reaching conclusions similar to Trent's and Medsker's was not as careful about controlling for these variables: reported in *The New York Times* by Nadine Brozan, "Widening Gap in Views Is Registered Between College and Noncollege Women," May 22, 1974, p. 45; and by Richard Severo, "College Students Showing Reduced Sense of Alienation," May 22, 1974, pp. 45, 86.

9. The idea that people continue to grow and develop in a patterned way into and beyond early adulthood has now begun to find expression in even the popular media. As examples, see Gail Sheehy, "Catch-30 and Other Predictable Crises of Growing Up Adult," *New York Magazine*, February 18, 1974, pp. 30–44; idem, "Why Mid Life Is Crisis Time for Couples," *New York Magazine*, April 29, 1974, pp. 31–35. See also Gerald Gurin, "Impact During College," Withey et al., eds., *A Degree and What Else?*, pp. 14–32.

10. Erik Erikson, *Childhood and Society*, 2d ed. (New York: W. W. Norton & Co., 1963), pp. 247 ff.

11. Joseph Axelrod and associates have written very well on this process of developmental unfolding: *Search for Relevance* (San Francisco: Jossey-Bass, 1969), pp. 18 ff.

12. Kenneth Keniston and Mark Gerzon summarize some of this very well, and I am indebted to them in what follows. See their "Human and Social Benefits," in Logan Wilson, ed., *Universal Higher Education* (Washington, DC.: American Council on Education, 1972) pp. 63 ff.

13. *Forms of Intellectual and Ethical Development in the College Years* (New York: Holt, Rinehart and Winston, 1970).

14. Lawrence Kohlberg, "State and Sequence: The Cognitive-Developmental Approach to Socialization," in D. A. Goslin, ed., *Handbook of Socialization Theory Research* (Chicago: Rand McNally, 1969), pp. 347–48; idem, "The Child as Moral Philosopher," *Psychology Today*, September 1968, pp. 25–30; idem, "Moral Education in the Schools," *The School Review* 74 (Spring 1966): 1–30.

15. Nevitt Sanford, "The Freeing and Acting Out of Impulse in Late Adolescence," in R. White, ed., *The Study of Lives*

(New York: Atherton, 1963), pp. 4–39; Joseph Katz, "Four Years of Growth, Conflict and Compliance," in J. Katz et al., eds., *No Time For Youth* (San Francisco: Jossey-Bass, 1968), pp. 3–73.

16. Nevitt Sanford, "Developmental Status of the Entering Freshman," in Sanford, ed., *The American College*, p. 266.

17. "Perspectives on Open Admissions," in Wilson, ed., *Universal Higher Education*, pp. 365–86.

18. *The Student in Higher Education* (New Haven: The Hazen Foundation, 1968).

19. Ibid., p. 32.

20. Joseph Katz, "Recommendations for Policy and Philosophy," in J. Katz et al., eds., *No Time For Youth*, p. 419.

21. Gerald Weinstein and Mario Fantini, *Toward Humanistic Education: A Curriculum of Affect* (New York: Praeger Publishers, 1970), p. 27.

22. *The Student in Higher Education*, p. 61.

23. Weinstein and Fantini, *Toward Humanistic Education*, p. 28. See also Sylvia Scribner and Michael Cole, "Cognitive Consequences of Formal and Informal Education," *Science* 182 (November 9, 1973): 553–59.

24. August Hollingshead, for example, in his classic sociological study *Elmtown's Youth* (New York: Science Editions, 1961), p. 286, found that 41 percent of low-S.E.S. high-school youth had no crystalized image of themselves in future life roles whereas only 3 percent of high-S.E.S. students had this problem.

25. Seventy-four percent of the Columbia College class of 1974 graduated in four years; an additional number finished earlier: "Shaky Economy Lures Record Number at Columbia to Law and Medicine: Trend Irks Some Students," *New York Times*, May 16, 1974, pp. 43, 68.

26. Erikson, *Childhood and Society*, p. 306.

27. This capacity to plan may well be essential for a relatively healthy life in a future-shock society. Alvin Toffler puts it this

way: generalized if tentative life-plans "help orient the individual in the midst of hurricaning change. In this way the future becomes intensely personal, instead of remote." See "The Psychology of the Future," in A. Toffler, ed., *Learning for Tomorrow: The Role of the Future in Education* (New York: Vintage Books, 1974), p. 18. See also Benjamin Singer, "The Future-Focused Role-Image," ibid., pp. 19–32.

28. See for example, John Roueche, *Salvage, Redirection, or Custody?: Remedial Education in the Community Junior College* (Washington, D.C.: American Association of Junior Colleges, 1968). See also, Anita Summer and Barbara Wolfe, "Which School Resources Help Learning? Efficiency and Equity in Philadelphia Public Schools," *Business Review* (Federal Reserve Bank of Philadelphia, Pennsylvania, 1975).

29. Joe Rempson, "Minority Access to Higher Education in New York City," *The City Almanac* no. 7, August 1972, p. 12.

30. Alexander Astin and Jack Rossman, "The Case for Open Admissions: A Status Report," *Change*, Summer 1973, pp. 35–37.

31. For an excellent source of information on how the affective content of classroom culture influences learning and nonlearning, see Richard Mann et al., *The College Classroom: Conflict, Change and Learning* (New York: John Wiley & Sons, 1970).

32. *The Student in Higher Education*, p. 44.

33. Ronald Swofford and Joyce Swofford, for example, surveyed forty Virginia and North Carolina two-year colleges and found forty different kinds of remedial programs: "Developmental Studies in North Carolina and Virginia: A Constant Search for Anything that Will Work," (E.R.I.C. no. ED 082 727, 1974). See also "The Open Door, or the Revolving Door: Which Way, Texas?" (Austin: Texas State Legislature, January 9, 1973); *Teaching English in Two-Year Colleges: Three Successful Programs* (Urbana, Ill.: National Council of Teachers of English, 1974). These last three programs, at least, appear to be partially based upon the assumption that more than grammar and punctuation have to be dealt with—

students' prior education and their negative self-images also have to be considered.

34. *Islands of Innovation Expanding: Changes in the Community College* (Beverly Hills, Cal.: Glencoe Press, 1969), pp. 230 ff.

35. John Roueche and Wade Kirk, *Catching Up: Remedial Education* (San Francisco: Jossey-Bass, 1973). See also Sara Chalghian, "Success for Marginal Students," *Junior College Journal* 39 (1969): 28–30, for a detailed description of another successful remedial ghetto.

36. Roueche and Kirk, *Catching Up*, p. 59. In "Implementing a Curriculum for Provisional Students," mimeographed, (Los Angeles City College), Hope Powell quotes John Lombardi, well-known president of Los Angeles City College: " . . . remedial classes are not the answer. Because fewer than 5 in 100 will ever qualify for the transfer or the technical program." She doesn't, however, reveal the answer.

37. Frank Riessman and Alan Gartner, "The New Hereditarians," *Change*, February 1974, pp. 56–59.

38. See J. R. Clarke, "A Curriculum Designed for Disadvantaged Community Junior College Students," (Ph.D. diss., University of Florida, 1966); A. A. Kunsisto, *Report of the Conference on Two-Year Colleges and the Disadvantaged* (Albany: State University of New York and the State Education Department, 1966).

39. J. Richard Johnston, review of *Catching Up* by J. Roueche and W. Kirk, in *Community College Frontiers* 2 (Fall 1973): 52–53.

40. Boston: Houghton Mifflin Co., 1951.

41. Ibid., p. 45.

42. Ibid., p. 427.

43. Ibid., p. 399.

44. See Leonard Lansky, "Changing the Classroom," and Roger Harrison, "Classroom Innovation: A Design Primer,"

both in P. Runkel, R. Harrison, and M. Runkel, eds., *The Changing College Classroom* (San Francisco: Jossey-Bass, 1969), pp. 292–301, 302–40 respectively.

45. *Toward A Psychology of Being*, 2d ed. (New York: Van Nostrand, 1968), p. 30.

46. "Teaching and Learning: Whose Goals Are Important Around Here?" in C. Dobbins and C. Lee, eds., *Whose Goals for American Higher Education?* (Washington, D.C.: American Council on Education, 1968), pp. 19–38. See also Michael Rossman, "Learning and Social Change: The Problem of Authority," in Runkel, Harrison, and Runkel, eds., *The Changing College Classroom*, pp. 20–32; Pressley McCoy, "Johnston College: An Experimenting Model," in Paul Dressel, ed., *The New Colleges: Toward an Appraisal* (Iowa City: American College Testing Program, 1971), pp. 53–87.

47. Steven Zwerling, "Circle Students On Probation," mimeographed, (Staten Island, N.Y.: Staten Island Community College, October 23, 1974).

48. Gene Mulcahy, "Evaluation of Circle 73," mimeographed, (Staten Island, N.Y.: Staten Island Community College, May 17, 1974).

NOTES TO CHAPTER 8

1. Donald Super, *The Psychology of Careers: An Introduction to Vocational Development* (New York: Harper & Row, 1957).

2. Eli Ginzberg et al., *Occupational Choice: An Approach to a General Theory* (New York: Columbia University Press, 1951).

3. Ibid., pp. 134, 154.

4. Ibid., pp. 60, 90, 105. We also seem to deliver a confounding mixed message to young people when we tell them, on the one hand, that they are free to choose their curricula and their careers but then, on the other hand, tell them that freedom to choose has to be earned. For example, they must

work for external rewards (grades and later money) in order to achieve the freedom or capacity for more intrinsic rewards: Harold Korn, "Careers: Choice, Chance, or Inertia," in J. Katz, ed., *No Time For Youth* (San Francisco: Jossey-Bass, 1969), pp. 207–38. We find too that though we expect students to make lifelong choices, they tend to do so with little knowledge of the day-to-day work expected in different occupations. About all they know is the status and lifestyle of various careers: David Beardslee and Donald O'Dowd, "Students and the Occupational World," In Nevitt Sanford, ed., *The American College* (New York: John Wiley & Sons, 1962), pp. 597–626.

5. James Davis, *Undergraduate Career Decisions: Correlates of Occupational Choice* (Chicago: Aldine-Atherton, 1965), p. 45.

6. See Davis, *Understanding Career Decisions*, p. 32, for evidence of college's limited impact and J. Katz, ed., *No Time For Youth*, pp. 441–42, for what can and does occur.

7. See page 138 herein.

8. See J. W. Wilson, "Survey of Cooperative Education, 1972," *Journal of Cooperative Education*, November 1972, pp. 9–15.

9. For a fuller discussion see J. D. Dawson, *New Directions for Cooperative Education* (New York: National Commission for Cooperative Education), pp. 1–3. When Ann Heiss discusses experiential education at two- and four-year colleges, she distinguishes between the "internships" of four-year colleges and the "apprenticeships" of two-year colleges. "Internship" carries the aura of the postgraduate experience of lawyers, doctors, architects, etc. "Apprenticeship" is something usually identified with workers: printers, construction workers, plumbers, etc. Thus, even for off-campus work, tracking is built right into the language: *An Inventory of Academic Innovation and Reform* (New York: McGraw-Hill Book Co., 1973), pp. 42–43.

10. "The Role of the Teacher in Cooperative Education," *Journal of Cooperative Education*, May 1969, pp. 18–20.

11.   San Francisco: Jossey-Bass, 1973.

12.   Ibid., p. 41.

13.   There is even some not-surprising evidence that off-campus internships are helpful in increasing student motivation and academic standing. A report of a three-year-long program of cooperative education sponsored by five California community colleges claims that the retention rate of participants improved by a factor of more than two to one: "Community College Vocational Cooperative Education," (Costa Mesa, Cal.: Coast Community College District, September 1973, E.R.I.C. no. ED 080 108).

14.   The traditional curriculum for education majors is a reverse of the practice I am advocating. Teacher-training programs usually offer two or three years of on-campus course work (Philosophy of Education, History of Education, Adolescent Psychology, various "methods" courses, etc.) before getting their education majors out into the field, into the classroom.

15.   Barry Heermann, *Cooperative Education in the Community College* (San Francisco: Jossey-Bass, 1973), p. 111.

16.   J. W. Wilson's survey of cooperative education programs reveals that as of 1972 63.9 percent of community college programs had students alternating terms of on- and off-campus work. Another 20.3 percent had students on campus half a day and working off-campus the other half. I suppose we at Staten Island fall into the remaining 15.8 percent: Wilson, "Survey," p. 12. Incidentally, we've come to feel good about this structure in which students, in a sense, simultaneously work on- and off-campus: by having both kinds of work run concurrently there is less chance of reinforcing our unfortunate social dichotomy between learning and working.

17.   Heermann, *Cooperative Education*, pp. 141, 145.

18.   Among others: M. Barlow, *A Survey of Junior College Work Experience Education Programs* (Los Angeles: Division of Vocational Education, U.C.L.A., 1963). G. Hayes, *Junior*

College Work Experience Education (Los Angeles: E.R.I.C. Clearinghouse for Junior Colleges, 1969).

19. An article in *The New York Times Magazine* about Bronx Community College reveals that only 4 percent of the fall 1970 open-admissions students received their associate's degree in two years: Gene Maeroff, "This Side of Paradise: A Kind of Higher Education," May 27, 1973, p. 17.

NOTES TO CHAPTER 9

1. That this is a nationwide problem is confirmed by Warren Willingham in his monograph *The No. 2 Access Problem: Transfer to the Upper Division* (Washington, D.C.: American Association for Higher Education, 1972). He concludes: "Important problems that students encounter in transferring seem traceable to their not being informed early about admission and financial aid procedures" (p. 44). Frederick Kintzer surveyed two thousand community college students regarding the help they received in the transfer process. He concludes that neither the sending community colleges nor the receiving senior colleges provided much preparation: "Catalogs are no help. Usually [the student] picks up information and misinformation from other students, and is otherwise left to make his own adjustments": "The Transfer Student Dimension of Articulation," in *College Transfer: Working Papers and Recommendations from the Airlie House Conference, December 2–4, 1973* (New York: Association Transfer Group, April 30, 1974), pp. 72–106.

2. The "articulation" problem continues to dominate most discussions of transfer. See for example Warren Willingham, "Transfer Standards and the Public Interest," in *College Transfer: Working Papers*, pp. 26–49. See also Edmund Gleazer and Roger Yarrington, eds., *Coordinating State Systems* (San Francisco: Jossey-Bass, 1974). They indicate that only one-half the states have articulation agreements because many senior-college faculty members do not believe community colleges provide "quality education."

3. Clyde Blocker, Robert Plummer, and Richard Richardson, for example, write:

It is in this technical training that the opportunity so manifestly exists for the two-year college to make its unique contribution. . . . In the future, requirements for technicians may increase geometrically as more and more highly skilled persons are graduated from the universities. No other agency of education is so well equipped as the two-year college to serve the function of legitimation with respect to technicians.

The Two Year College: A Social Synthesis (Englewood Cliffs, N.J.: Prentice-Hall, 1965), p. 4.

4. Dorothy Knoell and Leland Medsker, *From Junior to Senior College* (Washington, D.C.: American Council on Education, 1965), p. 61.

5. Ibid., p. 41; see also D. Knoell and L. Medsker, *Articulation Between Two-Year and Four-Year Colleges* (Berkeley: Center for the Study of Higher Education, 1964), p. 76.

6. Frederick Kintzer's *Middlemen In Higher Education* (San Francisco: Jossey-Bass, 1975) is the most recent and comprehensive treatment of the history of this developing flexibility: He shows how articulation, until very recently, has been a one-way situation, a series of policies and procedures dictated by senior institutions. Before 1960, for example, coordinated efforts to improve the plight of the transfer student were almost nonexistent. Up until 1955, acceptance of credits and courses were provisional; there were no guarantees: credits were transferable only on an individual review by registrars of four-year colleges. And only exactly parallel courses were considered (pp. 5, 12).

7. Ibid., p. 13.

8. Ibid.

9. Minutes of the April 3, 1973 meeting. See also "Report of the University Faculty Senate Task Force on the Educational Mission of the City University of New York," (New York: City

University Faculty Senate, 1974). Bruce Dearing puts the problem of the acceptability of transfer credits this way: "Most serious discussion is distorted by implicit suggestions that transfer students are somehow alien, immigrant, adopted, *nouveau riche*, converted, or Johnnies-come-lately whose claims and credentials are subordinate, inferior or suspect.": "Substantive Issues in the Transfer Problem," in *College Transfer: Working Papers*, p. 50.

10.   *College Transfer: Working Papers*, pp. 18, 25, 27. Others who feel that two-year colleges are doing quite well with regard to their transfer programs include Charles Monroe:

> Community colleges are meeting the goal of providing adequate transfer programs.

Profile of the Community College (San Francisco: Jossey-Bass, 1972), p. 63.

Arthur Cohen:

> Transfer students seem to be in an increasingly favorable position in the university and, insofar as transfer admissions is concerned, the junior college model is working very well.

A Constant Variable (San Francisco: Jossey-Bass, 1971), p. 70. And Warren Willingham and N. Findikyan:

> The junior college model is working very well with respect to transfer admissions. . . . There are good indications that the model can succeed in making higher education available to a much larger proportion of the population without simultaneously generating artificial administrative barriers.

"Transfer Students: Who's Moving from Where to Where, and What Determines Who's Admitted?" *College Board Review* 72 (Summer 1969): 11.

11. Blocker, Plummer, and Richardson, *The Two Year College*, p. 288.

12. Knoell and Medsker, *From Junior to Senior College*, footnote, pp. 3–4. A. J. Jaffe and W. Adams in a later study present evidence that although California boasts one of the highest rates of high-school graduation (80 percent) and college entrance (68 percent), it has the second lowest proportion of students going on to attain B.A.'s of the nation's nine census divisions: "In short, other parts of the nation, in which open enrollment was far less prevalent, provided four or more years of college to a larger proportion of the total college age group than did California.": "Two Models of Open Enrollment," in Logan Wilson, ed., *Universal Higher Education* (Washington, D.C.: American Council on Education, 1972), pp. 229 ff.

13. Actually, until recently there was little or no decline in transferred students' grades. Both Leonard Koos in 1924 and William Crosby Eells in 1931 found they did at least as well and sometimes better than native students: L. Koos, *The Junior College Movement* (Boston: Ginn and Co., 1924); W. C. Eells, *The Junior College* (Boston: Houghton Mifflin Co., 1931). Through the 1930s into the 1940s and even up to the middle 1950s, studies continued to show this pattern, including among terminal students who changed their minds and went on to senior colleges: D. D. Grossman, "Junior College Transfers at Illinois," *Junior College Journal* 4, (1934): 297–303; W. C. Eells, "Success of the Transferring Graduates of Junior College Terminal Curricula," *American Association of Collegiate Registrars Journal* 13 (1943): 372–98; J. P. Bogue, *The Community College* (New York: McGraw-Hill Book Co., 1950); C. H. Siemans, "Predicting Success of Junior College Transfers," *Junior College Journal* 13 (1943): 24–26; H. P. Rodes, "Successful Transfer in Engineering," *Junior College Journal* 19 (1949): 121–27; S. V. Martorama and L. L. Williams, "Academic Success of Junior College Transfers at the State College of Washington," *Junior College Journal* 24 (1954): 402–15; L. M. De Ridder, "Comparative Scholastic Achievement of Native and Transfer Students," *Junior College Journal* 21 (1951): 83. It wasn't until the mid 1960s that

Knoell, Tillery, Medsker, and others began to show that junior-college transfers were not doing all that well academically. This happens to correspond with the diversion of more and more students away from the four- to the two-year colleges: Dorothy Knoell, "Focus on the Transfer Program," *Junior College Journal* 35 (1965): 5; Dale Tillery, "Differential Characteristics of Entering Freshmen at the University of California and their Peers at California's Junior Colleges," (Ph.D. diss., University of California, Berkeley, 1964); John Hills, "Transfer Shock: The Academic Performance of the Junior College Transfer Student," *The Journal of Experimental Education* 33 (1965): 201–15.

14. The Panel on Financial-Need Analysis of the College Scholarship Service, in its review of the past fifteen years of financial aid practices, indicates that a good deal more than economic need affects the allocation of financial aid: "A cherished myth of educators and the general public is that student financial aid today is primarily based on relative need. However, when source and application of all aid funds (including the G.I. Bill, Social Security, athletic grants, and scholarships from restricted funds) are considered, the greater amount of student aid appears to be beyond institutional control and is *commonly awarded on the basis of criteria other than need.*" (my italics): *New Approaches to Student Financial Aid* (New York: College Entrance Examination Board, 1971), p. 9. This lack of correlation between need and award extends even to federally funded loan and work/study programs which *by law* require that awards be determined by a means test. Further, as usual, community college students *with equivalent financial needs* are frequently less than half as likely to receive aid as their public or private four-year college counterparts—yet another example of institutional commitment to failure: *Financial Aid for New York State Students* (Albany: New York State Education Department, March 1974), pp. 52–58.

15. Ruth Payne, "The Question of Financial Assistance at Mount Holyoke," *Mount Holyoke Alumnae Quarterly,* Spring 1973, p. 12.

16.   Knoell and Medsker, *From Junior to Senior College*, pp.
71–72. In addition, financial aid funds are not even available to
middle-income students. As *The New York Times* reported
recently, families beyond the $12,000 to $15,000 range are
almost entirely excluded from four of the five federally-funded
programs in which financial need is the sole criterion. The
only aid available is student loans, but parents are apparently
reluctant to permit their youngsters to apply because of the
detailed information on assets that must be divulged to the
college. As a result, the amount of money loaned is down 41
percent from the previous year: Gene Maeroff, "Middle-
Income Student Finds it Difficult to Get U.S. Aid," *New York
Times*, September 4, 1974, pp. 1, 24.

17.   In *The Hidden Injuries of Class* (New York: Alfred A.
Knopf, 1972), Jonathan Cobb and Richard Sennett have
written about how people from lower-class backgrounds learn
to deal better with failure than success: self-alienation from
one's own competence and power is a defense that wards off
the humiliation of failure.

18.   During the first three years of the transfer program at
S.I.C.C., 89 percent of the students who took the Transfer
Seminar went on to four-year colleges. Of these, over 90
percent have graduated or are continuing their pursuit of the
baccalaureate degree. Students who transferred to colleges
outside the City University system received an average of
more than $3,000 per year in scholarships and other forms of
financial aid. All of these figures are significantly higher than
the national averages: Elinor Azenberg, "Transfer Seminar
Report 1974–75," mimeographed, (Staten Island, N.Y.: Staten
Island Community College, July 1975).

19.   Willingham and Findikyan, "Transfer Students," p. 9.
They note that though 30 percent of all new freshmen
received financial aid, only 14 percent of transfers did. And
Willingham, in another report three years later, writes: "In a
selected sample of senior institutions only two in five report
that proportionately as many transfers as freshmen receive
financial aid." Obviously, things haven't changed very much
in the interim: *The No. 2 Access Problem*, p. 47.

20.   Kintzer, *Middlemen In Higher Education*, p. 103.

NOTES TO CHAPTER 10

1.   The City University of New York, for one, has been experimenting with what it calls a CUNY-BA degree. Admission to the program enables students, with a faculty committee's approval, to create courses for themselves that combine on- and off-campus work at *any* of the twenty individual units of the City University. At the completion of their work, students receive a degree awarded by the university itself and not from any of the separate colleges as is the policy if students complete all of their work at a single college.

The idea to present a single degree to all CUNY graduates was proposed by William Birenbaum to the central administration of CUNY in 1969 while they were considering various plans for the implementation of open admissions. He felt such a single degree would reduce the inequalities he saw to be inherent in the plans under consideration, including the one finally accepted and implemented. Birenbaum's proposal was eventually rejected and with the exception of the relatively small CUNY-BA program, individual colleges continue to offer their own distinct degrees.

2.   "Reflections of a Cosmic Apple Juice Drinker," in Norman Harris, ed., *Updating Occupational Education* (San Francisco: Jossey-Bass, 1974), p. 111.

3.   Patricia Cayo Sexton also deals with the question: What if "everyone" had a B.A.? See her provocative answers in "The *Inequality* Affair: A Critique of Jencks," *Social Policy*, September/October 1973, pp. 53–61.

4.   Quoted in Iver Peterson, "Cheap Public Colleges and Career Training in Demand," *New York Times*, April 17, 1975, p. 34. Additional evidence of increasing college enrollments comes from the Office of Education's projections for the 1975–76 academic year. According to their figures, enrollments in both public and private colleges will continue to increase. For example, they expect 7.1 million students to be enrolled in public colleges compared to 6.8 million for the

previous year: Iver Peterson, "Enrollments Drop as Costs Rise," *New York Times,* September 3, 1975, p. 33.

5. Iver Peterson, "Job Problems Stir Doubts About College," *New York Times,* June 6, 1975, pp. 1, 12. But by September, the *Times* headlined that these same "June Graduates Find More Jobs Than Expected": Seth King, *New York Times,* September 21, 1975, pp. 1, 39.

6. "The Reserve Army of the Underemployed: The Role of Education," *Change,* June 1975, pp. 26–33, 60–62.

7. "1,000 Apply for 90 Tutoring Jobs at Bronx College," *New York Times,* April 25, 1975, p. 39.

8. "1974–75 College Freshman Is Found More Conservative Politically," *New York Times,* January 16, 1975, p. 20. See also William Brazziel, *Quality Education for All Americans* (Washington, D.C.: Howard University Press, 1974).

9. Quoted in Iver Peterson, "Job Problems," p. 12.

10. Murray Bookchin, *Post-Scarcity Anarchism* (San Francisco: Ramparts Press, 1971).

11. There is more than irony in Patricia Sexton's perception that although schools are often considered to be essential to instructing the young in how to participate in our democracy's institutions, and although in a democracy people are supposed to serve as their own authority (an essential element of intellectual freedom is the questioning of all authority), in spite of this, in our hierarchically structured schools students are denied any genuine authority in the conduct of this institution which so powerfully governs their young lives and shapes their adult future: *The American School: A Sociological Analysis* (Englewood Cliffs, N.J.: Prentice-Hall, 1967), p. 68. See also Miriam Wasserman, *The School Fix, N.Y.C., U.S.A.* (New York: Outerbridge & Dienstfrey, 1970).

For more on the schools' role in teaching participation in democracy, see Rush Welter, *Popular Education and Democratic Thought in America* (New York: Columbia University Press, 1962).

12. See also Stanley Aronowitz, "The Trap of Environmentalism," *Social Policy*, September/October 1972, pp. 34–38.

13. *Deschooling Society* (New York: Harper & Row, 1970), p. 40.

14. *Social Mobility in Industrial Society* (Berkeley: University of California Press, 1959).

15. *The American Occupational Structure* (New York: John Wiley & Sons, 1967), p. 437.

16. Ibid., p. 440.

17. For more on how schools ritualize our ideology, see Everett Reimer, *School Is Dead: An Essay on Alternatives in Education* (Harmondsworth, England: Penguin Books, 1971), pp. 45 ff.

18. Leo Munday and Nancy Cole, "Evaluation and the New Colleges: Assessment for Student Development," in Paul Dressel, ed., *The New Colleges: Toward An Appraisal* (Iowa City: The American College Testing Program, 1971), pp. 301–07.

19. "The Problems of Evaluation," in Dressel, ed., *The New Colleges*, pp. 1–24.

20. See Gary MacDonald, ed., *Five Experimental Colleges* (New York: Harper-Colophon, 1973). On the limitations of revolutionary love as a tool for social change see Steven Bhaerman and Joel Denker, *No Particular Place to Go: The Making of a Free High School* (New York: Simon and Schuster, 1972).

21. Philip Werdell, "Futurism and the Reform of Higher Education," in Alvin Toffler, ed., *Learning for Tomorrow: The Role of the Future in Education* (New York: Vintage Books, 1974), pp. 272–311.

22. Robert Reinhold, "At Brown, Trend Is Back to Grades and Tradition," *New York Times*, February 24, 1974, pp. 1, 47. There are of course challenges to the idea that the movement is all back to grades and tradition. Recently, a thousand

students occupied the administration building at the State University of New York at New Paltz protesting, in part, the "trend back to more traditional methods": "New Paltz Students Stage Office Sit-In to Protest Policies," *New York Times*, March 27, 1974, p. 45.

23. Ann Heiss, *An Inventory of Academic Innovation and Reform* (New York: McGraw-Hill Book Co., 1973).

24. Ibid., p. 25.

25. Ibid., p. 15. For other examples of the machine orientation of innovative two-year-college programs see B. Lamar Johnson, *Islands of Innovation Expanding: Changes in the Community College* (Beverly Hills, Cal.: Glencoe Press, 1969).

26. At ghetto two-year colleges, experimentation is often even less than second best. Barry Castro reveals how the misplaced learning assumptions of administrators and faculty at innovative Hostos Community College led to chaos and third-rate results: "Hostos: Report from a Ghetto College," *Harvard Educational Review*, May 1974, pp. 270–94.

27. Carnegie Commission on Higher Education, *Toward a Learning Society: Alternative Channels to Life, Work, and Service* (New York: McGraw-Hill Book Co., 1973).

28. *The Junior College: Progress and Prospect* (New York: McGraw-Hill Book Co., 1960).

29. *1968 Master Plan of the Board of Higher Education for the City University of New York*, draft, (New York: Board of Higher Education, 1968, pp. 16–18.

30. In other places I've indicated how the very fact of going to a community college reduces a student's chance for academic success. A recent report from the City University of New York reveals how students of *equivalent ability* (equal high-school averages) do worse at community than at four-year colleges; the reverse of what one might expect since two-year colleges purport to specialize in teaching and counseling: David Lavin and Richard Silberstein, "Student Retention Under Open Admissions at the City University of New

York: September 1970 Enrollees Followed Through Four Semesters" (New York: Office of Program and Policy Research, City University of New York, February 1974).

31. Michael Brick, *Forum and Focus for the Community College Movement* (New York: Teachers College Press, 1963), pp. 78 ff. The most fervent advocate of the 6-4-4 plan was Leonard Koos. His *Junior College Movement* (Boston: Ginn and Co., 1925) in a sense is a lengthy essay in its behalf.

32. The third part of Eells's *Junior College* (Boston: Houghton Mifflin Co., 1931) is virtually an assault on the 6-4-4 concept as well as an attempt to point out the dangers reality poses for theory.

33. Stephen Reichert, Jr., "The End of the Four-Year Junior College in California," in W. K. Ogilvie and M. R. Raines, eds., *Perspectives On the Community-Junior College* (New York: Appleton-Century-Crofts, 1971), pp. 110–15.

34. Harold Hodgkinson, *Institutions in Transition: A Profile of Change in Higher Education* (New York: McGraw-Hill Book Co., 1971). It is often argued that two-year colleges are particularly important for people who cannot, for one reason or another, reside at a four-year college. This assumes that senior colleges cannot or do not meet the needs of commuters. This assumption is untrue: Most college students, four- as well as two-year, do not live on campus. In addition, even residential students as long ago as 1961, on the average, went to college rather close to home; seniors, for example, within four hours driving distance of their homes. And this distance has been shrinking ever since as the result of the expansion of state university systems: James Davis, *Great Aspirations: The Graduate School Plans of America's College Seniors* (Chicago: Aldine-Atherton, 1964), p. 2.

There's a cruel irony involved in encouraging the expansion of two-year *commuter* colleges. Much evidence suggests that living at college, in and of itself, significantly contributes to students' chances of persisting at school and doing well academically. Commuting and dropping out appear to be directly correlated: Arthur Chickering, *Commuting Versus Resident Students: Overcoming the Educational Inequalities of Living Off Campus* (San Francisco: Jossey-Bass, 1974). See also Alexander Astin, *Preventing Students From Dropping Out* (San Francisco: Jossey-Bass, 1975), pp. 164–65.

35. Hodgkinson, *Institutions in Transition*, pp. 204–05.

36. See Frederick W. Taylor, "The Principles of Scientific Management" (1911) and "Shop Mnagement" (1903), both included in his *Scientific Management* (New York: Harper & Row, 1947).

37. London: Allen & Unwin, 1943.

38. See chapter 5 herein.

39. *Motivation and Personality* (New York: Harper & Row, 1970), p. xv.

40. Ibid., p. 37.

41. For examples of worker discontent and worker revolts see *Work in America* (Washington, D.C.: U.S. Department of Health, Education, and Welfare, 1973).

42. *Participation and Democratic Theory* (London: Cambridge University Press, 1970), p. 105.

43. *Job Power: Blue and White Collar Democracy* (Garden City, N.Y.: Doubleday & Co., 1973). See also Thomas Gordon, "Group-Centered Leadership and Administration," in Carl Rogers, ed., *Client-Centered Therapy* (Boston: Houghton Mifflin Co., 1951), pp. 320–83.

44. "What Future Spaceship Earth?" *Social Policy*, November/December, 1973, pp. 17–21. In *More Equality* (New York: Pantheon Books, 1973), Herbert Gans argues that although there has not been an increase in economic equality during most of this century, various social and cultural movements (students, women, blue-collar workers) have created changes in values that may very well lead to more equality—without violence and without sacrificing our sense of either individualism or liberty.

45. The academic benefits of cooperation as compared with competition are discussed in James Coleman, "Academic

Achievement and the Structure of Competition," *Harvard Educational Review*, Fall 1959, 330–51; and in Morton Deutsch, "The Effects of Cooperation and Competition Upon Group Process," in D. Cartwright and A. Zander, eds., *Group Dynamics* (Evanston, Ill.: Row Peterson, 1953), pp. 319–53.

46. For more on this see Frank Ricssman and Alan Gartner, "The New Hereditarians," *Change*, February 1974, pp. 56–59. See also Talcott Parsons, "The Problem of Controlled Institutional Change," in T. Parsons, *Essays in Sociological Theory* (New York: Free Press, 1954), pp. 238–74.

47. For evidence that homeostasis is different from a theory of rest or equilibrium see Charlotte Buhler, "Maturation and Motivation," *Dialectica* 5 (1951): 312–61. Theories of rest call simply for the removal of tension and assume that zero tension is best. Homeostasis means coming to an optimum, not zero, level: sometimes this means reducing tension; sometimes it means increasing it.

For some examples of both successes and failures of this homeostatic method of educational reform see Jerry Gaff and associates, *The Cluster College* (San Francisco: Jossey-Bass, 1970). For other evidence that the decentralized cluster-college approach improves the collegiate learning environment see *The Study Commission Newsletter* (Lincoln: University of Nebraska, June 1973), p. 1. And on the educational value of smallness, see Jonathan Gallant and John Prothero, "Weight Watching at the University," *Science*, January 1972, pp. 381–88. Finally, for some insight into the value of such disruption for institutional change, but in a different context, see Eli Glogow, "The 'Bad Patient' Gets Better Quicker," *Social Policy*, November/December 1973, pp. 72–76.

NOTES TO THE APPENDIX

1. See for example Alexis Lange, "The Junior College— What Manner of Child Shall This Be?" *School and Society* 7 (1918): 211–18.

2. *Profile of the Community College* (San Francisco: Jossey-Bass, 1972), p. 37.

3. New York: McGraw-Hill Book Co., 1960.

4. Ibid., p. 51.

5. Ibid., p. 114.

6. D. Bushnell, *Organizing for Change: New Priorities for Community Colleges* (New York: McGraw-Hill Book Co., 1973).

7. Edmund Gleazer, Jr., *Project Focus: A Forecast Study of Community Colleges* (New York: McGraw-Hill Book Co., 1973).

8. Bushnell, *Organizing for Change*, p. 45.

9. Gleazer, *Project Focus*, p. 88.

10. Ibid., p. 107.

11. For other examples of official reform-without-reform proposals see Joseph Cosand, "The Community College in 1980" in Alvin Eurich, ed., *Campus 1980: The Shape of the Future in American Higher Education* (New York: Delta Books, 1968), pp. 134–48; and Marvin Feldman, "Opting for Career Education: Emergence of the Community College," in Roman Pucinski and Sharlene Hirsch, eds., *The Courage to Change: New Directions for Career Education* (Englewood Cliffs, N.J.: Prentice-Hall, 1971), pp. 109–20.

12. San Francisco: Jossey-Bass, 1970.

13. Ibid., pp. 174, 181 ff.

14. San Francisco: Jossey-Bass, 1971. For another view of Cohen's work, see left-official critic Frank Jennings, "The Two-Year Stretch: Junior Colleges in America," *Change*, March/April 1970, pp. 15–25.

15. Washington, D.C.: U.S. Government Printing Office, 1971.

16. Ibid., p. vii.

17. Ibid., p. 17.

18. Ibid., p. 57.

19. Garden City, N.Y.: Doubleday & Co., 1968.

20. Ibid., pp. 485–86.

21. New York: Herder and Herder, 1970, p. 313. This echoes the kind of thing one hears from official critics such as B. Lamar Johnson. For example: "The junior college seems to me to offer the best chance to stimulate genuinely fresh investigations, and then to do something about the answers. Free of the rigid traditions which tie most schools and colleges to their administration and instructional arrangements, junior colleges can tinker with all sorts of new ideas and put them to work in their classrooms.": "Encouraging Innovation In Teaching," *Junior College Journal* 38 (March 1968): 34.

22. "The More We Change the Worse We Get," *Social Policy*, May/June 1971, p. 10.

23. New York: Delacorte Press, 1969, pp. 159–60.

24. Ibid., p. 34.

25. *Change*, September 1972, pp. 30–35.

26. *Harvard Educational Review* 42 (November 1972): 521–62.

27. Ibid., pp. 540–41. On this, see also D. M. Anthony, "The Relationship of Certain Socioeconomic Factors to Student Choice of Occupation and Programs in the Public Junior College," (Ph.D. diss., University of Texas, 1964); and Robert Fenske, "Who Selects Vocational-Technical Post-High School Education?" in *The Two-Year College and Its Students: An Empirical Report* (Iowa City: The American College Testing Program, 1969), pp. 89–99.

BIBLIOGRAPHY

Adams, Walter, and Jaffe, A. J. "Economic Returns on the College Investment," *Change*, November 1971, pp. 8–9, 60.

Agnew, Spiro. "Address to the Convention of the American Association of School Administrators," Washington, D.C., February 16, 1972.

————. "Toward a 'Middle Way' in College Admissions." *Educational Record*, Spring 1970, pp. 106–11.

"Ancient History." *The Junior College Journal* 1 (May 1931): 503–4.

"Ancient History." *The Junior College Journal* 6 (December 1935):143.

Angell, James. "The Junior College Movement in High Schools." *The School Review* 23 (1915): 289–302.

Anthony, D. M. "The Relationship of Certain Socioeconomic and Academic Factors to Student Choice of Occupation and Program in the Public Junior College." Ph.D. dissertation, University of Texas, 1964.

Aronowitz, Stanley. "The Trap of Environmentalism," *Social Policy*, September/October 1972, pp. 34–38.

Astin, Alexander. *College Dropouts: A National Profile*. American Council on Education Research Reports, vol. 7, no. 1. Washington, D.C.: American Council on Education, 1972

————. *Predicting Academic Performance in College*. New York: Free Press, 1971.

————. *Preventing Students From Dropping Out*. San Francisco: Jossey-Bass, 1975.

————, et al. *The American Freshmen: National Norms for Fall 1973*. American Council on Education, U.C.L.A., n.d.

————, and Rossman, J. E. "The Case for Open Admissions: A Status Report." *Change*, Summer 1973, pp. 35–37.

Averch, Harvey, et al. *How Effective Is Schooling? A Critical Review and Synthesis of Research and Findings*. Santa Monica, Cal.: Rand Corporation, 1972.

Axelrod, Joseph; Freedman, M.; Hatch, W.; Katz, J.; and Sanford, N. *Search for Relevance*. San Francisco: Jossey-Bass, 1969.

Azenberg, Elinor. "Transfer Seminar Report 1974–75." Mimeographed. New York: Staten Island Community College, July 1975.

Baird, Leonard. "Cooling Out and Warming Up in the Junior College." *Measurement and Evaluation in Guidance* 4 (October 1971): 160–71.

——. "Patterns of Educational Aspirations." *American College Testing Research Report* 32. Iowa City, December 1969.

Ballard, Allen. *The Education of Black Folk: The Afro-American Struggle for Knowledge in White America.* New York: Harper & Row, 1973.

Barlow, M. *A Survey of Junior College Work Experience Education Programs.* Los Angeles: Division of Vocational Education, U.C.L.A., 1963.

Beardslee, David, and O'Dowd, D. "Students and the Occupational World." In *The American College,* edited by Nevitt Sanford, pp. 597–626, New York: John Wiley & Sons, 1962.

Benoit, Emile. "What Future Spaceship Earth?" *Social Policy,* November/December 1973, pp. 17–21.

Berg, Ivar. *Education and Training: The Great Training Robbery.* New York: Praeger Publishers, 1970.

Berger, Peter; Berger, B.; and Kellner, H. *The Homeless Mind: Modernization and Consciousness.* New York: Random House, 1973.

Bhaerman, Steve, and Denker, Joel. *No Particular Place to Go: The Making of a Free High School.* New York: Simon and Schuster, 1972.

Birenbaum, William. *Overlive: Power, Poverty and the University.* New York: Delacorte Press, 1969.

——. "The More We Change the Worse We Get. *Social Policy,* May/June 1971, pp. 10–13.

Birnbaum, Norman. "The Politics of the Future." *Change,* November 1973, pp. 28–37.

Blank, Arthur, et al. *The Graduates Restudied: A Comparison of the Follow-Up of New York City High School Graduates of 1970 and 1971.* New York: City University of New York, Center for Social Research, the Graduate School and University Center, September 1972.

Blau, Peter, and Duncan, O. *The American Occupational Structure.* New York: John Wiley & Sons, 1967.

Blaug, Mark. *An Introduction to the Economics of Education.* Harmondsworth, England: Penguin Books, 1970.

Blocker, Clyde; Plummer, R.; and Richardson, R. *The Two-Year Colleges: A Social Synthesis.* Englewood Cliffs, N.J.: Prentice-Hall, 1965.

Bloom, Benjamin; Davis, A.; and Hess, R. *Compensatory Education for Cultural Deprivation.* New York: Holt, Rinehart and Winston, 1965.

Bogue, Jesse Parker. *The Community College.* New York: McGraw-Hill Book Co., 1950.

Bookchin, Murray. *Post Scarcity Anarchism.* San Francisco: Ramparts Press, 1971.

Boutwell, George. *Twenty-First Annual Report of the Massachusetts Board of Education,* Boston, 1859.

Bowen, Howard. *Who Benefits from Higher Education and Who Should Pay?* Washington, D.C.: American Association for Higher Education, 1972.

Bowles, Samuel. "Cuban Education and the Revolutionary Ideology." In *Schooling In A Corporate Society,* edited by Martin Carnoy, pp. 272–303. New York: David McKay Co., 1972.

————. "Schooling and Inequality from Generation to Generation." In *Investment in Education: The Equity-Efficiency Quandary,* edited by T. Schultz, pp. 219–51. Chicago: University of Chicago Press, 1972.

————. "The Integration of Higher Education Into the Wage System." Mimeographed. Harvard University and the University of Massachusetts, 1972.

————, and Gintis, Herbert. "I.Q. and the U.S. Class Structure." *Social Policy,* November/December 1972—January/February 1973, pp. 65–96.

Brazziel, William. *Quality Education for All Americans.* Washington, D.C.: Howard University Press, 1974.

Brick, Michael. *Forum and Focus for the Junior College Movement: The American Association of Junior Colleges.* New York: Teachers College Press, 1963.

Brozan, Nadine. "Widening Gap in Views Is Registered Between College and Noncollege Women." *New York Times,* May 22, 1974, p. 45.

Brubacher, John, and Rudy, W. *Higher Education In Transition: A History of American Colleges and Universities, 1636–1968.* New York: Harper & Row, 1968.

Brue, E. J.; Engen, H. B.; and Maxey, E. J. "How Do Community College Transfer and Occupational Students Differ?" *American College Testing Program Report 41,* Iowa City, 1971.

Brunner, Ken August. "Historical Developments of the Junior College Philosophy." *Junior College Journal* 40 (April 1970): 30–34.

————. "The Training of Subprofessional Personnel in the United States." Mimeographed. International Conference on Middle Level Manpower, San Juan, Puerto Rico, October 10–12, 1962.

Buhler, Charlotte. "Maturation and Motivation." *Dialectica* 5 (1951): 312–61.

Bureau of the Census. "Men With College Degrees: March 1967." *Current Population Reports,* 1967, pp. 46–60.

————. *The American Almanac.* New York: Grosset & Dunlap, 1971.

Bushnell, David. *Organizing for Change: New Priorities for Community Colleges.* New York: McGraw-Hill Book Co., 1973.
——, and Kievit, M. B. "Community Colleges: What is Our Job?" *Change,* April 1974, pp. 52–53.
Butts, R. Freeman. *The Education of the West: A Formative Chapter in the History of Civilization.* New York: McGraw-Hill Book Co., 1973.
California Student Resources Survey, 1972. Sacramento: California State Scholarship and Loan Commission, 1972.
Campbell, Doak. "Effects of the Depression," *Junior College Journal* 3 (April 1933): 381–82.
Carnegie Commission on Higher Education. *Higher Education: Who Pays? Who Benefits? Who Should Pay?* New York: McGraw-Hill Book Co., 1973.
——. *The Open-Door Colleges: Policies for Community Colleges.* New York: McGraw-Hill Book Co., 1970.
——. *Toward a Learning Society: Alternative Channels to Life, Work, and Service.* New York: McGraw-Hill Book Co., 1973.
——. *Tuition.* New York: McGraw-Hill Book Co., 1974.
Carnegie Foundation for the Advancement of Teaching. *More Than Survival: Prospects for Higher Education In A Period of Uncertainty.* San Francisco: Jossey-Bass, 1975.
Carnoy, Martin. Introduction to *Schooling in a Corporate Society: The Political Economy of Education in America,* edited by M. Carnoy. New York: David McKay Co., 1972.
Carter, C. F. "Cost and Benefits of Mass Higher Education." Mimeographed. Lancaster, England: University of Lancaster, 1972.
Castro, Barry. "Hostos: Report from a Ghetto College." *Harvard Educational Review,* May 1974, pp. 270–94.
Chalghian, Sara. "Success for Marginal Students." *Junior College Journal* 39 (1969): 28–30.
Chickering, Arthur. *Commuting Versus Resident Students: Overcoming the Educational Inequalities of Living Off Campus.* San Francisco: Jossey-Bass, 1974.
——. *Education and Identity.* San Francisco: Jossey-Bass, 1969.
Cicourel, Aaron, and Kitsuse, John. *The Educational Decision-Makers.* Boston: Bobbs-Merrill Co., 1963.
Clark, Burton. "The 'Cooling-Out' Function in Higher Education." *American Journal of Sociology* 65 (1960): 569–76.
——. *The Open Door College.* New York: McGraw-Hill Book Co., 1960.
Clarke, J. R. "A Curriculum Designed for Disadvantaged Community Junior College Students." Ph.D. dissertation, University of Florida, 1966.

Cobb, Jonathan, and Sennett, Richard. *The Hidden Injuries of Class*. New York: Alfred A. Knopf, 1972.

Cohen, Arthur M. *Dateline '79: Heretical Concepts for the Community College*. Beverly Hills: Glencoe Press, 1969.

————, and associates. *A Constant Variable*. San Francisco: Jossey-Bass, 1971.

————, and Brawer, Florence. "The Community College in Search of Identity." *Change*, Winter 1971–72, pp. 55–59.

————. *Student Characteristics: Personality and Dropout Propensity*. Washington, D.C.: American Association of Junior Colleges, 1970.

Cohen, David, and Lazerson, M. "Education and the Corporate Order." *Socialist Revolution* 2 (May/June 1971): 14–46.

Coleman, James. "Academic Achievement and the Structure of Competition." *Socialization and Schools*, Reprint Series no. 1, *Harvard Educational Review*, 1968, pp. 1–22.

————, et al. *Equality of Educational Opportunity*. Washington, D.C.: U.S. Government Printing Office, 1966.

Collins, Charles. *Junior College Student Personnel Programs: What They Are and What They Should Be*. Washington, D.C.: American Association of Junior Colleges, 1967.

Collins, R. "Functional and Conflict Theories of Educational Stratification." In *Education: Structure and Society*, edited by B. R. Cosin, pp. 175–99. Harmondsworth, England: Penguin Books, 1972.

Colvert, C. C. "Terminal Education and the National Defense." *Junior College Journal* 11 (May 1941): 16–19.

Committee on the Student in Higher Education. *The Student in Higher Education*. New Haven, Conn.: The Hazen Foundation, 1968.

"Community College Vocational Cooperative Education." Costa Mesa, Cal.: Coast Community College District, September 1973.

Conant, James B. *The Citadel of Learning*. New Haven: Yale University Press, 1956.

————. "The Community College." In *Perspectives on the Community-Junior College*, edited by William Ogilvie and Max Raines, pp. 36–42. New York: Appleton-Century-Crofts, 1950.

Cook, Joseph; Hoss, Marvin; and Vargas, Robert. *The Search for Independence*. Belmont, Cal.: Brooks/Cole Publishing Co., 1968.

Cooley, William, and Becker, Susan. "The Junior College Student." *Personnel and Guidance Journal* 44 (January 1966): 464–69.

Corcoran, Thomas. "Community Colleges: The Coming Slums of Higher Education." *Change*, September 1972, pp. 30–35.

Cosand, Joseph. "The Community College in 1980." In *Campus 1980: The Shape of the Future in American Higher Education.* edited by Alvin Eurich, pp. 134–48. New York: Delta Books, 1968.

Cottle, Thomas. "What Tracking Did to Ollie Taylor," *Social Policy,* July/August 1974, pp. 21–24.

Cross, K. Patricia. "Higher Education's Newest Student." In *Student Development Programs in the Community Junior College,* edited by Terry O'Banion and Alice Thurston, pp. 26–35. Englewood Cliffs, N.J.: Prentice Hall, 1972.

———. *Beyond The Open Door: New Students to Higher Education.* San Francisco: Jossey-Bass, 1971.

———. *The Junior College Student: A Research Description.* Princeton, N.J.: Educational Testing Service, 1968.

Davis, James. *Great Expectations: The Graduate School Plans of America's College Seniors.* Chicago: Aldine Publishing Co., 1964.

———. *Undergraduate Career Decisions: Correlates of Occupational Choice.* Chicago: Aldine Publishing Co., 1965.

Dawson, J. D. *New Directions for Cooperative Education.* New York: National Commission for Cooperative Education, April 1971.

Dearing, Bruce. "Substantive Issues in the Transfer Problem." In *College Transfer: Working Papers and Recommendations from the Airlie House Conference, December 2–4, 1973,* pp. 50–71. New York: Association Transfer Group, April 30, 1974.

DeRidder, L. M. "Comparative Scholastic Achievement of Native and Transfer Students." *Junior College Journal* 21 (1951): 83.

Deutsch, Monroe; Douglass, Aubrey; and Strayer, George. *A Report of the Survey of the Needs of California in Higher Education.* Berkeley: University of California Press, 1948.

Deutsch, Morton. "The Effects of Cooperation and Competition Upon Group Process." In *Group Dynamics,* edited by D. Cartwright and A. Zander. Evanston, Ill.: Row Peterson, 1953.

Dreeben, Robert. "The Contribution of Schooling to the Learning of Norms." *Harvard Educational Review,* Spring 1967, pp. 211–37.

———. *On What Is Learned in School.* Reading, Mass.: Addison-Wesley, 1968.

Dressel, Paul. "The Problems of Evaluation." In *The New Colleges: Toward an Appraisal,* edited by P. Dressel, pp. 1–24. Iowa City: The American College Testing Program, 1971.

Eckaus, Richard. *Estimating the Returns to Education.* Berkeley: Carnegie Commission on Higher Education, 1973.

Eckland, Bruce. "Social Class and College Graduation: Some Misconceptions Corrected." *American Journal of Sociology,* July 1964, pp. 36–50.

Eddy, Edward Danforth. *College for Our Land and Time: The Land-Grant Idea in American Education.* New York: Harper & Row, 1957.

Education Beyond High School: The Regents Statewide Plan for the Development of Post Secondary Education. New York: The State Education Department, 1972.

Eells, William Crosby. "Executive Secretary's Report." *Junior College Journal* 11 (May 1941): 503.

————. "Success of Transferring Graduates of Junior College Terminal Curricula." *American Association of Collegiate Registrars Journal,* 1943, pp. 372–98.

————. *The Junior College.* Boston: Houghton Mifflin Co., 1931.

————. *Why Junior College Terminal Education?* Monograph no. 3. Washington, D.C.: American Association of Junior Colleges, 1941.

El-Khawas, Elaine, and Bisconti, A. *Five and Ten Years After College Entry: 1971 Followup of 1961 and 1966 College Freshmen.* Research Report vol. 9, no. 1. Washington, D.C.: American Council on Education, 1974.

Erickson, Frederick. "Gatekeeping and the Melting Pot: Interaction in Counseling Encounters." *Harvard Educational Review,* February 1975, pp. 44–70.

Erikson, Erik. *Childhood and Society.* New York: W. W. Norton & Co., 1958.

————. *Young Man Luther.* New York: W. W. Norton & Co., 1958.

Eskow, Seymour, "The Uneasy Adolescence of Our Junior Colleges." *Change,* January/February 1969, pp. 44–47.

Eurich, Alvin. "Higher Education in the 21st Century." In *Campus in the Modern World,* edited by John Margolis, pp. 101–12. New York: MacMillan Co., 1969.

Fallows, Marjorie. "Goodbye Pygmalion." *Change,* March 1975, pp. 52–53.

Feldman, Kenneth, and Newcomb, T. *The Impact of College on Students.* San Francisco: Jossey-Bass, 1973.

Feldman, Marvin. "Opting for Career Education: Emergence of the Community College." In *The Courage to Change: New Directions for Career Education,* edited by Roman Pucinski and Sharlene Hirsch, pp. 109–20. Englewood Cliffs, N.J.: Prentice Hall, 1971.

Felty, John. *A Feasibility and Planning Study for an Experimental Two-Year Community College for Rural and Urban Youth.* Washington, D.C.: Office of Education, 1969.

Fenske, Robert. "Who Selects Vocational-Technical Post-High

School Education?" In *The Two Year College and Its Students: An Empirical Report*, pp. 88–99. Iowa City: American College Testing Program, 1969.

Fields, Ralph. *The Community College Movement*. New York: McGraw-Hill Book Co., 1962.

Financial Aid for New York State Students. Albany: New York State Education Department, 1974.

Fiske, Edward. "Education Uncertainty." *New York Times*, April 18, 1975, p. 36.

Fitch, Robert. "An Investigation of the 'Cooling Out' Process in the Junior College as Indicated by Changes of Major." Seminar paper, E.R.I.C. no. ED 039 868, U.C.L.A. Graduate School of Education, 1969.

Five Years of Progress: Florida's Community Junior Colleges. A Report to the State Board of Education by the State Junior College Advisory Board. Tallahassee: Florida State Department of Education, 1963.

Folger, John; Astin, H.; and Bayer, A. *Human Resources and Higher Education*. New York: Russell Sage Foundation, 1970.

Freedman, Mervin. *Impact of College. New Dimensions in Higher Education*, no. 4, edited by Winslow Hatch. Washington, D.C.: U.S. Government Printing Office, 1960.

Freeman, Richard, and Holloman, J. H. "The Declining Value of College Going." *Change*, September 1975, pp. 24–31, 62.

Fretwell, Elbert. *Founding Public Junior Colleges: Initiative in Six Communities*. New York: Teachers College Press, 1954.

Gaff, Jerry, and associates. *The Cluster College*. San Francisco: Jossey-Bass, 1970.

Gallant, Jonathan, and Prothero, J. "Weight Watching at the University." *Science*, January 1972, pp. 381–88.

Gans, Herbert. *More Equality*. New York: Pantheon Books, 1973.

———. *The Urban Villagers*. New York: Free Press, 1962.

Gardner, John. *Excellence: Can We Be Equal and Excellent Too?* New York: Harper & Row, 1961.

———. "National Goals in Education." In *Goals for Americans: The Report of the President's Commission on National Goals and Chapters Submitted for the Consideration of the Commission*. New York: Spectrum Books, 1960.

———. "Quality in Higher Education." In *Current Issues in Higher Education—1958*, pp. 8–13. Washington, D.C.: Association for Higher Education, September 1958.

Ginzberg, Eli. "Education and National Efficiency in the U.S.A." In *Education, Economy, and Society*, edited by A. H. Halsey, Jean

Floud, and C. A. Anderson, pp. 68–79. New York: Free Press, 1965.

———, et al. *Occupational Choice: An Approach to a General Theory.* New York: Columbia University Press, 1951.

Gittell, Marilyn. "Education and Equality: Social Darwinism Revisited." In *What Nixon is Doing to Us*, edited by A. Gartner, C. Greer, and F. Reissman. New York: Harrow Books, 1973.

Gleazer, Edmund. *Project Focus: A Forecast Study of Community Colleges.* New York: McGraw-Hill Book Co., 1973.

———. *This Is the Community College.* Boston: Houghton Mifflin Co., 1968.

———. "Analysis of Junior College Growth." *Junior College Directory.* Washington, D.C.: American Association of Junior Colleges, 1961.

———, and Yarrington, Roger, eds. *Coordinating State Systems.* San Francisco: Jossey-Bass, 1974.

Glogow, Eli. "The 'Bad Patient' Gets Better Quicker." *Social Policy*, November/December 1973, pp. 72–76.

Goffman, Erving. "On Cooling the Mark Out: Some Aspects of Adaption to Failure." *Psychiatry*, November 1952, pp. 45–63.

Goldberg, L., and Dailey, J. T. "Research on Academic Degree Projections: The Identification and Development of Talents of 1960 High School Graduates." Unpublished manuscript. Palo Alto: Project TALENT, 1963.

Goodwin, Gregory. *A Social Panacea: A History of the Community Junior College Ideology.* E.R.I.C. no. ED 093 427, September 1973.

Gordon, Thomas. "Group-Centered Leadership and Administration." In *Client-Centered Therapy*, edited by Carl Rogers, pp. 320–83. Boston: Houghton Mifflin Co., 1951.

Gray, A. A. "The Junior College in California." *School Review* 23 (1915): 465–73.

Greer, Colin. *The Great School Legend: A Revisionist Interpretation of American Public Education.* New York: Basic Books, 1972.

Gross, Alan. "Communiversity—A New Approach." E.R.I.C. no. ED 100 471, 1974.

Grossman, D. D. "Junior College Transfers at Illinois." *Junior College Journal* 4 (1934): 297–303.

Gurin, David. "Impact During College." In *A Degree and What Else?*, edited by E. Withey. New York: Dryden Press, 1943.

Halsey, A. H. "British Universities and Intellectual Life." In *Education, Economy, and Society*, edited by A. H. Halsey, Jean Floud, and C. A. Anderson, pp. 502–12. New York: Free Press, 1965.

————. "The Changing Functions of Universities in Advanced Industrial Societies." *Harvard Educational Review,* Spring 1960, pp. 119–27.

Hamilton, Richard. *Class and Politics in the United States.* New York: John Wiley & Sons, 1972.

Hansen, W. Lee, and Weisbrod, B. *Benefits, Costs, and Finance of Public Higher Education.* Chicago: Markham Publishing Co., 1969.

————, and Witmer, D. R. "Economic Benefits of Universal Higher Education." In *Universal Higher Education,* edited by Logan Wilson and Olive Mills, pp. 19–39. Washington, D.C.: American Council on Education, 1972.

Harper, William Rainey. "President's Annual Report, University of Chicago, July 1902," *Decennial Publications of the University of Chicago,* vol. 1. Chicago: University of Chicago Press, 1902.

————. "The High School of the Future." *School Review* 11 (1903): 1–3.

————. "The Small College: Its Prospects." *Journal of Proceedings and Addresses,* National Education Association, 39th Annual Meeting, July 7–13, 1900, pp. 74–80.

————. *The Trend in Higher Education.* Chicago: University of Chicago Press, 1905.

Harris, Norman. "Major Issues in Junior College Technical Education." *The Educational Record,* Spring 1964, pp. 128–38.

————. "Reflections of a Cosmic Apple Juice Drinker." In *Updating Occupational Education,* edited by N. Harris, pp. 105–13. San Francisco: Jossey-Bass, 1974.

Harrison, Roger. "Classroom Innovation: A Design Primer." In *The Changing College Classroom,* edited by Philip Runkel, Roger Harrison, and Margaret Runkel, pp. 302–40. San Francisco: Jossey-Bass, 1969.

Hartman, Robert. "A Comment on the Pechman-Hansen-Weisbrod Controversy." *Journal of Human Resources,* Fall 1970, p. 521.

Hausman, Louis. "Pressures, Benefits, and Options." In *Universal Higher Education,* edited by Logan Wilson and Olive Mills, pp. 1–15. Washington, D.C.: American Council on Education, 1972.

Hayes, G. *Junior College Work Experience Education.* Los Angeles: E.R.I.C. Clearinghouse for Junior Colleges, 1969.

Healy, Timothy. "The Case for Open Admissions: New Problems— New Hopes." *Change,* Summer 1973, pp. 24–29.

Hechinger, Fred. "Class War Over Tuition." *New York Times,* February 5, 1974.

Heerman, Barry. *Cooperative Education in Community Colleges: A*

Sourcebook for Occupational and General Educators. San Francisco: Jossey-Bass, 1973.

Heiss, Ann. *An Inventory of Academic Innovation and Reform.* New York: McGraw-Hill Book Co., 1973.

Heist, Paul, and Yonge, G. *Omnibus Personality Inventory: Manual.* New York: The Psychological Corporation, 1968.

Henry, Jules. *Culture Against Man.* New York: Vintage Books, 1965.

Higher Education for American Democracy, 6 vols. New York: Harper and Brothers, 1947–48.

Hills, John. "Transfer Shock: The Academic Performance of the Junior College Transfer Student." *The Journal of Experimental Education,* 1965, pp. 201–15.

Hillway, Tyrus. *The American Two-Year College.* New York: Harper and Brothers, 1958.

Hodgkinson, Harold. *Institutions in Transition: A Profile of Change in Higher Education.* New York: McGraw-Hill Book Co., 1971.

Hollingshead, August. *Elmtown's Youth.* New York: Science Editions, 1961.

Hoyt, Donald, and Munday, L. "Academic Description and Prediction in Junior Colleges." In *The Two-Year College and Its Students.* pp. 108–20. Iowa City: The American College Testing Program, 1969.

Hyman, Herbert. "The Value Systems of Different Classes." In *Class, Status, and Power,* edited by Semour M. Lipset and R. Bendix, pp. 488–99. New York: Free Press, 1966.

Illich, Ivan. *Deschooling Society.* New York: Harper & Row, 1970, 1971.

"Illinois Public Junior College System: A Program Review." Springfield, Ill.: Illinois Economic and Fiscal Commission, January 1973.

"It Pays to Teach at S.I.C.C.; Scale is 15th in Nation." *Staten Island Advance,* June 29, 1975, pp. 1, 2.

Jackson, Philip. *Life in Classrooms.* New York: Holt, Rinehart and Winston, 1968.

Jacob, Philip. *Changing Values in College.* New York: Harper and Brothers, 1957.

Jaffe, A. J., and Adams, W. "Two Models of Open Enrollment." In *Universal Higher Education,* edited by Logan Wilson and Olive Mills, pp. 223–51. Washington, D.C.: American Council on Education, 1972.

Jencks, Christopher. "Social Stratification and Higher Education." *Harvard Educational Review,* Spring 1968, pp. 277–316.

———, et al. *Inequality: A Reassessment of the Effect of Family and Schooling in America.* New York: Basic Books, 1972.

————, and Riesman, David. *The Academic Revolution.* New York: Doubleday & Co., 1968.

Jenkins, David. *Job Power: Blue and White Collar Democracy.* Garden City, N.Y.: Doubleday & Co., 1973.

Jennings, Frank. "The Two-Year College Stretch: Junior Colleges in America." *Change,* March/April 1970, pp. 15–25.

Jerome, Judson. *Culture Out of Anarchy.* New York: Herder and Herder, 1970.

Johnson, B. Lamar. "Encouraging Innovation In Teaching." *Junior College Journal* 38 (March 1968): 18–22.

————. *Islands of Innovation Expanding: Changes in The Community College.* Beverly Hills: Glencoe Press, 1969.

Johnston, J. Richard. Review of John Roueche and W. Kirk, *Catching Up: Remedial Education. Community College Frontiers,* Fall 1973, pp. 52–53.

Kaestle, Carl. *The Evolution of an Urban System: New York City, 1750–1850.* Cambridge,Mass.: Harvard University Press, 1973.

Kahl, Joseph. "'Common Man' Boys." In *Education, Economy, and Society,* edited by A. H. Halsey, Jean Floud, and C. A. Anderson, pp. 348–66. New York: Free Press, 1965.

Karabel, Jerome. "Community Colleges and Social Stratification." *Harvard Educational Review,* November 1972, pp. 521–62.

————. "Perspectives on Open Admissions." In *Universal Higher Education,* edited by Logan Wilson and Olive Mills, pp. 265–86. Washington, D.C.: American Council on Education, 1972.

————. "Protecting the Portals: Class and the Community College." *Social Policy,* May/June 1974, pp. 12–18.

Katz, J. M. "The Educational Shibboleth: Equality of Opportunity in a Democratic Institution, The Public Junior College." Ph.D. dissertation, U.C.L.A., 1967.

Katz, Joseph. "Four Years of Growth, Conflict, and Compliance." In *No Time For Youth: Growth and Constraint in College Students,* edited by J. Katz, pp. 3–73. San Francisco: Jossey-Bass, 1969.

Katz, Michael. *Class, Bureaucracy, and Schools: The Illusion of Educational Change in America.* New York: Praeger Publishers, 1971.

————. *The Irony of Early School Reform: Educational Innovation in Mid-Nineteenth Century Massachusetts.* Boston: Beacon Press, 1968.

Kaufman, Barry, and Botwinick, R. "Student Retention and Graduation at the City University of New York: Fall 1970 to Spring 1974." New York: City University of New York, Office of Program and Policy Research, June 1975.

Kaufman, Michael. "City U. Division of Plastics Lacks Nothing But Students." *New York Times*, May 2, 1974, p. 49.

Kelly, Henry. "The Modern School in Retrospect." In *The Modern School of Stelton*, pp. 115–19. Stelton, N.J., 1925.

Keniston, Kenneth, and Gerzen, M. "Human and Social Benefits." In *Universal Higher Education*, edited by Logan Wilson and Olive Mills, pp. 49–74. Washington, D.C.: American Council on Education, 1972.

Kennedy, Gail, ed. *Education for Democracy: The Debate Over the Report of the President's Commission on Higher Education.* Lexington, Mass.: D. C. Heath & Co., 1952.

Kerr, Clark, et al. *Industrialism and Industrial Man.* Cambridge, Mass.: Harvard University Press, 1960.

King, Seth. "June Graduates Find More Jobs Than Expected." *New York Times*, September 21, 1975, pp. 1, 39.

Kintzer, Frederick. *Middlemen In Higher Education.* San Francisco: Jossey-Bass, 1973.

————. "The Community College Transfer Student." In *Understanding Diverse Students*, edited by Dorothy Knoell, pp. 1–14. San Francisco: Jossey-Bass, 1973.

————. "The Transfer Student Dimension of Articulation." In *College Transfer: Working Papers and Recommendations for the Airlie House Conference, December 2–4, 1973*, pp. 72–106. New York: Association Transfer Group, April 30, 1974.

Knoell, Dorothy. "Focus on the Transfer Program." *Junior College Journal* 35 (1965): 5.

————, and Medsker, Leland *Articulation Between Two-Year and Four-Year Colleges.* Berkeley: Center for the Study of Higher Education, 1964.

————. *From Junior to Senior College.* Washington, D.C.: American Council on Education, 1965.

Kohlberg, Lawrence. "Moral Education in the Schools." *School Review* 74 (Spring 1966): 1–30.

————. "State and Sequence: The Cognitive-Developmental Approach to Socialization." In *Handbook of Socialization Theory and Research*, edited by R. Goslin, pp. 347–48. Chicago: Rand McNally, 1969.

————. "The Child as Moral Philosopher." *Psychology Today*, September 1968, pp. 25–30.

Kolko, Gabriel. *Wealth and Power in America: An Analysis of Social Class and Income Distribution.* New York: Praeger Publishers, 1962.

Koos, Leonard. *The Community College Student.* Gainesville: University of Florida Press, 1970.

———. *The Junior College Movement.* Boston: Ginn and Co., 1925.
———. *Secondary Education in California—A Preliminary Survey.* Sacramento: California State Department of Education, 1929.
Korn, Harold. "Careers: Choice, Chance, or Inertia." In *No Time For Youth*, edited by Joseph Katz, pp. 207–38. San Francisco: Jossey-Bass, 1969.
Kunsisto, A. A. *Report of the Conference on Two-Year Colleges and the Disadvantaged.* Albany: State University of New York and the State Education Department, 1966.
Lange, Alexis. "The Junior College." *Sierra Educational News* 16 (1920): 483–86.
———. "The Junior College as an Integral Part of the Public School System." *School Review* 25 (1917): 465–79.
———. "The Junior College Department of Civic Education." *School and Society* 2 (1915): 442–48.
———. "The Junior College—What Manner of Child Shall This Be?" *School and Society* 7 (1918): 211–18.
———. "The Junior College, With Special Reference to California." *Proceedings of the National Education Association*, Washington, D.C., 1915, pp. 119–24.
Lansing, John; Lorimer, Thomas; and Moriguchi, Chikashi. *How People Pay For College.* Ann Arbor, Mich.: Study Research Center, 1960.
Lansky, Leonard. "Changing the Classroom." In *The Changing College Classroom*, edited by Philip Runkel, Roger Harrison, and Margaret Runkel, pp. 292–301. San Francisco: Jossey-Bass, 1969.
Lauter, Paul, and Howe, F. *The Conspiracy of the Young.* New York: Meridian Books, 1971.
Lavin, David. "Student Retention and Graduation at the City University of New York: September 1970 Enrollees Through Seven Semesters." Mimeographed. New York: City University of New York, 1974.
———, and Silberstein, R. "Student Retention Under Open Admissions at the City University of New York: September 1970 Enrollees Followed Through Four Semesters." New York: City University of New York, Office of Program and Policy Research, February 1974.
Lazerson, Marvin. "Revisionism and American Educational History." *Harvard Educational Review*, May 1973, pp. 269–83.
Levison, Andrew. *The Working-Class Majority.* New York: Coward, McCann & Geoghegan, 1974.
Lipset, Seymour, and Bendix, R. *Social Mobility in Industrial Society.* Berkeley: University of California Press, 1959.

Lipsitz, Louis. "Working Class Authoritarianism: A Reevaluation." *American Sociological Review*, February 1965, pp. 27–43.

MacDonald, Gary, ed. *Five Experimental Colleges.* New York: Harper Colophon Books, 1973.

McCoy, Pressley. "Johnston College: An Experimenting Model." In *The New Colleges: Toward an Appraisal*, edited by Paul Dressel, pp. 53–87. Iowa City: American College Testing Program, 1971.

McDermott, John. "Campus Missionaries: The Laying On of Culture." *The Nation*, March 10, 1969, pp. 296–301.

McDonald, Donald. "A Six Million Dollar Misunderstanding." *The Center Magazine* 6 (September/October 1973): 32–50.

McDowell, F. M. *The Junior College.* Bureau of Education Bulletin 32. Washington, D.C.: U.S. Government Printing Office, 1919.

McLane, C. L. "The Fresno Junior College." *California Weekly*, July 15, 1910, p. 539.

———. "The Junior College, or Upward Extension of the High School." *School Review* 21 (1913): 166–67.

Maeroff, Gene. "City U. Open Admissions Held a Success." *New York Times*, March 17, 1974, pp. 1, 52.

———. "Colleges Face Year of Economic Worry." *New York Times*, September 7, 1974, p. 1, 30.

———. "Middle-Income Student Finds It Difficult to Get U.S. Aid." *New York Times*, September 4, 1973, pp. 1, 24.

———. "Study of College Degree Finds Its Value Declining." *New York Times*, August 14, 1975, pp. 1, 35.

———. "This Side of Paradise: A Kind of Higher Education." *New York Times Magazine*, May 27, 1973, pp. 12–13, 15–24.

The Management and Financing of Colleges. New York: Committee for Economic Development, October 1973.

Mann, Richard, et al. *The College Classroom: Conflict, Change, and Learning.* New York: John Wiley & Sons, 1970.

Martorama, S. V., and Williams, L. L. "Academic Success of Junior College Transfers at the State Colleges of Washington." *Junior College Journal* 24 (1954): 402–15.

Maslow, Abraham. *Motivation and Personality.* New York: Harper & Row, 1970.

———. *Toward A Psychology of Being*, 2d ed. New York: Van Nostrand Reinhold Co., 1968.

Master Plan Survey Team. *A Master Plan for Higher Education in California. 1960–1975.* Sacramento: California State Department of Education, 1960.

Matching Needs and Facilities in Higher Education. State of New York Legislative Document no. 31. Albany, N.Y., 1948.

Mayhew, Lewis. *The Carnegie Commission on Higher Education.* San Francisco: Jossey-Bass, 1973.

Medelman, John. "Does Your Husband Know You're Bisexual?" *Playboy,* January 1975, pp. 145–46, 252–61.

Medsker, Leland. *The Junior College: Progress and Prospect.* New York: McGraw-Hill Book Co., 1960.

————, and Tillery, D. *Breaking the Access Barriers: A Profile of Two-Year Colleges.* New York: McGraw-Hill Book Co., 1971.

Miller, Herman. *Rich Man, Poor Man.* New York: Thomas Y. Crowell Co., 1964.

Mills, C. Wright. *White Collar: The American Middle Classes.* New York: Oxford University Press, 1951.

Milner, Murray. *The Illusion of Equality.* San Francisco: Jossey-Bass, 1972.

"Minorities Drop in U.S. Colleges: First Slash Since Mid-60's Linked to Economics." *New York Times,* February 3, 1974, p. 34.

Monahan, Anthony. "Making It at the Inner-City's Proving Grounds." *Chicago Tribune Magazine,* April 16, 1968, pp. 22–23, 38–44.

Monroe, Charles. *Profile of the Community College.* San Francisco: Jossey-Bass, 1972.

Moore, William. *Against the Odds: The High Risk Student in the Community College.* San Francisco: Jossey-Bass, 1970.

Mulcahy, Gene. "Evaluation of Circle 73, Staten Island Community College." Mimeographed. New York: Staten Island Community College, May 17, 1974.

Munday, Leo. "Evaluation and the New Colleges: Assessment for Student Development." In *The New Colleges: Toward an Appraisal,* edited by Paul Dressel, pp. 301–7. Iowa City: American College Testing Program, 1971.

New Approaches to Student Financial Aid. New York: College Entrance Examination Board, 1971.

Newcomb, T. M. *Personality and Social Change: Attitude Formation in a Student Community.* New York: Dryden Press, 1943.

Newman, Frank, et al. *Report On Higher Education.* Washington, D.C.: U.S. Government Printing Office, 1971.

"New Paltz Students Stage Office Sit-In to Protest Policies." *New York Times,* March 27, 1974, p. 45.

Niblett, W. R. "The Commission's Work: A View From Abroad." *Change,* November 1973, pp. 38–44.

"1974–75 College Freshman Is Found More Conservative Politically." *New York Times,* January 16, 1975.

1968 Master Plan of the Board of Higher Education for the City

University of New York. New York: City University of New York, 1968.

O'Connell, Thomas. *Community Colleges: A President's View.* Urbana: University of Illinois Press, 1968.

"1,000 Apply for 90 Tutoring Jobs at Bronx College." *New York Times*, April 25, 1975, p. 39.

Open Admissions: The Pros and Cons. Washington, D.C.: Council for Basic Education, 1972.

"The Open Door, or the Revolving Door: Which Way, Texas?" Austin: Texas State Legislature, January 9, 1973.

O'Toole, James. "The Reserve Army of the Underemployed: The Role of Education." *Change*, June 1975, pp. 26–33, 60–62.

Parenti, Michael. "Politics of the Classroom." *Social Policy*, July/August 1973, pp. 67–70.

Parsons, Talcott. "The Problem of Controlled Institutional Change." In T. Parsons, *Essays in Sociological Theory*, rev. ed., pp. 238–74. New York: Free Press, 1954.

Pateman, Carole. *Participation and Democratic Theory.* London: Cambridge University Press, 1970.

Payne, Ruth. "The Question of Financial Assistance at Mount Holyoke." *Mount Holyoke Alumnae Quarterly*, Spring 1973, pp. 8–12.

Pechman, Joseph. "The Distributional Effects of Public Higher Education in California." *Journal of Human Resources*, Summer 1970, pp. 361–70.

Perry, William. *Forms of Intellectual and Ethical Development in the College Years.* New York: Holt, Rinehart and Winston, 1970.

Peterson, Iver. "College Textbooks Being Simplified to Meet the Needs of the Poor Reader." *New York Times*, November 7, 1974, p. 47.

———. "Enrollments Drop as Costs Rise." *New York Times*, September 3, 1975, p. 33.

———. "Job Problems Stir Doubts About College." *New York Times*, June 6, 1975, pp. 1, 12.

———. "Schools Use New Ways to 'Track' Students." *New York Times*, July 2, 1975, p. 38.

Pincus, Fred. "Tracking in the Community Colleges." Baltimore: Research Group One Report no. 18, 1974.

Plachta, Leonard. "The Role of the Teacher in Cooperative Education." *Journal of Cooperative Education*, May 1969, pp. 18–20.

"Pound Foolish." *New York Times*, September 12, 1974, p. 38.

Powell, Hope. "Implementing a Curriculum for Provisional Students." Mimeographed. Los Angeles: Los Angeles City College, n.d.

Raines, Max. "Characteristics of Junior College Students." In *Perspectives on the Community Junior College*, edited by William Ogilvie and Max Raines, pp. 178–82. New York: Appleton-Century-Crofts, 1971.

———. *Junior College Student Personnel Programs: Appraisal and Development*. Washington, D.C.: American Association of Junior Colleges, 1965.

Ravitch, Diane. "Moral Education and the Schools." *Commentary*, September 1973, pp. 62–68.

"Recruiters Snap Up Job-Trained 'Grads' of Two-Year Colleges." *Wall Street Journal*, June 10, 1965.

Reed, Lloyd Dell. *Jesse Parker Bogue: Missionary for the Two-Year College*. New York: Carlton Press, 1971.

Reichert, Stephen. "The End of the Four-Year Junior College in California." In *Perspectives on the Community Junior College*, edited by William Ogilvie and Max Raines, pp. 110–15. New York: Appleton-Century-Crofts, 1971.

Reimer, Everett. *School Is Dead: An Essay on Alternatives in Education*. Harmondsworth, England: Penguin Books, 1971.

Reinhold, Robert. "At Brown, Trend Is Back to Grades and Tradition." *New York Times*, February 24, 1974, pp. 1, 47.

Rempson, Joe. "Minority Access to Higher Education in N.Y.C." *The City Almanac* 7 (August 1972): 1–15.

Report of the Commission on Industrial and Technical Education. Boston: Commonwealth of Massachusetts, 1906.

Report of the Joint Committee On the Master Plan for Higher Education. Draft. Sacramento: California State Legislature, February 1973.

Report of the Temporary Commission on the Need for a State University. State of New York Legislative Document no. 30. Albany, N.Y., 1948.

"Report of the University Faculty Senate on the Educational Mission of the City University of New York." New York: City University Faculty Senate, October 1974.

Riessman, Frank, and Gartner, A. "The New Hereditarians." *Change*, February 1974, pp. 56–59.

Richards, J. M., and Braskamp, L. A. "Who Goes Where to Junior College?" In *The Two-Year College and Its Students: An Empirical Report*, pp. 72–86. Iowa City: American College Testing Program, pp. 72–86.

Rinehart, Richard. "Articulating Career Education at Associate-Degree and Baccalaureate-Degree Levels." In *Updating Occu-*

pational Education, edited by Norman Harris, pp. 93–103. San Francisco: Jossey-Bass, 1974.

Rogers, Carl. *Client-Centered Therapy: Its Current Practices, Implications, and Theory.* Boston: Houghton Mifflin Co., 1951.

Rogoff, Natalie. "Local Social Structure and Education Selection." In *Education, Economy, and Society,* edited by A. H. Halsey, Jean Floud, and C. A. Anderson, pp. 241–51. New York: Free Press, 1965.

Rosen, Bernard. "The Achievement Syndrome: A Psychocultural Dimension of Social Stratification." *American Sociological Review* 21 (April 1956): 203–11.

Rosen, David; Brunner, Seth; and Fowler, Steve, eds. *Open Admissions: The Promise and the Lie of Open Access to American Higher Education.* Lincoln: University of Nebraska Press, 1973.

Ross, Earle. *Democracy's College: The Land-Grant Movement in the Formative State.* New York: Arno Press and *The New York Times,* 1969.

Rossman, Michael. "Learning and Social Change: The Problem of Authority." In *The Changing College Classroom,* edited by Paul Runkel, Roger Harrison, and Margaret Runkel, pp. 20–32. San Francisco: Jossey-Bass, 1969.

————. *On Learning and Social Change: Transcending the Totalitarian Classroom.* New York: Vintage Books, 1972.

Roueche, John. *Salvage, Redirection, or Custody? Remedial Education in the Community Junior College.* Washington, D.C.: American Association of Junior Colleges, 1968.

————, and Kirk, W. *Catching Up: Remedial Education.* San Francisco: Jossey-Bass, 1973.

Sanford, Nevitt. "Developmental Status of the Entering Freshman." In *The American College,* edited by N. Sanford, pp. 253–82. New York: John Wiley & Sons, 1962.

————, "Higher Education as a Social Problem." In *The American College,* edited by N. Sanford, pp. 103–73. New York: John Wiley & Sons, 1962.

————, "The Freeing and Acting Out of Impulse in Late Adolescence." In *The Study of Lives,* edited by C. R. White, pp. 4–39. New York: Atherton Press, 1963.

Schelsky, H. "Family and School in Modern Society." In *Education, Economy, and Society,* edited by A. H. Halsey, Jean Floud, and C. A. Anderson, pp. 414–20. New York: Free Press, 1965.

Schmuck, Richard, and Schmuck, P. *Group Processes in the Classroom.* Dubuque, Iowa: William C. Brown Co., 1971.

Schonemann, Friedrich. "A German Looks at American Higher

Education." In *Higher Education Faces the Future*, edited by Paul Schilpp. New York: Liveright, 1930.

Schultz, Stanley. *The Culture Factory: Boston Public Schools, 1789–1860.* New York: Oxford University Press, 1973.

Schultz, Theodore. "Optimal Investment in College Instruction: Equity and Efficiency." In *Investment in Education*, edited by T. Schultz, pp. 2–30. Chicago: University of Chicago Press, 1972.

Schumpeter, Joseph. *Capitalism, Socialism and Democracy.* London: Allen and Unwin, 1943.

Scribner, Sylvia, and Cole, M. "Cognitive Consequences of Formal and Informal Education." *Science* 180 (November 1973): 553–59.

Seashore, Carl. *The Junior College Movement.* New York: Holt, Rinehart and Winston, 1940.

Seashore, Harold. "Academic Abilities of Junior College Students." *Junior College Journal* 28 (October 1958): 74–80.

Seibel, Dean. *A Study of the Academic Ability and Performance of Junior College Students.* Princeton, N.J.: Educational Testing Service, 1965.

Severo, Richard. "College Students Showing Reduced Sense of Alienation." *New York Times*, May 22, 1974, pp. 45, 86.

Sexton, Patricia Cayo. *The American School: A Sociological Analysis.* Englewood Cliffs, N.J.: Prentice Hall, 1967.

———. "The Inequality Affair: A Critique of Jencks." *Social Policy*, September/October 1973, pp. 53–61.

"Shaky Economy Lures Record Number at Columbia to Law and Medicine: Trend Irks Some Students." *New York Times*, May 16, 1974, pp. 43, 68.

Sheehy, Gail. "Catch-30 and Other Predictable Crises of Growing Up Adult." *New York Magazine*, February 18, 1974, pp. 30–40.

———. "Why Mid Life Is· Crisis Time for Couples." *New York Magazine*, April 29, 1974, pp. 31–35.

Siemens, C. H. "Predicting Success of Junior College Transfers." *Junior College Journal* 19 (1949): 121–27.

Simon, Laura. "The Cooling-Out Function of the Junior College." *Personnel and Guidance Journal*, June 1967, pp. 973–78.

Singer, Benjamin. "The Future-Focused Role-Image." In *Learning for Tomorrow: The Role of the Future in Education*, edited by Alvin Toffler, pp. 19–32. New York: Vintage Books, 1974.

Somers, Gerald. *The Effectiveness of Vocational and Technical Programs.* Madison, Wisc.: Center for Studies in Vocational and Technical Education, 1971.

Spindler, George, ed. *Education and Culture: Anthropological Approaches.* New York: Holt, Rinehart and Winston, 1963.

Spring, Joel. *Education and the Rise of the Corporate State.* Boston: Beacon Press, 1972.

Sproul, Robert. *Before and After the Junior College.* Los Angeles: The College Press, 1938.

Steinitz, Victoria, et al. "Ideological Development in Working-Class Youth." *Harvard Educational Review,* August 1973, pp. 333–61.

The Study Commission. Lincoln: University of Nebraska, 1973.

Summer, Anita, and Wolfe, B. "Which School Resources Help Learning? Efficiency and Equity in Philadelphia Public Schools." *Business Review.* Philadelphia: Federal Reserve Bank of Philadelphia, 1975.

Super, Donald. *The Psychology of Careers: An Introduction to Vocational Development.* New York: Harper & Row, 1957.

Swofford, Ronald, and Swofford, J. "Developmental Studies in North Carolina and Virginia: A Constant Search for Anything That Will Work." E.R.I.C. no. ED 082 727, 1974.

Tappen, Henry. *The Progress of Educational Development, A Discourse Delivered Before the Literary Societies of the University of Michigan.* Ann Arbor: University of Michigan Press, 1855.

Taylor, Frederick. "The Principles of Scientific Management" and "Shop Management." In F. Taylor, *Scientific Management.* New York: Harper & Row, 1947.

Teaching English in Two-Year Colleges: Three Successful Programs. Urbana, Ill.: National Council of Teachers of English, 1974.

Thernstrom, Stephen. *Poverty and Progress: Social Mobility in a Nineteenth Century City.* Cambridge, Mass.: Harvard University Press, 1964.

Thomas, Frank. "A Study of Functions of the Public Junior College and the Extent of the Realization in California." Ph.D. dissertation, Stanford University, 1926.

Thornton, James. *The Community Junior College.* New York: John Wiley & Sons, 1972.

Thurow, Lester. "Education and Economic Equality." *The Public Interest,* Summer 1972, pp. 66–81.

Tillery, Dale. "Differential Characteristics of Entering Freshmen at the University of California and their Peers at California Junior Colleges." Ph.D. dissertation, University of California, Berkeley, 1964.

———. "Report to the Conference for Chief Student Personnel Administrators on Implementing the Open Door." Mimeographed. Pacific Grove, Cal., January 10, 1964.

Toffler, Alvin. "The Psychology of the Future." In *Learning for Tomorrow: The Role of the Future in Education*, edited by A. Toffler, pp. 3–18. New York: Vintage Books, 1974.

Trent, James, and Medsker, L. *Beyond High School: A Psychosociological Study of 10,000 High School Graduates*. San Francisco: Jossey-Bass, 1968.

Trimberger, Ellen Kay. "Open Admissions: A New Form of Tracking?" *Insurgent Sociologist* 4 (Fall 1973): 29–43.

Trow, Martin. "The Second Transformation of American Secondary Education." In *Class, Status, and Power: Social Stratification in Comparative Perspective*, edited by Seymour M. Lipset, and R. Bendix, pp. 437–49. New York: Free Press, 1966.

———. "Toward An Empirical Typology of Junior College Subcultures." E.R.I.C. no. ED 013 076, 1967.

Tubbs, Walter. "Minority Students and the Experimental Colleges." In *Toward a Community of Seekers: A Report on Experimental Education*, edited by W. Tubbs, pp. 162–84. Lincoln: University of Nebraska, Nebraska Curriculum Development Center, 1972.

Venn, Grant. *Man, Education and Work: Postsecondary Vocational and Technical Education*. Washington, D.C.: American Council on Education, 1964.

Ward, Phebe. *Terminal Education in the Junior College*. New York: Harper and Brothers, 1947.

Warren, J. R. *Patterns of College Experience*. U.S.O.E. Cooperative Research Project S-327. Claremont, Cal.: College Student Personnel Institute and Claremont Graduate School and University Center, October 1966.

Wasserman, Miriam. *The School Fix, N.Y.C., U.S.A.* New York: Outerbridge & Dienstfrey, 1970.

Wax, Murray; Diamond, S.; and Gearing, F., eds. *Anthropological Perspectives on Education*. New York: Basic Books, 1972.

Welter, Rush. *Popular Education and Democratic Thought in America*. New York: Columbia University Press, 1962.

Werdell, Philip. "Futurism and the Reform of Higher Education." In *Learning for Tomorrow: The Role of the Future in Education*, edited by Alvin Toffler, pp. 272–311. New York: Vintage Books, 1974.

———. "Teaching and Learning: Whose Goals Are Important Around Here?" In *Whose Goals for American Higher Education?* edited by Charles Dobbins and Calvin Lee, pp. 19–38. Washington, D.C.: American Council on Education, 1968.

White, Joseph. *Twenty-Eighth Annual Report of the Massachusetts Board of Education*. Boston, 1866.

Willingham, Warren. *The No. 2 Access Problem: Transfer to the Upper Division.* Washington, D.C.: American Association for Higher Education, 1972.

————. "Transfer Standards and the Public Interest." In *College Transfer: Working Papers and Recommendations from the Airlie House Conference, December 2–4, 1973,* pp. 26–49. New York: Association Transfer Group, April 30, 1974.

————, and Findikyan, N. "Transfer Students: Who's Moving from Where to Where, and What Determines Who's Admitted?" *College Board Review* 72 (Summer 1969): 4–12.

Wilms, Wellford. *Public and Proprietary Vocational Training: A Study of Effectiveness.* Berkeley: University of California Center for Research and Development in Higher Education, 1974.

Wilson, J. W. "Survey of Cooperative Education, 1972." *Journal of Cooperative Education,* November 1972, pp. 9–15.

Windham, Douglas. *Education, Equality and Income Redistribution.* Lexington, Mass.: D. C. Heath & Co., 1970.

Withey, S., et al, eds. *A Degree and What Else? A Review of the Correlates and Consequences of a College Education.* New York: McGraw-Hill Book Co., 1971.

Wolfe, Alan. "Carnegie Again." *Social Policy,* November/December 1974, pp. 60–63.

————. "Reform Without Reform: The Carnegie Commission on Higher Education." *Social Policy,* May/June 1971, pp. 18–27.

————. "Working With the Working Class." *Change,* February 1972, pp. 24–29.

Work In America. Washington, D.C.: U.S. Government Printing Office, 1973.

Wrenn, Gilbert. *The Counselor in a Changing World.* Washington, D.C.: American Personnel and Guidance Association, 1962.

Yankelovich, Daniel. *The New Morality: A Profile of American Youth in the 70's.* New York: McGraw-Hill Book Co., 1974.

Yarrington, Roger, ed. *Junior Colleges: 50 States/50 Years.* Washington, D.C.: American Association of Junior Colleges, 1969.

Young, Michael. *The Rise of the Meritocracy.* Harmondsworth, England: Penguin Books, 1958.

Zwerling, L. Steven. "Circle Students On Probation." Mimeographed. New York: Staten Island Community College, October 23, 1974.

————. "Experiential Education at a Community College." In *New Directions for Higher Education: Implementing Field Experience Education,* edited by John Duley, pp. 1–12. San Francisco: Jossey-Bass, 1974.

————. "On Community Colleges." *Social Policy,* August 1973, pp. 124–28.

————. Review of W. L. Hansen and B. Weisbrod, *Benefits, Costs and Finance of Public Higher Education* and D. Windham, *Education, Equality and Income Redistribution*. *School Review* 81 (August 1973): 643–49.

————. "Second-Class Education at the Community College." In *New Directions for Community Colleges: From Class to Mass Learning*, edited by William M. Birenbaum, pp. 23–37. San Francisco: Jossey-Bass, 1974.

————. "The Community College: Cooling-Out or Heating-Up?" *Community College Frontiers*, Spring 1974, pp. 4–8.

————, and Park, Dabney, Jr. "Curriculum Comprehensiveness and Tracking: The Community College's Commitment to Failure." *Community College Review*, Spring 1974, pp. 10–20.

INDEX

375

Environment, as factor in success, xiv, xv
E.R.I.C. Clearinghouse for Junior Colleges, 285
Erikson, Erik, 160, 180–181, 185, 198
Ethnic identity, and education, 162–164
Eskow, Seymour, 226
Etzioni, Amitai, 35, 36
Excellence (Gardner), 64, 65
Expectations, teachers', xv, xvi

Failure, as socially programmed, 9, 37
Fallows, Marjorie, 135, 136
Feldman, Kenneth, 178, 179
Financial aid, 3, 22–23
and grades, 236–267
First Amendment, 23
Fitch, Robert, 74, 102–103
Flunking out, xviii
Folwell, W. W., 45
Ford Foundation, 255
Four-year colleges, xviii
Franconia College, 13
Franklin Pierce College, 197, 198
Freire, Paulo, 161
Fresno, Board of Education, 49–51
Friends World College, 244
From Junior to Senior College (Knoell and Medsker), 234–237

Gardner, John, 64–65, 140
Ghettos, 12
remedial, 200
G.I. Bill, 62
Ginsberg, Allen, 147

Gintis, Herbert, 59, 80, 130–131
Ginzberg, Eli, 210–212
Glatt, Erwin, 99–101
Gleazer, Edmund, Jr., 85–86, 283–284
Goals for Americans (Eisenhower Commission), 63, 64
Goddard College, 13
Goffman, Erving, 83–84, 88
G.P.A.s, 77–78, 237, 245, 247
Grading systems, 172
Graduates Restudied, The (Blank et al.), 163
Gratifications, delay of, 11–13
"Great School Legend," 27
Greer, Colin, 27, 161
Guillou, Wendy, viii
Gymnasium, 44

Hadas, Moses, viii
Hansen, W. Lee, 112–161
confirmation of data of, 117–119
Harper, William Rainey, 45–47
Harris, Norman, 25–26, 252–253
Harvard University, 66, 98, 265
Heermann, Barry, 215
Heist, Paul, 133, 134
Henry, Jules, 13, 158
"Hidden curricula," 13
Hierarchicality, 250–251, 269, 273,
and attempted reform, 257, 259–263, 271–277
and B.A. degrees, 252–256
and ideological egalitarianism, 258–259
and Taylorism, 267–268
Hierarchy of needs, 269

About the Author

About the Author

L. Steven Zwerling was born and raised in Brooklyn, New York. After obtaining both his B.A. and M.A. in English from Columbia University, he continued to do graduate work at Rutgers University. In addition to his articles on education that have appeared in *Social Policy* and the University of Chicago's *School Review*, Mr. Zwerling has had stories and poems published in various magazines. Currently the director of an innovative inner college at Staten Island Community College, Mr. Zwerling conducts a weekly radio program in New York City on WRVR called "Metroscope," which deals with the city, its people, and its problems.

DATE DUE
